The Religion of Jesus the Jew

Also by Geza Vermes
and published by Fortress Press

The Dead Sea Scrolls: Qumran in Perspective

Jesus the Jew: A Historian's Reading of the Gospels

The Religion of
Jesus the Jew

Geza Vermes

FORTRESS PRESS   MINNEAPOLIS

First Fortress Press edition published 1993.

Copyright © Geza Vermes 1993

Library of Congress Cataloging-in-Publication data available
ISBN 0-8006-2797-0

AF 1-2797

Manufactured in Great Britain
98 97 96 95 94 93   1 2 3 4 5 6 7 8 9 10

If ever a day should come and this ethical code be stripped of its wrappings . . . , the Book of the Ethics of Jesus will be one of the choicest treasures in the literature of Israel for all times.

Joseph Klausner, *Jesus of Nazareth* (1925)

I am more than ever certain that a great place belongs to [Jesus] in Israel's history of faith.

Martin Buber, *Two Types of Faith* (1951)

After the First World War, some Jewish historians . . . devoted studies directly to Jesus . . . All these attempts are to be accorded serious attention by Christian theologians engaged in the study of Christology.

Pontifical Biblical Commission, *Scripture and Christology* (1983)

Modern biblical scholarship is increasingly becoming a joint enterprise between Jews and Christians . . . Some Jews have become very aware of Jesus as part of their own history, and their writings have brought home to Christians his Jewishness. Renewed study of Jewish sources by Christian scholars has led them to see first-century Judaism in a new and more positive light.

Lambeth Conference of the Anglican Communion, *Inter-faith Dialogue* (1988)

Contents

Preface

The present volume completes a trilogy which started in 1973 with *Jesus the Jew* and continued ten years later with the appearance of *Jesus and the World of Judaism*.

Like its predecessors, *The Religion of Jesus the Jew* is one man's reading of the Synoptic Gospels of Mark, Matthew and Luke. It does not offer readers a *status quaestionis*, a general sketch of scholarly views, nor does it engage in a systematic discussion with proponents of different theories. Opinions of other writers are presented only when they have actually inspired me or challenged me to a fruitful debate.

This book is primarily addressed to readers whose expertise lies outside the Bible, the New Testament and theology, viz. students of ancient religions, history and culture, Judaism in particular, though I hope biblical scholars and theologians will also at least glance at it. Christian readers, untrained in the academic study of the origins of their faith, may find many of these pages, most of all the final chapter, disturbing, but I trust thought-provoking too.

For the benefit of those unacquainted with the Gospels and/or with the non-scriptural books of ancient Judaism, literary evidence will always be cited rather than alluded to in references.

Over the years, when lecturing on Jesus the Jew, I have often encountered an objection, usually raised at the very beginning of the discussion, which runs like this. If Jesus was neither a political agitator, nor a teacher attacking fundamental tenets of the Jewish religion, why was he put to death? Without rehearsing the argument set out in the Preface of *Jesus and the World of Judaism* (pp. viii–ix), I would like to summarize my view very briefly.

The arrest and execution of Jesus were due, not directly to his words and deeds, but to their possible insurrectionary consequences feared by the nervous authorities in charge of law and order in that powder-keg of first-century Jerusalem, overcrowded with pilgrims. Had Jesus not caused an affray in the Temple by overturning the tables of the merchants and money-changers, or had even chosen to do so at a time other than Passover – the moment when the hoped-for Messiah, the final liberator of the Jews, was expected to reveal himself – he would most probably have escaped with his life. He died on the cross for having done the wrong thing (caused a commotion) in the wrong place (the Temple) at the wrong time (just before Passover). Here lies the real tragedy of Jesus the Jew.

The late Professor Sir Godfrey Driver, having caught me out some twenty-five years ago making a mistake in English, asked: 'How come that when you write, your English is faultless?' The answer was easy: 'I have an English wife who co-operates with me', I said. Indeed, over thirty-five years Pam and I have been working out together both the substance and the form of articles and books. Her very considerable help, despite ill-health, has greatly improved *The Religion of Jesus the Jew* and enabled me to meet the publishers' deadline. To her is offered the whole fruit of our common creative labour.

Oxford
15 October 1992   G.V.

I

Jesus the Jew and his Gospel

In the optimistic era preceding the outbreak of the First World War, most New Testament scholars firmly believed that by means of a rational and critical enquiry they could rediscover the Jesus of history. Ernest Renan's *The Life of Jesus* (*La vie de Jésus*, 1863) and Albert Schweitzer's *The Quest of the Historical Jesus* (issued in German in 1906 and in English in 1910) are the two important landmarks in this field. Hand in hand with this naive expectation went the equally candid assurance that a comprehensive presentation of his message was no less possible. *L'évangile de Jésus-Christ* by Marie-Joseph Lagrange, the renowned French Dominican founder of the Ecole Biblique in Jerusalem, and here in Britain T. W. Manson's *The Teaching of Jesus*, published respectively in 1929 and 1931 may be seen as the last examples of this type of literature.

Clouds of doubt began to gather after 1914 and 1926 marked the start of a new period of deep-seated pessimism with the appearance of a booklet, *Jesus* (*Jesus and the Word*, 1934 in English), in which Rudolf Bultmann, the scholar who was to dominate the New Testament scene for years, declared that the life and personality of Jesus lay beyond the realm of historical knowledge because 'the early Christian sources' – viz. the Gospels – 'show no interest in either' (op. cit., p. 14).

In Bultmann's view, the Gospels voice, not the thought and yearnings of Jesus, but the spiritual and organizational needs of the primitive church which was responsible for their redaction and transmission. No doubt, some of the teachings are authentic, but beside them in the same documents stand utterances issued by Christian 'prophets' as Paul calls them, (I Cor 12.28; 14.29, 32, etc.) speaking in the name and on behalf of the 'risen' Lord in church gatherings during worship. Form criticism or

Formgeschichte, Bultmann's discipline, sets out to distinguish the literary constituents of the accounts and determine their nature by identifying the role they were to fulfil in the life of early Christianity. With the help of the parallel attestations in the Synoptic Gospels, his ambition was to find the prehistory of every tradition, leading, in his words, 'in a very few cases' to Jesus himself.[1] Since his expertise lay in the Greek rather than the Semitic (Hebrew-Aramaic) domain, such a result was not altogether surprising.

Owing to the colossal influence of Bultmann on German, and subsequently through his former students on North American, New Testament learning, the clock of real historical research stopped for almost half a century, but in the 1950s a modest 'new quest' was launched in Germany and in 1956 a Bultmann pupil, Günther Bornkamm, dared to publish a book entitled, *Jesus of Nazareth*.

In an era still dominated by form criticism, this endeavour must have appeared fool-hardy. Indeed, Bornkamm's nervousness in face of much potential hostility may account for his opening sentence, which seemingly contradicts the aim of his book: 'No one is any longer in the position to write a life of Jesus.'[2]

Of course, the Gospels fall far short of the requirements needed for a real biography of Jesus, or for a full, detailed and systematic account of his teaching. But that is a far cry from Bultmann's claim and that of his fellow sceptics that we can know 'almost nothing' concerning him. The sensible question to ask is whether we can grasp *something significant and central* about his life and personality and about his message. Several books written during the last twenty years, three of them in Oxford, assert that we can.

---

[1] *The History of the Synoptic Tradition* [hence *HST*] (1963), 105. Though I often disagree with its historical inferences, *HST* will be regularly used in this volume on account of its high standard of literary analysis.

[2] *Jesus von Nazareth* (1956). [English translation: *Jesus of Nazareth* (1960)]. From the point of view of Bornkamm's understanding of Jesus, the book constituted no novelty at all. It echoes, in fact, a very familiar tune, the until recently traditional antipathy of German scholarship towards Judaism. Bornkamm felt constrained to admit that Jesus appears within the Jewish world, but claimed that he unmistakably stands outside it as a stranger because narrow and hardened post-exilic Judaism was a perversion of the Israelite religion. Under the influence of scribes and Pharisees, it developed into a formalistic legalism, a foretaste of the Talmudic religion against which Jesus stood out in sharp contrast!

Unlike Bultmann and his followers, the authors of this latest historical quest, while investigating the subject from within the (Synoptic) Gospels, pay not mere lip service to the essential contribution of post-biblical Jewish literature to a genuine perception of Jesus, but in their various ways make substantial use of it. But before turning to them, it may be salutary to peruse the wise words of my successor in Oxford, Martin Goodman, an expert on Galilean Judaism as well as an outstanding ancient historian, who puts the incoherence of the Bultmannian line of thinking into proper perspective:

> Whatever the problems in reconstructing the life and career of Jesus (and they are immense), it is more plausible than otherwise that the general outline of his career as presented in the Gospel biographies is correct, simply because the hypothesis that these accounts were entirely composed, rather than partially altered, to make a theological point is more implausible than the belief that the outlines of Jesus' career are correctly described. Among other objections to the former (and commonly held) view are the survival within each Gospel of contradictory views of Jesus and the oddness of biography as a vehicle for theological didacticism.[3]

Leaving *Jesus the Jew* (1973), of which the present volume and the earlier *Jesus and the World of Judaism* (1983) are the sequels, to the end of the list, let me start with works of two close friends and ex-Oxford colleagues, A. E. Harvey and E. P. Sanders.

In *Jesus and the Constraints of History* (1982), Harvey, while concurring to some extent with common academic scepticism in regard to the general historical reliability of the Gospels, admits welcome fresh air into the study of the life of Jesus when he writes: 'There are also certain facts about Jesus which, by any normal criterion of historical evidence, it would be altogether unreasonable to doubt. Such facts are that Jesus was known in both Galilee and Jerusalem; that he was a teacher; that he carried out cures of various illnesses, particularly demon-possession, and that these were widely regarded as miraculous; that he was involved in controversy with fellow-Jews over questions of the

---

[3]*The Ruling Class of Judaea* (1987), 22f. See also his *State and Society in Roman Galilee, A.D. 132–212* (1983).

Law of Moses; and that he was crucified in the governorship of Pontius Pilate.' (p. 6).

On the other hand, while stipulating limited historical genuineness regarding the Gospels, with most theologians he denies the possibility of knowing 'anything that really matters', e.g. Jesus' 'messianic consciousness, his moral perfection or his relationship with his heavenly father' (ibid.). In other words, he accepts traits of Jesus' biographical sketch, but declares himself totally doubtful in matters which for him are of the gravest doctrinal import.

Ed Sanders is definitely not a theologian and much less hesitant at venturing into the dangerous field of Jesus' religious message. In *Jesus and Judaism* (1985), he classifies Gospel teachings and grades them as certain, highly probable, probable, possible, conceivable and incredible (i.e. negatively certain). To his first category belong, among others, the arguments that Jesus proclaimed the Kingdom of God to all, including the wicked; that he preached in an eschatological setting; that neither his, nor his disciples' aim in bringing in the Kingdom was political; and that he did not explicitly oppose the Law of Moses (p. 326).

My own first contribution, *Jesus the Jew*, is based on a double conviction: (1) that historians have the right and duty to pursue their research independent of belief, and (2) that it is possible to extract, thanks to our considerably increased knowledge of Palestinian-Jewish realities of the time of Jesus, historically reliable information from non-historical sources, such as the Gospels.

Research has to be restricted to Mark, Matthew and Luke and to exclude John because, despite the occasional historical detail it contains, its Jesus portrait is so evolved theologically as to be wholly unsuitable for historical investigation. By contrast, a reading, devoid of doctrinal preconceptions, of the Synoptic Gospels has disclosed a figure of Jesus as a popular teacher, healer and exorcist, who fits perfectly into the first-century Galilee known directly from Josephus, and indirectly from rabbinic literature. He represents the charismatic Judaism of wonder-working holy men such as the first-century BC Honi and Jesus' younger contemporary, Hanina ben Dosa, modelled on the biblical prophets such as Elijah and Elisha. They feed the hungry, cure disease, physical and mental, both often attributed to demonic possession.

The enquiry in the second half of *Jesus the Jew* is centred on the titles conferred on Jesus in the Gospels: Prophet, Lord, Messiah, Son of Man and Son of God. Their philological and historical analysis has indicated that with the exception of the Aramaic phrase, 'son of man', no titular use of which is attested in extant Jewish literature, and 'Messiah' which Jesus did not seem to have claimed or accepted, they applied easily to holy men who could be addressed or described as Prophet, Lord and even figuratively 'Son of God'. Thus, the thaumaturge Honi's relationship with God is compared to that between a son and his father, and Hanina ben Dosa, like Jesus at the moment of his baptism, is described as 'my son' by a *bat qol* or divine voice from heaven (*JJ* 206–10).

The chief finding of *Jesus the Jew* is the recognition of Jesus within the earliest Gospel tradition, prior to Christian theological speculation, as a charismatic prophetic preacher and miracle-worker, the outstanding 'Galilean Hasid' who, thanks to the 'sublimity, distinctiveness and originality' of his ethical teaching (Joseph Klausner),[4] stood head and shoulders above the known representatives of this class of spiritual personality. Powerful positive and negative support for such a perception comes from the first-century Jewish historian, Flavius Josephus' characterization of Jesus as a 'wise man' and a 'performer of astonishing deeds' (*Ant.* xviii. 63), a description which expressed in neutral terms the positive Gospel portrait, and in its negative mirror image, the later hostile Talmudic picture of Jesus, 'seducer' and 'sorcerer'.[5]

Scholarly research published during the intervening years has

[4]Exactly seventy years ago, Joseph Klausner, the first modern Jewish scholar to devote a book to Jesus, concluded his volume with the highest praises for the moral teaching of Jesus: 'In his ethical code there is a sublimity, distinctiveness and originality in form unparalleled in any other Hebrew ethical code; neither is there any parallel to the remarkable art of his parables. The shrewdness and sharpness of his proverbs and his forceful epigrams serve, in an exceptional degree, to make ethical ideas a popular possession. If ever the day should come and this ethical code be stripped of its wrappings of miracle and mysticism, the Book of the Ethics of Jesus will be one of the choicest treasures in the literature of Israel for all time.' (*Jesus of Nazareth: His Life, Times and Teaching* (1925), 414.

[5]For a full bibliographical survey of the *Testimonium*, see L. H. Feldman, *Josephus and Modern Scholarship 1937–1980* (1984), 673–99. Cf. also my study, 'The Jesus Notice of Josephus re-examined', *JJS* 38 (1987), 1–10. My hypothetical reconstruction of the *Testimonium* reads: 'At about this time lived Jesus, a wise man . . . He accomplished astonishing (literally, paradoxical) deeds . . . He won over many Jews . . . He was [called] Christ. When Pilate, upon

in different ways and to varying degrees confirmed my basic
theory. J. B. Segal has furnished a broader historical context for
the 'charismatic Hasid' as another manifestation of the familiar
'man of God' figure, well-attested in popular Judaism of the
biblical and post-biblical era.[6] In their detailed examination of
the traditions relating to Honi the Circle-drawer and Hanina ben
Dosa, W. S. Green and the late B. M. Bokser have clarified and
supplemented my presentation of the rabbinic evidence.[7] Seán
Freyne and Martin Goodman have improved our knowledge of
ancient Galilee and thus furnished a more refined framework for
the historical understanding of Jesus and the Gospels.[8] Though
helpful and complementary in many ways, I find J. D. Crossan's
chapter on 'Magician and Prophet' in his recent book historically
insensitive since the title 'magician' applied to Jesus (*pace* Morton
Smith) is quite unsuitable, as is the epithet, 'peasant' in the
subtitle of the volume.[9]

But all in all, when it comes to identifying the character of the
historical Jesus, my choice of charismatic healer – teacher –
prophet is now supported by almost the self-same short defini-
tions given in the works of two of the foremost New Testament
experts of today, Martin Hengel and E. P. Sanders.[10] Needless to
say, the present enquiry into the religion of Jesus will take this
understanding as its starting-point.

Pursuit of the authentic teaching of Jesus is in a sense even more
hazardous than an attempt to discover his historical contours.
Indeed, the only point on which students agree is that the Gospels
include much that did *not* originate with him. My first but

---

the indictment brought by the principal men among us, condemned him to the
cross, those who loved him from the very first did not cease to be attached to
him . . . And the tribe of the Christians, so called after him, has to this day not
disappeared' (*Ant.* xviii. 63f.).

[6]'Popular Religion in Ancient Israel', *JJS* 27 (1976), 1–22.

[7]Green, 'Palestinian Holy Men: Chrismatic Leadership and Rabbinic Tradition', *ANRW* ii. 19.2 (1979), 619–37; Bokser, 'Wonder-working and Rabbinic
Tradition. The Case of Hanina ben Dosa', *JSJ* 16 (1985), 42–92.

[8]Freyne, *Galilee from Alexander the Great to Hadrian* (1980); *Galilee, Jesus
and the Gospels* (1988); Goodman, *State and Society in Roman Galilee, AD
132–212* (1983).

[9]*The Historical Jesus: The Life of a Mediterranean Jewish Peasant* (1991),
137–67. Cf. Smith, *Jesus the Magician* (1978).

[10]Hengel, *The Charismatic Leader and his Followers* (1981); Sanders, *Jewish
Law from Jesus to the Mishnah* (1990), 3.

rudimentary and schematic venture to disentangle the true from the inauthentic resulted in *The Gospel of Jesus the Jew*, consisting of my three Riddell Memorial Lectures delivered at the University of Newcastle upon Tyne in 1981, and published under that title in the same year. They are included, slightly revised, in *Jesus and the World of Judaism*, chapters 2–4 (1983). Some guide-lines are laid down there to assist in the search, along a very rough path, for the genuine message of Jesus, and they comprise certain principles borrowed from form criticism, adapted and supplemented where necessary (*JWJ* 21–25). It would be quite inappropriate, however, to attach to these guide-lines the grandiloquent, but highly fashionable, label of *methodology*. In my opinion, research aiming to be innovative should not be bound by strict, predetermined rules. Indeed, although the claim coming from someone born in Hungary, educated in Belgium and France and citizen of the United Kingdom by naturalization only, may strike a faintly amusing note, I pride myself on being a true *British* pragmatist.[11]

Methodology, no doubt irrationally, makes me see red perhaps because more than once I have been rebuked by trans-Atlantic dogmatists for illegitimately arriving at the *right* conclusion, following a path not sanctioned by my critics' sacred rule book. My preferred procedure, which will be adhered to in the forthcoming pages too, starts with fixing the outer limits of a problem, before attempting to fill in, piece by piece, often after much trial and error, the blank areas within those boundaries. The only time in the past that I was involved in a quest bordering on the methodological, was when I wanted to clarify my own mind rather than lay down universally binding laws.[12]

I knew from personal experience that rabbinic literature, judiciously and sensitively handled, can throw valuable and sometimes unique light on the study of the Gospels. Indeed, its use for such a purpose has been customary since the seventeenth century, ever since John Lightfoot's *Horae Hebraicae et Talmudicae* (1658–78) saw the light of day, and especially after

[11]When Sir Isaiah Berlin, former President of my College, was told some years ago that I had just been described in a lecture in those terms, even mentioning my liking for 'muddling through', he muttered in my direction: 'The graft has taken, eh? It sometimes does.'

[12]'Jewish Studies and New Testament Interpretation', *JWJ* 74–88, 173–5. Originally published in *JJS* 33 (1982), 361–76.

the publication between 1922 and 1928 of the notorious four-volume Commentary to the New Testament from Talmud and Midrash (*Kommentar zum Neuen Testament aus Talmud und Midrasch*) by Hermann Strack and Paul Billerbeck. This work seemed to enjoy an authority almost greater than the Gospels themselves among New Testament scholars; they had no scruples about criticizing the latter, but not the *Kommentar*. However, more recently it has lost much of its reputation (*JWJ* 62–64). It has been known for a long time that comparison between the New Testament, dating to the late first century AD, and rabbinic literature, compiled roughly between 200 and 500, meets a serious chronological snag. Is it legitimate, one must ask, to use the more recent Mishnah, Talmud and Midrash in interpreting the older New Testament? The dilemma is felt more acutely today because with the Dead Sea Scrolls, scholarship now possesses a considerable body of comparative material contemporaneous with the first Christian writings or only slightly predating it, whereas prior to 1947 no such documentation was extant.

In the new circumstances, is it still justifiable to turn to Mishnah, Tosefta, Talmud, Midrash or Targum for help in establishing the meaning of the Gospels? No, reply unanimously the pan-Qumranists. Only the Scrolls belong to the right era; the rabbis should be ignored. Since a good many (most?) of the partisans of this school are largely unfamiliar with Talmudic texts, they are only too eager to welcome this blanket dispensation from the need to acquaint themselves with such difficult writings!

To clarify the issue, one must proceed step by step. Is it permissible to use later rabbinic literature to explain the earlier Gospels? The answer is clearly negative if the material contained in rabbinic documents definitely postdates by a century or more the New Testament in substance and not only in formulation or redaction, or if the similarity between them is due to the rabbis' dependence on the evangelists.

However, it is most unlikely, indeed unthinkable, that the Jewish sages would directly borrow from the Gospels. Indeed, with sporadic and questionable exceptions, no rabbinic awareness of the Gospels, let alone willingness to learn from them, can be proved. Even negative reactions to the New Testament are rare and belong to a relatively late period, the third or rather the fourth century, when the Christian church already constituted a threat to Judaism. Equally improbable is the theory that all the contents recorded in the rabbinic compilations were created in the Talmudic age. Both the evidence included in the writings themselves, and critical scholarship, tend to show that these documents largely consist of teachings dating from earlier centuries and handed down, often re-shaped and re-edited, by the redactors of the Talmud, etc.

Moreover, as it is impossible to assert with any degree of confidence that Jewish works similar or identical in form and content to rabbinic Targum and Midrash existed in writing in the first century AD or before, it would be wholly unsound to postulate that the evangelists used such purely conjectural literature, and further assume that they were substantially the same as the much more recent texts known to us.

The hypothesis I prefer would envisage a common *source*, written or oral – it may be called Jewish (doctrinal, legal, exegetical) tradition – firm in substance but variable in shape, on which both the evangelists and the later rabbis depended.

If, furthermore, the New Testament, in particular the Synoptic Gospels, and rabbinic literature cease to be viewed as self-contained and autonomous entities, and are held to be parts of a continuously evolving Jewish religious and literary creativity, then the message of Jesus and its reverberations on Palestinian soil can be perceived dynamically as a first-century AD stage of a long process of development where Bible, Apocrypha, Pseudepigrapha, Dead Sea Scrolls, Philo, New Testament, Josephus, Mishnah, Tosefta, Targum, Midrash, Talmud, liturgy and early Jewish mysticism mutually supplement, correct, enlighten and explain each other.

In brief, instead of elevating the New Testament to the status of an independent, and doctrinally superior corpus, with centrality, finality and ultimacy, as theologians are often inclined to do, and downgrading rabbinic literature to a mere ancillary role, we shall treat it in this enquiry into the religion preached and practised by Jesus as one particular sector on the general map of Jewish cultural history. And if it works, perhaps someone will be tempted to extricate from it general methodological principles for further use!

*

The task facing us is new, at least relatively speaking, for after Bultmann's revolution, the thought of Jesus was deemed as inaccessible as his life. Scholars shied away from reconstructing the teaching of the Master and set out instead to investigate the *theology* of the New Testament. (In Bultmann's own *Theologie des Neuen Testaments* (^{5}1965) the preaching of Jesus, the presupposition and not part of that theology, is covered in 34 out of the volume's 620 pages.) More recently, an even less adventurous tendency has prevailed and instead of enquiring into the teaching of the whole New Testament, attention has been narrowed to focus only on individual evangelists or Paul.

Our investigation will be pursued in three stages. First Jesus' relationship to the living Judaism of his age, and the nature, style and content of his own preaching will be presented in the light of a detailed historical analysis (chapters 2, 3 and 4). Next, the idea of God as King and Father will be considered in the atmosphere of Jesus' eschatological enthusiasm (chapters 5–6), this leading naturally to the chapter entitled, 'Jesus, the Religious Man'. Finally, a brief epilogue is intended to bring into sharp relief the difference between that religion and historic, ecclesiastical Christianity.

2

Jesus and the Law: The Judaism of Jesus

Any study of Jesus undertaken within the framework of traditional New Testament scholarship is sooner or later bound to confront his attitude to 'the Law'. Did he, or did he not, observe the Torah of Moses? More importantly, did he envisage it as still enduring, or did he intend to abrogate, replace or transform it? These questions are taken to be so simple, and the answers so predictable, that few writers bother to enquire what they really entail, and as a result a largely ill-conceived, often misleading, and by definition confused debate ensues.

I The Meaning of 'the Law'[1]

Let us face the facts. The Law of Moses is not restricted to ritualistic minutiae, but encompasses the entire sphere of Jewish life. It lays down rules for agriculture, commerce, and the ownership of immovable and movable property. It deals with matrimony and its financial implications; with compensations for material damages suffered by a person, or for bodily harm inflicted on him by men or by beasts owned by men. The Torah legislates about theft, rape, homicide and many other civil and criminal matters over which judges and tribunals had competence. In brief, a charter for civilized life constitutes the bulk of the Mosaic laws. Did Jesus reject these? The Synoptic Gospels, our primary witnesses, give no support to such a theory. Moreover, since it is nowhere stated or implied in them that Jesus failed to pay his debts, beat up his opponents or committed adultery, it is

[1] On the general problem, see J. D. M. Derrett, 'Law and Society in Jesus' World', *ANRW* 25.1 (1982), 477–564 and, especially, E. P. Sanders, *Jewish Law from Jesus to the Mishnah: Five Studies* (1990).

reasonable to infer that he accepted, respected and observed the laws and customs regulating private and public existence which were in force among his compatriots in his age.[2]

In addition to these sectors of social life which today we would call secular, though the Jews and other peoples in antiquity believed them to be governed by divine statutes, the Torah concerned itself also with 'religious' matters. These include, to begin with, the Temple with its sacrifices, and not surprisingly, the tithes, cultic taxes and other contributions to priests and Levites. Since they were the chief organizers of Jewish society in the biblical age, their offices, rights and privileges received much attention in scripture, and subsequently gained seemingly exaggerated importance in the eyes of the sacerdotal redactors of the Pentateuch and its later priestly and lay interpreters. Ritual cleanness and the dietary rules were also essentially associated with the cult. People who came into contact with a *niddah* (a menstruating woman) or with a corpse, or simply indulged in legitimate sex, were not obliged to appear before a court of law. The consequence of such acts or infringements was that the persons involved were excluded, or more precisely excluded themselves, from participation in Temple worship until they regained a state of purity, usually by means of a ritual bath, although no ceremony of cleansing is prescribed in the Bible for eating forbidden food (cf. Sanders, *Jewish Law*, 24).

The Sabbath legislation basically belongs to the same cultic domain, although it is not directly linked to the Jerusalem Temple. Nevertheless, it represents an entirely different category since according to the Bible and post-biblical law, Sabbath breakers, or rather some of them, were liable to the death penalty.[3]

---

[2]While the historical authenticity of the Gospel polemics with Pharisees and other groups is more than doubtful, it is, nevertheless, highly significant for the general portrayal of Jesus that when asked whether Jews should pay taxes to Rome, he is presented as advocating compliance with the imperial demands (Mark 12.17; Matt. 22.21; Luke 20.25).

[3]The Decalogue (Ex. 20.8–11; Deut. 5.12–15) simply prohibits work on the Sabbath. The forbidden acts are specified only incidentally in the Bible: travel (Ex. 16.29), ploughing (Ex. 34.21), lighting fire (Ex. 35.3), gathering sticks (Num. 15.32–36) and engaging in commerce (Neh. 10.31). The penalty for not keeping the Sabbath is indicated only once in the particular case of the man collecting firewood in the desert (Num. 15.35–36). We have to wait until the Book of Jubilees (50.6–9) in mid-second century BC, and the statutes of the

How Jesus distinguished between the licit and the illicit on the seventh day will have to be discussed later; but it may be remarked at once that there is no record of him being denounced to the authorities in charge of Jewish criminal law on account of public misbehaviour in this respect. He is not even criticized openly for healing on the Sabbath. The nearest comment reported in this regard is a rebuke addressed by the president of a Galilean synagogue to his congregants for asking to be cured on the Sabbath rather than on any of the six weekdays (Luke 13.14). If, as is often claimed, the evangelists aimed at inculcating, in a fictional account of the life of Jesus, Christian doctrine such as the annulment of the Sabbath legislation, to members of the Gentile church, they did a pitiful job which falls far short of proving their alleged thesis.

II   The Gospel Image of Jesus as an Observant Jew

More positively, the general picture of Jesus emerging from the Synoptic Gospels is that of a Jew who conforms to the principal religious practices of his nation. It is not essential at this juncture to investigate the authenticity of the passages in question. What matters most is the overall impression given by the narrators, all the more so since it conflicts with the Pauline church's antipathy towards all forms of 'Judaizing'.

To begin with, Jesus is regularly associated with synagogues, the centres of worship and teaching. There are general references to his frequenting them in Galilee, sometimes specifically on the Sabbath. Two of these synagogues, one at Capernaum (Mark 1.21; Luke 4.31) and the other at Nazareth (Luke 4.15), are explicitly named. He was, it seems, a familiar figure in those circles, a much sought-after teacher and preacher of great originality, as well as a highly admired charismatic healer and exorcist (Mark 1.39; Matt. 4.23; Luke 4.44, etc.).[4]

Damascus Document (10.14–12.6) half a century later, before encountering the first attempts at systematization, and until the relevant section of the Mishnah (Shab. 7.2) before receiving a detailed list of thirty-nine classes of proscribed action. Both Jubilees (50.8) and the Mishnah (Sanh. 7.4) declare Sabbath breaking to be punishable by death, viz. by stoning at the end of a trial according to the Mishnah. See further Sanders, *Jewish Law*, 16–19.

[4] Cf. *JJ*, 22–31.

If one relies on the Synoptic Gospels, leaving aside the
unhistorical infancy narrative of Luke, the link between Jesus and
the Jerusalem temple is tenuously documented since only a single
visit to the capital is mentioned there. Even so, he appears in all
three Gospels as a man who, in obedience to biblical law,
attended the pilgrim festival of the Passover. He visited the
sanctuary, where the unholy atmosphere reigning in the
merchants' quarter provoked him to a violent intervention which
may have substantially contributed to sealing his fate. Nevertheless, once he calmed down, he is said to have taught every day,
outwardly unmolested, though probably not unwatched by the
authorities, in the Temple courtyard (Mark 11.15; 14.49; Matt.
21.12; 26.55; Luke 19.45; 22.53, etc.).

It may be worth noting that he is nowhere presented as participating in acts of worship. In fact, this applies also to his
attendance at the synagogue with one exception. Luke 4.16–21
reports an episode in Nazareth where Jesus took public part in the
service: he read the prophetic portion of the Bible (Isa. 61), and
followed this with a fulfilment interpretation of the passage
reminiscent of the kind of Bible exegesis for which the Dead Sea
Scrolls are famous (cf. below, 'Jesus the Teacher', 61–66). In both
Temple and synagogue he played the role of a teacher, and
although all three Synoptics ascribe to him the prophetic doctrine
identifying the sanctuary as a house of prayer (Mark 11.17; Matt.
21.13; Luke 19.46), nowhere do we find mention of his having
recited there, or for that matter in a synagogue, the usual psalms
and benedictions.

Anticipating our examination of the place of prayer in the
religious behaviour of Jesus, it should be pointed out that the
Gospel writers seek to describe him, probably correctly, as chiefly
interested in non-communal prayer. We mostly find Jesus
addressing God in solitary places, or at least at some distance
from other people: in the desert (Mark 1.35; Luke 5.15), on a
mountain (Mark 6.46; Matt. 14.23; Luke 6.12), in the garden of
Gethsemane away from his disciples (Mark 14.32–41; Matt.
26.36–44; Luke 22.41–45). His only non-liturgical blessing in
public follows the laying on of his hands on children, but even
here prayer is referred to only in Matthew 19.13, not in the
corresponding verses of Mark and Luke. This consistent omission of cultic worship is attributable to Jesus' stress on the

private, unostentatious and even secret character of prayer (Matt. 6.5–6; Mark 12.40; Matt. 23.14; Luke 20.47). By contrast, after the Ascension, the apostles 'were continually in the Temple blessing God' (Luke 24.53); 'day by day attending the Temple together' (Acts 2.46); 'Peter and John were going up to the Temple at the hour of prayer' (Acts 3.1). However, the most conservatively Jewish of them all was Paul, who not only prayed in the sanctuary (Acts 22.17), but is the only Christian to be described as undergoing a ceremonial purification and presenting an offering in the Temple (Acts 21.26)!

In addition to being a synagogue-goer and a Temple pilgrim, Jesus is pictured as an observer of particular commandments of ritual import. Chief among these is his keeping, or more concretely eating, the Passover (Mark 14.12–16; Matt 26.17–19; Luke 22.7–15). This was a home or family celebration, though in the Second Temple era it was also linked to the sanctuary where the Passover lamb was slaughtered. So, despite the problems it raises for the chronology of the crucifixion, the evangelists did not hesitate to impress on their readers that Jesus faithfully performed the commandments relating to this festival.[5]

At this juncture, it should be noted that the historicity of the Last Supper as a Passover meal is a hotly debated subject, the solution of which does not directly concern us here. The fact that the three synoptists assert that Jesus gave instructions for the preparation of the paschal ritual suffices to prove that they considered him to be Law-abiding. John, it is true, does not refer to the event; nevertheless, he mentions several Passover pilgrimages by Jesus, which would imply that his observance of the essential rites of the festival was taken for granted.

In parenthesis, the historical authenticity of the establishment of the eucharist as a permanent institution depends not only whether the meal was really a Passover supper celebrated on the correct date – with the ensuing problem of the crucifixion taking place on the feast day, but also on whether he ever envisaged the creation of an enduring church (cf. *JWJ*, x, 50–51, and

---

[5]For a detailed study of the festival, cf. J. B. Segal, *The Hebrew Passover from the Earliest Time to A.D. 70* (1963). If Jesus partook of the Passover supper on the correct date, his trial and execution, aided and abetted by Jewish officialdom, occurred on the feast-day itself, a quasi impossible eventuality.

pp. 188–94, 214–15 below). In any case, the imagery of eating a man's body and especially drinking his blood (Mark 14.22–24; Matt. 26.26–28; Luke 22.17–20), even after allowance is made for metaphorical language, strikes a totally foreign note in a Palestinian Jewish cultural setting (cf. John 6.52). With their profoundly rooted blood taboo, Jesus' listeners would have been overcome with nausea at hearing such words.

Two other Gospel passages, one containing a descriptive feature and the other conveying a story, will further contribute to the general definition of the religious leanings of Jesus. On separate occasions, the evangelists reveal, as it were fortuitously, that in conformity with the Mosaic precept (Num. 15.38–40), he wore a garment the hem of which was fitted with 'tassels' (*kraspeda* = *tsitsiyot*). In both cases, we are dealing with healing narratives (Matt. 9.20; Luke 8.44 and Mark 6.56; Matt. 14.36). Whether the mention of the touching of the lower extremity of the charismatic's clothes simply indicates humility and awe on the part of the person seeking a supernatural cure, or whether in the popular imagination the tassels were endowed with miraculous power, need not be determined here.[6]

Another incidental pointer to Jesus' observance of the Law, viz. the duty to pay the half-shekel Temple tax, occurs in Matthew 17.24–27. The episode is introduced as of secondary importance; it appears in only one Gospel and is told, if I am not mistaken, with poker-faced humour. The first fish Peter would catch would hold in its mouth a shekel coin sufficient for both Jesus and Peter to acquit themselves of their obligation so that the collectors would not be scandalized. Whether historical or not in its essence, the story portrays Jesus as willingly contributing, like (in principle at least) all the Jewish adult men of Palestine and the diaspora, to the legally ordained upkeep of the Temple of Jerusalem.[7]

---

[6]The children requesting the charismatic miracle-worker Hanan, grandson of Honi the circle-drawer, to end a drought, seized the fringe of his mantle (*shippule gelimeh*) and cried, 'Abba, Abba, give us rain!' (bTaan. 23b). A rabbinic anecdote preserved in the Tannaitic midrash Sifre on Numbers 115 (ed. S. H. Horovitz, 128–9) and in the Talmud (bMen. 44a), recounts how a young Jew, getting ready to go to bed with a beautiful high-class prostitute, was prevented from sinning by the miraculous intervention of the tassels of his garment.

[7]On the half-shekel tax, see *HJP* II, 271–2. For the additional Qumran evidence, see *DJD* VII (4Q513) and *DSSE*(3), 297–8. Cf. also Sanders, *Jewish Law*, 49–51.

III   The Authentic and Presumed Teaching of Jesus
on the Law

Substantial libraries have been written on the problem of how to
discern the genuine teaching of Jesus, separating the authentic
message from sayings formulated by the early church and placed
on the lips of the Master. Criteria have been devised to distinguish
the two, though professional New Testament scholarship during
the last fifty or sixty years has tended to be pessimistic about such
a possibility and has shown more interest in the theology of the
New Testament or in that of an individual evangelist than in the
pristine teaching of Jesus himself.[8]

Admitting that certainty in most cases is beyond the student's
reach, and that the best he can usually hope for is to demonstrate
a high degree of verisimilitude, I would like to preface my enquiry
with two basic assumptions. Both derive, positively or negatively,
from the *cui bono* principle: Does anyone stand to gain from
inventing the teaching in question? A saying which serves the
interest of early, especially Gentile, Christianity and is not in
harmony with the overall outlook of Jesus, is likely to be a
product of the primitive church. By contrast, if we are faced with
a doctrine contrary to, and impossible to reconcile with, ecclesiastical needs, a good case can be made out for its historical
authenticity.

Many of the utterances of Jesus on the Law demonstrably
belong to this category provided that an objection specially raised
against their genuineness is discarded. A good proportion of
Jesus' pertinent doctrine has survived in Matthew alone. But, it is
sometimes argued, this writer of a Judaeo-Christian Gospel
superimposed Jewish colouring on certain sayings of Jesus
originally uttered in universal terms. Though such an understanding of the doctrinal development in Palestinian Christianity
is, in my opinion, intrinsically unsound, I will not reject it without
further ado, but will first seek to establish Jesus' view with the
help of sources not exclusively Matthaean, and examine afterwards how the special material transmitted by this evangelist
relates to the tradition preserved in the other sources.

---

[8]Cf. *JWJ*, 18–25. For an interesting, though not entirely successful attempt,
see N. Perrin, *Rediscovering the Teaching of Jesus* (1967).

1. *Jesus' adherence to the cultic Law (Mark 1.44; Matt. 8.64; Luke 5.14)*

In addition to the portrayal of Jesus as a Torah-observing Jew, including such non-ethical details as the wearing of tassels or the payment of the Temple-tax, all three Synoptic Gospels report that after curing a leper, he enjoined him to appear before a priest for examination, and when declared by him 'clean', to perform the sacrificial rites prescribed in Leviticus 14.1–7.

> See that you say nothing to anyone; but go, show yourself to the priest, and offer for your cleansing what Moses commanded (Mark 1.44).

The picture reflects perfectly the situation obtaining in one of the Dead Sea Scrolls where special emphasis is laid on the priestly monopoly of the treatment of leprosy (CD 13.3–7). Jesus expressly instructs the man not merely to present himself before a priest *qua* public health official, but also to attend the appropriate Mosaic ceremony. The episode, despite the mention by Matthew (8.1), in an editorial phrase (cf. *HST*, 351), of the presence of 'great crowds', appears to have taken place without outside observers; otherwise the secrecy injunction would be meaningless. Hence, the only logical inference is that Jesus freely insisted, even in a purely ritual context, on strict adherence to the Torah.[9]

2. *The validity of the Torah as a whole*

The so-called source Q (cf. *IDBS*, 715–6), consisting of doctrinal statements, lacking in Mark but common to Luke and Matthew, though often appearing in different contexts, contains a proverbial saying of Jesus which, *prima facie* irreconcilably contradicts Pauline and Christian antinomianism. Not surprisingly, the redactors of both Gospels attempt to weaken its impact, but the very continuance of the saying implies that Jesus did not envisage any possible cancellation, whether fully or in part, of the Mosaic dispensation during the limited future which in his

[9]The correctness of this interpretation is supported by the noticeable differences in Luke's account of the healing of ten lepers (Luke 17.11–19) which contains no reference to the observance of the ritual prescriptions. Typical of Luke is also the remark that only the one Samaritan, and not the nine Jews, returned to thank Jesus.

view belonged to the then present age. Luke's version (16.17) reads:

> It is easier for heaven and earth to pass away than for one tittle of the Law to drop.

The logion asserts the permanence of the smallest detail of the Torah.[10] Luke's statement is absolute; in the divinely predetermined world-order, the disintegration of the cosmos is less difficult to envisage than the loss of a single 'tittle' of the Law. Since apart from Judaeo-Christianity, which the third evangelist could not conceivably represent, no branch of the primitive church would have welcomed a straight assertion of the permanency of the Law, it is truly astonishing that it has survived in its blunt simplicity. Luke did not interfere editorially with the saying itself but, as will be seen presently, sought by other means to set a limit to the duration of the Law's validity.

In his parallel formulation, Matthew declares:

> For truly I say to you, till heaven and earth pass away, not an iota nor a tittle will pass from the Law until all is accomplished (Matt. 5.18).

Here the evangelist, in addition to supplying what appears to be a more idiomatic Jewish phrase, despite its Hellenized form (*iota*),[11] has introduced a further temporal clause: 'until all is accomplished'.

Taken separately, the logion 'until all is accomplished', may simply stress the continuously binding nature of the Torah, which would suit perfectly the needs of the Palestinian church. So also

---

[10]For Greek use, see Philo, *Flacc.* 131. The term alludes to artistic embellishments of Hebrew letters used by Bible scribes and known as *qots* (thorn, hook) or *keter* (crown). An ironical story, preserved in the Babylonian Talmud (bMen. 29b), describes God as a Torah-scribe adding 'crowns' to the letters. He explains to Moses that the purpose of the decorations is to enable the future Rabbi Akiba in the second century AD to attach heaps of legal refinements to each and every 'hook'.

[11]The iota and the tittle, or *yod* and *qots* in Hebrew, appear side by side in a rabbinic story, independent of the Gospel tradition, in which king Solomon is portrayed as meddling with the Law. 'He said: Why did the Holy one blessed be he say (regarding the king), "He shall not multiply (*yrbh*) wives for himself" (Deut. 17.17)? Only in order that "his heart may not go astray". *I* will multiply (*'rbh*) them but my heart will not go astray. Our rabbis said: At that moment the letter *yod* rose and prostrated itself before the Holy one blessed be he and said: Lord of the universe, did you not say that not a letter shall ever be destroyed from the Torah? Behold, Solomon arose and destroyed me (sub-

does the following verse, which is generally held to be a Jewish-Christian creation: 'Whoever relaxes one of the least of these commandments and teaches men so, shall be called least in the kingdom of heaven; but he who does them and teaches them shall be called great in the kingdom of heaven' (Matt. 5.19). However, within the wider framework of Gentile Christianity which provided the lasting home for this Gospel, the phrase is likely to have been perceived as alluding either to the end of the Torah of the Old Testament by virtue of the establishment of the New Covenant, or to a Judaeo-Christian situation prevailing after the destruction of Jerusalem in AD 70, when a substantial segment of the Law, all the Temple legislation, ceased to be practicable.[12]

Luke, as has been noted, reproduces in his Gospel an unconditional declaration concerning the continuity of the Law, thus creating a serious difficulty for the Gentile church. He then endeavours to bypass it by linking it to a separate saying aimed at determining the position of John the Baptist, and that of the Torah, in the eschatological order:

> The Law and the Prophets were until John; since then the good news of the kingdom of God is preached, and every one enters it violently (Luke 16.16).

This would mean that in the post-John period the Torah pertains to the past, and thus the shocking impact of the following verse is to a large extent preempted. Matthew 11.13 is similar but more expertly formulated in that it envisages the Law as playing a prophetic role: 'For all the prophets and the Law prophesied until John.' A similar prophetic fulfilment idea is incorporated into Matthew's introductory phrase prefixed to 5.18. 'Think not that I have come to abolish the Law and the Prophets; I have come not to abolish them but to fulfil them' (Matt. 5.17).[13]

------

stituting an *aleph* for a *yod*, i.e., changing *yrbh* to *'rbh*). One (letter) today, another tomorrow until the entire Torah is destroyed. The Holy one blessed be he said to it: Solomon and a thousand like him may (set out to) destroy, but I will not let one tittle from you be destroyed.' (Ex. R. 6.1).

[12]Cf. W. D. Davies, *The Sermon on the Mount* (1964), 334; *JWJ*, 161, n. 16.

[13]Cf. *JWJ*, 161, n. 16. The 'abolish'/'fulfil' antonyms correspond to the Hebrew-Aramaic *lebattel-lebattela/leqayyem-leqayyema*. A good parallel is furnished by the Mishnah: 'Whoever fulfils the Torah in poverty, will fulfil it later on in wealth; and whoever abolishes the Torah (i.e. disregards it as though null and void) in wealth, will abolish it later on in poverty' (mAb. 4.9).

In sum, bearing in mind the obvious sense of the words in Luke 16.17 (and in Matthew 5.18), compared to the confused artificiality of Luke's effort to eviscerate it, and to the Matthean redactor's learned contrivance to provide it with meaning in the post-destruction Jewish-Christian world of the late first century AD, the historically-minded reader of the passage is bound to conclude that some kind of restriction of the universal and permanent obligatory nature of the Mosaic Law was an absolute necessity for the primitive church and that in consequence the only acceptable explanation for its unconditional inclusion in Luke, and even in Matthew, is that it was an authentic dictum of Jesus which the evangelist felt unable to suppress. Obliged to hand it down, he did so in an 'interpreted' form.

3. Did Jesus ever contradict the Law?

A straight answer to this question must be firmly negative. (The question of equating forgiveness of sins with blasphemy will be dealt with later (pp.191–2). Nowhere in the Gospels is Jesus depicted as deliberately setting out to deny or substantially alter any commandment of the Torah *in itself*. The controversial statements turn either on conflicting laws where one has to override the other, or on the precise understanding of the full extent of a precept. Both classes may have ritual as well as ethical-religious ingredients.

To be more explicit, Jesus' attitude to Sabbath legislation, especially in connection with healing, but also in the episode of the disciples' plucking corn, gave rise, as has been noted, to some concern. Likewise, his view on *kashrut*, i.e. precepts relating to clean and unclean food, is often held by modern Christian interpreters of the Gospels to be untraditional. Moving from the ritual to the moral domain, his order to a would-be disciple to follow him at the expense of his duty to bury his father, is also construed by New Testament scholars as impiety from a Jewish point of view. Finally, the contrast between, 'You have heard that it was said', introducing a biblical commandment, and, 'but I say to you', is seen as proof that he was in fact prepared to disregard the Torah, or more gravely still, to abolish the 'old' Law and replace it with a new code.

(a) Jesus and ritual laws

(i) The Sabbath

Healings said to have been performed by Jesus on the Sabbath day are few and far between. Of the three events recorded, the case of the man with a wasted hand is attested by all three Synoptic evangelists (Mark 3.1–6; Matt. 12.9–14; Luke 6.6–11), but the cure of the woman with a curved spine (Luke 13.10–17) and that of a man suffering from dropsy are witnessed by Luke alone (Luke 13.10–17; 14.1–6). Conservative and unfriendly observers found Jesus' behaviour disturbing, though not patently illegal. Hence questions had to be raised. According to the Gospel accounts, they were formulated either by his critics, 'Is it lawful to heal on the Sabbath?' (Matt. 12.10), or by Jesus himself for didactic purposes, 'Is it lawful to do good or to do harm, to save life or to kill?' (Mark 3.4; Luke 6.9; cf. Luke 14.3).[14]

We are faced here with the habitual conflict between commandments, and with the question of which of the two outweighs the other. The general principle has never been in doubt in Judaism: the saving of life always has priority. In connection with Ex. 31.13–16, the Tannaitic midrash, Mekhilta de Rabbi Ishmael (ed. Lauterbach III, 197–9) poses the question, 'Whence do we know that the duty of saving life supersedes the Sabbath laws?' Two second-century AD rabbis answer in the affirmative by means of *a fortiori* reasonings: circumcision affecting only one part of the body is licit on the Sabbath day (Eleazar ben Azariah); execution of a murderer (i.e. the *taking* of life) supersedes the Temple service; Temple service has precedence over the Sabbath (R. Akiba); how much more so the *saving* of the whole body, of life. Or more straightforwardly, 'Regard for life overrules the Sabbath' (bYoma 85b). Moreover, in the case of any lingering doubt concerning the potential severity of an illness, legal presumption favours intervention and the Mishnah (Yoma 8.6) cites the principle: 'Whenever there is doubt concerning life being in danger (the case discussed is a sore throat!), this overrides the

---

[14]The question is rhetorical and the antithetic formula is almost self-explanatory. It is never permitted, on the Sabbath or any other day, to do harm or to kill. The emphasis must therefore lie on the positive act: to do good, i.e. to save life. Indeed, by implication those who abstain from the latter become guilty of murder.

Sabbath.' Whether Jesus himself felt it necessary to defend his actions verbally, or more likely, his Jewish-Christian followers did so at a later stage, his own basic attitude and his, or his disciples', arguments are the same as those of the rabbis: a Jew may lift a sheep fallen into a pit on the Sabbath; *a fortiori* human life may be saved (Matt. 12. 11–12); he may pull out of a well both his son and his ox (Luke 14.5).[15]

In brief, according to the words placed by Matthew (12.12) on the lips of Jesus, 'It is lawful to do good on the Sabbath.' The whole debate seems to be, however, a storm in a tea-cup since none of the Sabbath cures of Jesus entailed 'work', but were effected by word of mouth, or at most, by the laying on of hands or other simple physical contact.[16]

It is worth noting that in Luke's account (13.10–17), the healing of a woman suffering from curvature of the spine, portrayed in the language of magic as someone 'bound' by the devil, is described as an act of 'loosing': 'Does not each of you on the Sabbath untie his ox or his ass from the manger, and lead it away to water it? And ought not this woman, a daughter of Abraham whom Satan bound for eighteen years, be loosed from this bond on the Sabbath day?' Here, interestingly, the metaphorical idiom, to bind and to loose, is used as an *a fortiori* argument against the customary tying and untying of domestic animals on the Sabbath, although in principle both acts are characterized as work in the Mishnah (Shab. 7.2).

The second allegation that Jesus contradicted common opinion in the same domain of sabbatical rest is linked with an episode, no doubt didactic rather than historical, which figures in all three Synoptics (Mark 2.23–28; Matt. 12.1–8; Luke 6.1–5). Crossing a field on the Sabbath, his disciples, not Jesus himself, plucked ears of corn, possibly even rubbed them in their hands (Luke 6.1), and ate them. Whilst doing this in someone else's field did not amount to theft according to biblical law (Deut. 23.25), it could be understood as breaking the Sabbath rules which, together with

---

[15]Such was, it would seem, the middle of the way opinion. The Damascus Document suggests that the Essenes, noted for their rigoristic Sabbath observance, adopted a much harsher line of action, prohibiting help to an animal when it gives birth, and forbidding its rescue from a cistern or a pit on the sacred day of rest (CD 11.13–14). Cf. L. H. Schiffman, *The Halakhah at Qumran* (1975), 122–3.

[16]Cf. *JWJ*, 46–7; Sanders, *Jewish Law*, 19–23.

thirty-eight other acts of 'work', prohibit 'harvesting' (mShab. 7.2) under which heading plucking corn may be listed. The main argument, preserved in the three synoptics (Mark 2.25–26; Matt. 12.3–4; Luke 6.3–4), by which the breach of the Sabbath is excused is that hunger (which may lead to starvation and thus to death) falls into the category of danger to life. Hence the relief of hunger, i.e. the safeguarding of life, overrides the Sabbath law, in the same way as it sets aside, in the case of David and his hungry soldiers, the ban on laymen on eating the bread of Presence destined to priests only (cf. Lev. 24.5–9 and I Sam. 21. 1–7).[17]

The short answer attributed to Jesus in Mark 2.27, 'The Sabbath was made for man, not man for the Sabbath', is also firmly rooted in rabbinic thought. Still in the same Mekhilta extract, uninfluenced by the New Testament, R. Simeon ben Menasiah, a late second-century AD Tannaitic teacher, voices the same doctrine, in connection with Ex. 31.14, 'You shall keep the Sabbath for it is holy *to you*': 'The Sabbath is delivered up *to you* and not you to the Sabbath'. The same exegesis is handed down in the name of R. Jonathan ben Joseph, a pupil of R. Ishmael (bYoma 85b). The saying put in Jesus's mouth is surely not the source of the rabbinic dictum: it rather suggests that the idea had been current for some time before second-century Tannaim furnished it with exegetical justification. Generally speaking, Sabbath observance in the second century, and probably also in the first, was subservient to the essential well-being of a Jew. In the words of Rabbi Nathan, 'Behold it is said, "Therefore the children of Israel shall keep the Sabbath to observe it throughout their generations" (Ex. 31.16) – one Sabbath may be profaned that he may keep many (further) Sabbaths' (Mekhilta, ed. Lauterbach III, 198–9).

(ii) The food laws

Leaving aside the controversy in Mark 7 and Matthew 15

---

[17]Matt. 12.5 introduces another justification: plucking ears of corn for a valid purpose is no greater infringement of the Sabbath than the 'work' done by the priests in the Sanctuary on days of rest. In the Mekhilta passage quoted above (p. 22), R. Akiba puts forward the same argument, namely that Temple service countermands the Sabbath rules. Finally in Matt. 12.7, the famous prophetic axiom is invoked whereby demands of morality take precedence over ceremonial rules: 'I desire mercy, and not sacrifice' (Hos. 6.6).

concerning traditional rules relating to the washing of hands before meals which may be due to a higher esteem for the Bible than for ancestral customs – the culprits are once more some of the disciples, not Jesus himself – attention may be focussed on the crucial assertion of Mark that Jesus declared all foods clean (Mark 7.19), and thereby annulled a substantial segment of the Torah of Moses (cf. *JWJ*, 46 and n. 19). The debate is not yet closed and learned arguments continue to be deployed with a view to determining Jesus' standpoint vis-à-vis the halakhah current in his age.[18] But it would seem that New Testament scholars involve themselves here in discussions which are beside the point. On the one hand, they envisage Jesus as though he were a rabbi concerned with legal niceties, when any serious reading of the Gospels should reveal that he did not belong to that ilk. More particularly, whatever he meant to convey by 'Hear and understand: not what goes into the mouth defiles a man, but what comes out of the mouth, this defiles a man' (Matt. 15.11–12; Mark 7.14–15), a maxim excellently interpreted by Sanders (*Jewish Law*, 28), it was surely not an abrogation of the dietary laws. Indeed, if the clause 'purifying all foods', figuring in Mark 7.19, but not in Matthew 15.17, is correctly paraphrased as 'Thus he declared all foods clean', it can only be seen as a gloss introduced by the redactor of Mark, having nothing to do with the original narrative, and even less with Jesus. This is all the more likely since the first generation of his followers lived in total ignorance of the revocation of the distinction beween clean and unclean food. Peter's reaction to the command by a heavenly voice, 'Kill and eat!', in the course of a vision of all kinds of animals held in a sheet, is an instinctive and explosive, 'No, Lord, for I have never eaten anything that is common or unclean' (Acts 10.13–14). Again, to the great annoyance of Paul and Barnabas, Peter 'and the rest of the Jews' in the Christian church of Antioch, felt obliged to abandon table fellowship with Gentile Christians which they had happily practised prior to the visit of 'men from James', i.e. strictly observant or 'Judaizing' members of the Jerusalem

[18]Roger P. Booth, *Jesus and the Laws of Purity: Tradition History and Legal History in Mark 7* (1986), and in particular, E. P. Sanders, *Jewish Law*, chapters I, III and IV.

community (Gal. 2.11–14). These accounts would make no sense
at all if Jesus had in fact 'declared all foods clean'.[19]

In sum, whether in the domain of the Sabbath laws, or in that of
dietary regulations, it cannot be maintained that Jesus opposed
their observance. His approach to the Torah and his perception
of its main message may have borne an individual mark, but
neither in general, nor on any particular point, can he be
identified as an antinomian teacher.[20]

(b) Jesus and moral laws

(i) Filial piety

The bulk of Jesus' teaching on ethical matters is linked to a
direct or indirect interpretation of the Decalogue. His implicit
adherence to the fifth commandment is manifest in his reproach
of irreligiosity addressed to a group of Jerusalem Pharisees or
scribes visiting Galilee (Mark 7.1; Matt. 15.1). They are charged
with having elevated the fulfilment of a vow requiring a donation
to the Temple, a traditional rule known as *qorban*, above the duty
of filial support of parents, although the latter derives from the
divine injunction, 'Honour your father and your mother' (Ex.
20.12; Deut. 5.16).[21]

---

[19]On the interpretation of Mark 7. 14–22, see *JJ*, 28–29, 232. Note also Julius
Wellhausen's exegesis where the Greek *aphedrōn*, like its substitute, *ochetos*, in
codex D, is taken in the sense of 'intestinal canal': 'Der Darmkanal reinigt die
Speisen, indem er das Unreine von ihnen ausscheidet. Naturalia non sunt turpia'
(*Das Evangelium Marci* (1903), 58).

[20]In the light of this discussion, one is stupefied to read in works written by
scholars of renown in New Testament circles statements such as the following:
'There can be no doubt that Jesus, through his entire conduct, again and again
ostentatiously transgressed the Old Testament commandment to observe the
Sabbath and had little concern for the Old Testament laws relating to ritual
purity (Eduard Schweizer, *Jesus* (1971), 32). The charge that Jesus committed
blasphemy by forgiving sins will be dealt with below, p. 192.

[21]The detail, unsolicited by the general run of the story, that the legal experts
were visitors from the capital, lends some verisimilitude to the historicity of the
narrative. In the first century AD, Pharisee presence was scarcely attested in
Galilee. Cf. *JJ*, 56–7. On the other hand, it may be pointed out that the problem
of *qorban* is a Jerusalem issue, which does not seem to be the most natural
thought-association for a Galilean popular teacher. Consequently in its present
form the argument probably derives from the anti-Pharisee polemics of the
Judaeo-Christian church (cf. Bultmann, *HST*, 17–18). On the *qorban* saying, see
JWJ, 78–9, 174.

Be this as it may, and notwithstanding Jesus' habitual emphasis on the essential character of the Ten Commandments (cf. below), there is no denying that three sayings are placed into his mouth which are hardly consonant with filial piety. Thus he proclaims that listening to the word of God overrides mere natural kinship, and alternatively, that mother and siblings have no special standing when the issue is the preaching of the Kingdom of heaven. Hence Jesus declares:

> Whoever does the will of God is my brother, and sister, and mother (Mark 3.35; cf. Matt. 12.50).

> My mother and my brothers are those who hear the word of God and do it (Luke 8.21).

Similarly, just as in rabbinic thought respect for one's master ranks next to that for Heaven (mAb. 4.12), according to Jesus, a teacher recognized as God's messenger must be preferred to family. Or, to follow Luke's pregnant formulation, which is likely to be the original Q logion, compared to Matthew's smoother version where 'to love more' is substituted for 'to hate':

> If any one comes to me and does not hate his own father and mother and wife and children and brothers and sisters, yes, and even his own life, he cannot be my disciple (Luke 14.26; cf. Matt. 10.37).

Though both these utterances can be read as being irremediably in conflict with the piety due to parents, it is the third – equally attributed to Q and generally acknowledged as a genuine Jesus saying – that has become in recent years the principal source from which scholars endeavour to deduce that Jesus disregarded one of the basic precepts of the Torah. This is the notorious command addressed to a would-be disciple who wishes to delay joining the company of Jesus until after he has buried his father.

> To another he (Jesus) said, 'Follow me.' But he said, 'Lord, let me first go and bury my father.' But he said to him, 'Leave the dead to bury their own dead; but as for you, go and proclaim the Kingdom of God.' (Luke 9.59–60; cf. Matt. 8.21–22)

A common opinion has established itself among New Testament exegetes to the effect that Jesus' words not only struck his contemporaries as shocking, but that they actually overruled the Torah. Since this view has been advanced not only by scholars belonging to the old school, but even by a writer as steeped in, and sympathetic to, Jewish learning and Judaism as E. P. Sanders, it demands to be considered seriously.[22]

Setting Jesus' 'Follow me' against the most fundamental duty, solidly and universally attested in Judaism and outside it, of ensuring that a deceased parent receives a reverent burial, Sanders is led, at the end of a detailed examination, to formulate a 'modest conclusion':

> At least once Jesus was willing to say that following him superseded the requirements of piety and the Torah. This may show that Jesus was prepared, if necessary, to challenge the adequacy of the Mosaic dispensation. (*J & J*, 255)

What Sanders and his colleagues envisage is the case of a man whose father has just died, and who is told by Jesus to join him at once without wasting the few hours necessary to prepare and execute the burial rites which were to be performed on the very day of death, before nightfall, even in the case of executed criminals (Deut. 21.23). Sanders distinguishes a positive and a negative thrust in the saying. The former, the 'call to discipleship . . . which overrides other responsibilities' (*J & J*, 253) is considered in the Gospel context as logical and self-explanatory. The latter, however, has deeper implications which are usually overlooked, namely that 'disobedience of the requirement to care for one's dead parents is actually disobedience to God' (ibid.).

Such a dichotomy is, I believe, greatly misleading. As before, we are faced with a clash of requirements: one must both honour (and thus bury) one's father, and volunteer to devote oneself to the speedy realization of God's Kingdom; for this is the real issue, and not simply affiliation with the band of Jesus' disciples. In the case of such conflicting duties, the responsibility

[22]Cf. in particular, A. Schlatter, *Der Evangelist Matthäus* (1929/1959), 288; N. Perrin, *Rediscovering the Teaching of Jesus* (1967), 144; M. Hengel, *Nachfolge und Charisma* (1968), 16 [ET *The Charismatic Leader and his Followers* (1981), 15]; A. E. Harvey, *Jesus and the Constraints of History* (1982), 59–61; E. P. Sanders, *Jesus and Judaism* (1985), 252–5. See also *JWJ*, 51, 167 (n. 57).

for the unavoidable 'disobedience' to one of the precepts can be laid only at God's doorstep.[23]

As for the choice to be made for the solution of the dilemma, the examples given above, as well as the whole teaching of Jesus relating to the Kingdom, leave us in no doubt about where in his opinion the priority should lie (see ch. 6 below). If in such a context Sanders's 'negative thrust' had been consciously felt, the evangelist might have dealt with it in the form of hostile questioning. But he failed to do so.

This being said, and the 'positive thrust' of the statement recognized as making good sense, I still wonder whether the literal understanding of the episode – the call by Jesus of a man who has just lost his father – should be accepted as self-evident. For despite the absence in both Luke and Matthew of circumstantial details, the assumed reality of the exchange requires a historically and psychologically valid context.

The man is unlikely to have been a total stranger bluntly accosted by Jesus; indeed Matt. 8.21 portrays him as a 'disciple'. But what was this person doing among the followers of Jesus when he should have been busying himself with funeral matters, as his father had to be laid to rest within hours. Could it be that the disciple's words had a less straightforward meaning? If in a slightly confused and timid manner he intended to suggest that he would not throw in his lot with Jesus at once, and used his eventual filial duty to bury his father (old and sick?) as an excuse for procrastination, Jesus' sharp rejoinder would surprise no one. Let the dead (i.e. the other members of your family who have shown no interest in seeking life in God's Kingdom) care for their dead.[24]

Whilst admittedly this exegesis cannot be taken as imperative, it certainly provides a no less, and probably a more, satisfactory sense than the commonly held interpretation. Needless to say, it rids us of the red-herring issue of Jesus' challenge to the 'adequacy of the Mosaic dispensation', or more exactly and even incredibly, to the validity of the Decalogue.

[23]Family disunion during the upheaval signalling the approach of the end is envisaged in the Elijah passages of Mal. 3.24 (=4.5) and Ecclus. 48.10. Cf. also Micah 7.6 and its use in Matt. 10.34–6; Luke 12.51–3, where it is asserted that father and mother will be divided against son and daughter.

[24]For the metaphorical use of 'the dead' for 'the ungodly', see yBer. 2,4c; I Tim. 5.6, etc.

(ii) The so-called antitheses

The Sermon on the Mount contains six sections (or five, if the maxims on adultery and divorce are taken as one) in which a biblical law, introduced by the phrase, 'You have heard that it was said to the men of old', or simply 'You have heard that it was said', is contrasted by Jesus' assertion, 'But I say to you'. The words in question are preserved in this form only by the evangelist Matthew. Scholarly attitude to them varies: their genuineness, complete or partial, is recognized by some, but doubted by others. Curiously, critical judgments are frequently based on the most unexpected reasons. The *antitheses* are held to be genuine by scholars who discover in them ammunition for their 'anti-Jewish' thesis, viz. that Jesus rejected the Torah, whereas some of those who occupy a 'pro-Jewish' stance declare them inauthentic because they reflect a portrait of Jesus not sufficiently distinct from that of a Pharisee.[25]

From our point of view, verbal authenticity does not really matter as long as we can satisfy ourselves that the essence of the teaching can safely be assigned to Jesus. In other words, we are more concerned with the message *ad sensum* than with the *ipsissima verba* of the messenger. Moreover, the principal task is to determine Jesus' stand vis-à-vis the Torah; the actual doctrinal slant revealed by these passages will be investigated later in the course of our attempt to sketch the portrait of his religious personality (cf. ch. 7).

Jesus on murder (Matt. 5.21–26)   The form of this saying, and of those which follow, is particular and without parallel either in the New Testament or elsewhere in ancient Jewish literature. The formula, 'You have heard, etc.', introduces a quotation from the Pentateuch, 'You shall not kill' (Ex. 20.13; Deut. 5.17), to which here (as in Matt. 5.43) a Targum-type paraphrastic supplement is appended: 'and whoever kills shall be liable to judgment'. The so-called antithesis is in fact not to be understood in its true meaning as a contradiction. Jesus is not reported as stating, after a solemn 'but I say to you', that

[25]Cf. as extreme opposites E. Käsemann, *Essays on New Testament Themes* (1964), 37–8 and E. P. Sanders, *Jesus and Judaism* (1985), 260–4. Three of the antitheses – murder, adultery and swearing of oaths – are more often recognized as traceable to Jesus: see Bultmann, *HST*, 147.

homicide is permissible, let alone obligatory, but that 'every one who is angry with his brother shall be liable to judgment'. He preempts, in other words, the likelihood of murder by outlawing its inward root-cause, anger which may lead first to verbal insult, and then to physical violence. The correctness of such an understanding is supported by a rabbinic model. A similar line of reasoning, formulated explicitly and by means of scripture quotations, figures in the Tannaitic midrash, Sifre on Deut. 19.10–11 (186–187):

> *Lest innocent blood be shed . . . and so the guilt of bloodshed be upon you . . . But if a man hates his neighbour, and lies in wait for him, and attacks him . . .* On this account it has been said: A man who has transgressed a light commandment will finish by transgressing a weighty commandment. If he has transgressed *You shall love your neighbour as yourself* (Lev. 19.18), he will finish by transgressing *You shall not take vengeance or bear grudge* (ibid.), and *You shall not hate your brother* (Lev. 19.17), and *That your brother may live beside you* (Lev. 25.36) until he comes to shedding blood.[26]

The panacea prescribed by Jesus to neutralize feelings of hostility and eliminate their sequel is quick reconciliation.

> So if you are offering your gift at the altar, and there remember that your brother has something against you, leave your gift there before the altar and go; first be reconciled to your brother, and then come and offer your gift. Make friends quickly with your accuser . . . (Matt. 5.23–25)

How these words of Jesus and the like could have been taken as tantamount to 'shattering the letter of the Law', the phrase is Ernst Käsemann's, cannot be accounted for on scholarly grounds alone.[27]

Incidentally, Jesus' antitheses do not differ structurally from that by which, according to Mark 7.10–13 (Matt. 15.4–6), the Pharisees are said to have propounded their doctrine concerning

[26]The implied sequence is that lack of love may lead to sentiments of revenge, then to hatred culminating in murder.

[27]Cf. op.cit. in n. 25. A Jewish exegetical understanding of the 'antithesis' is offered by D. Daube, *The New Testament and Rabbinic Judaism* (1956), 55–62. For the general import of the saying, cf. *JWJ*, 47.

qorban: 'Moses said ... but you say' (Mark), or even more strongly, 'God commanded ... but you say' (Matt.). One can, needless to say, debate the nature of the contrasts in question, but the point at issue is that if Jesus' teaching 'shatters the letter of the Law', that of the Pharisees seems to do the same, which is of course nonsense.[28]

Jesus on adultery (Matt. 5.27–30) Just as anger should be avoided or overcome before it leads to homicide, looking at a woman with sexual desire should equally be shunned not only because it is conducive to adultery, but because it already amounts to it in thought. Once again, the Torah (Ex. 20.14; Deut. 5.17) is reinforced, and as it were protected, rather than declared obsolete by implication.

In identifying guilt incurred through the imagination with that corresponding to the deed itself, Jesus reflects the basic religious, as distinct from the forensic, outlook of contemporary and later rabbinic Judaism. The idiom, 'to lust after their eyes', 'to walk after a sinful heart and lustful eyes', 'to follow after the guilty inclination and lustful eyes', signifying the radical source of sinful action, is familiar to readers of the Dead Sea Scrolls (1QpHab 5.7; 1QS 1.6; CD 2.16; 11QTS 59.14). The same viewpoint, couched in more general terms, is testified to also by Flavius Josephus when he writes in his summary of the Mosaic Law in *Contra Apionem* (ii. 183): 'To us ... the only wisdom, the only virtue consists in refraining from every action, *from every thought* that is contrary to the laws originally laid down.' And again (ibid. 217), 'The *mere intention* of doing wrong to one's parents or of impiety against God is followed by instant death.'[29]

The same turn of mind is reflected also in the later writings of the rabbis. 'To follow your eyes' is equated with 'fornication' by an anonymous exegete in Sifre on Num. 15.39 (115). Overstating the case, the Babylonian Talmud (Yoma 29a) represents lewd thoughts as more sinful than their realization. And the post-Talmudic tractate Kallah (1) produces the perfect formulation:

---

[28]In the words of a well-known New Testament scholar, the scribes and Pharisees were 'tampering with God's Law', whereas in the case of Jesus, it was a matter of 'the Son elucidating its real meaning' (C. E. B. Cranfield, *The Gospel according to Saint Mark* (1959), 237).

[29]Cf. G. Vermes, 'A Summary of the Law by Flavius Josephus', *NT* 24 (1982), 303.

'Whoever looks lustfully at a woman is like one who has had unlawful intercourse with her.'[30]

Jesus on divorce (Matt. 5.31–32)   The introductory formula, 'It was also said', preceding the paraphrase of the Mosaic injunction regarding the *get*, i.e. the document whereby divorce is effected (Deut. 24.1), is shorter than either of the two previous ones and may suggest, like a similar phrase, 'and that which He said', in the Qumran *pesher* commentaries, that the quotation is to be associated with the previous biblical passage. If so, Matt. 5.31–32 should be read in conjunction with verses 27–30, indicating that divorce is seen as a subdivision of adultery. For a fuller understanding, the passage needs to be considered together with the other Gospel statements on divorce in Matt. 19.3–12; Mark 10.2–12 (Luke 16.18) which have been subjected to frequent and thorough examination in the context of inter-testamental Jewish ideas on the subject.[31]

Without attempting to set out all the details of the argument, we should note that Jesus, like the Essenes according to the Damascus Document (CD 4.21), saw in Gen. 1.27 ('male and female he created them') and 2.24 ('they become one flesh') the quintessence of marriage established by a divine principle (Matt. 19.4–5; Mark 10.6–8). Remarriage following divorce funda-mentally conflicts with this quasi-metaphysical unity and, in an ideal world, amounts to adultery, i.e. the destruction of the original bond. It would seem that implicitly the same idea underlies the divorce legislation in Deut. 24.1–4, where the specific case of a man intent on remarrying his first wife who in the meanwhile has been married to, and divorced by, another husband, or has become a widow. No such reunion is permiss-ible, as a sexual link with the second spouse has defiled her in regard to the first, and thus made her unfit for the restoration of the marital ties.[32]

---

[30]Cf. *S-B* I, 298–301; I. Abrahams, *Studies in Pharisaism and the Gospels* II (1924), 205–6.

[31]For the most recent survey of the New Testament material, see Sanders, *J & J*, 256–60; cf. also *JWJ*, 70–71, 87; J. A. Fitzmyer, 'The Matthean Divorce Texts and some new Palestinian Evidence', *Theological Studies* 37 (1976), 197–226. On divorce in general, see D. Daube, *NTRJ* (1956), 362–72; Z. W. Falk, *Introduction to Jewish Law in the Second Commonwealth* II (1978), 307–16; J. D. M. Derrett, *The Law in the NT* (1979), 363–88.

[32]The same situation is verified in the story of Abraham and Sarah in the account of the Qumran Genesis Apocryphon. The patriarch beseeches God not

In the Marcan version (10.11–12), echoed by Paul, who gives his ruling as a command of the Lord (I Cor. 7.10–11), any second marriage to a new partner counts as adultery, whereas in Matthew's account, here and in 19.9, there is an exception clause, viz. the wife's prior adultery, through which the unity of the two has already been destroyed. In this case, Jesus is described by him as siding with the strict outlook of the school of Shammai, authorizing divorce only on the grounds of sexual misbehaviour, against the over-lenient teaching of the school of Hillel, allowing it for practically 'any cause' (Matt. 19.3).[33]

But whichever way Jesus himself regarded the marriage bond, whether he thought of it as absolutely, or conditionally indissoluble, his message as it stands can in no circumstance be equated with a condemnation of the divine concession of divorce, granted by God through Moses because of the weakness of human nature.[34]

Jesus on oaths (Matt. 5.33–37)   The commandment relating to perjury is even less directly quoted from the Bible than the law concerning murder. 'You shall not swear falsely, but perform to the Lord what you have sworn' is once more a Targum-type combined re-phrasing of Leviticus 19.12 ('You shall not swear by my name falsely') and Deuteronomy 23.24 (23) ('You shall be careful to do what has passed your lips, for you have voluntarily vowed to the Lord your God what you have promised with your mouth'). So strictly speaking, the 'antithesis' is not set against a Mosaic precept. In the final age, Jesus intends to discard all the paraphernalia connected with oaths as unnecessary. Hence he declares redundant the multitude of commonly used surrogate terms for God. These *kinnuyim*, as the rabbis called them, are

---

to allow Pharaoh to consummate his 'marriage' with Sarah, for the ensuing defilement would separate her from him (1QApGen 20.15). The author tacitly presumes Sarah's remarriage *following divorce* which would render illicit any eventual coming together of the original couple.

[33]Cf. mGit. 9.10; Josephus, *Ant.* iv. 253; *Life* 426; *JWJ*, 70.

[34]That Jesus' rejection of divorce was not held to be absolute may be deduced from Paul's willingness to permit it in the case of a marriage between a Christian and an 'unbeliever'. If the latter, male or female, was unwilling to live peacefully with the new convert, divorce was said to be in order, and since Paul did not expressly command that he or she must remain single (as in I Cor. 7.11), it would seem that he was prepared to permit, or at least tolerate, remarriage.

alluded to in the Damascus Rule (15.1); they were adopted by the Pharisees according to Matt. 23.16–22, and recommended, when oaths were unavoidable, by Philo (*Spec.Leg.* ii. 2–5). These extra protective measures were introduced to ensure that the divine name would never be taken in vain, not even by error or inadvertence. But the heart of Jesus' doctrine is that among truthful people no special solemnities are necessary: a 'yes' or a 'no' should be enough (James 5.12).

Deliberate abstention from oaths is not peculiar to Jesus' outlook. The same stance is attributed to the Essenes by both Philo and Josephus:

> They show their love of God . . . by abstinence from oaths, by veracity . . . (*Omnis probus* 84).

> Everything they say is more certain than an oath. Indeed swearing is rejected by them as being more evil than perjury. For anyone who does not merit belief without calling on God is already condemned (*War* ii. 135).

Furthermore, Philo represents the superfluity of oaths as part and parcel of the virtuous life, the natural sequel of morality:

> The good man's word . . . should be an oath, firm, unswerving, utterly free from falsehood, securely planted in truth (*Spec. Leg.* ii. 2; cf. *Decal.* 84).

The Israelites' acceptance of the Ten Commandments was signified, according to the rabbinic sages, by a solemn yea or yea yea, nay or nay nay. The words are believed to possess the binding force of an oath.[35] Once more, what is characteristic of Jesus is the supreme emphasis he lays on ideas which are present, but less absolutely attested, in ancient Jewish piety.

Jesus on retaliation (Matt. 5.38–42)   In a hyperbolical disavowal of vindictiveness, the age-old *lex talionis* – 'You have heard that it was said, An eye for an eye, a tooth for a tooth' (Ex. 21.24) – is contrasted not only with passive resistence – 'But I say to you, Do not resist one who is evil' – but with a kind of provocative submissiveness conveyed by the counsel to offer the left cheek to one who has hit you on the right cheek (cf. Luke

---

[35]Cf. Mekh. on Ex. 20.1–2 (II, 229–30); bShebu. 36a; see *S-B* I, 336–7.

6.29). The fact that the two further examples given in Matthew, one of them echoed in Luke 6.29, namely the surrender of a cloak to one asking only for a shirt, or walking double the distance demanded, indicates that supererogation is the central theme.

It is scarcely necessary to recall that in post-biblical Jewish teaching, Exodus 21.24 was not understood literally as requiring corresponding damage to be inflicted on a person guilty of causing bodily injury. Bloody revenge was replaced by a judicially established monetary compensation. Josephus is acquainted with it (*Ant.* iv. 280), and the principle is presupposed in the Mishnah (cf. mBQ 8.1). The Mekhilta on Ex. 21.24 (III, 67) simply equates 'an eye for an eye' with *mamōn*, i.e. (eye-)money. The Palestinian Targums provide a neat paraphrase: 'The value of an eye for an eye; the value of a tooth for a tooth; the value of a hand for a hand; the value of a foot for a foot', etc.[36]

For a better understanding of this impractical saying – after all, not even the New Testament in the person of the fourth evangelist makes Jesus comply with it literally, for when struck by a Temple policeman, he is not made to offer the other cheek but to protest with dignity (John 18.23) – it should be examined together with the next and last 'antithesis'. Indeed, in Luke 6.27–36 the two, 'offer the other cheek' and 'love your enemies', coalesce to form one doctrine within a single perspective.

Jesus on the love of one's enemies (Matt. 5.43–48)

> You have heard that it was said, 'You shall love your neighbour and hate your enemy.' But I say to you, 'Love your enemies . . . '

The scriptural verse quoted is Lev. 19.18, 'You shall love your neighbour'.[37] It is severed from its concluding part, 'like yourself', or perhaps, 'for he is like you', but is followed, on the other hand, by a complementary statement absent from the Bible, 'and hate your enemy'. The teaching derived from the precept in Matt.

[36]Josephus (loc. cit.) refers to indemnity as an option: 'unless the maimed man be willing to accept money'. His presentation may have been influenced by Roman law. Cf. D. Daube *NTRJ*, 256.

[37]For the understanding of this commandment in post-biblical Judaism, see Paola Pallais's Oxford MPhil. thesis, *Exegesis of Lev. 19.18 and the Love Command in Judaism: Variations on a Theme* (1988). It also contains valuable information concerning the Golden Rule, discussed below.

5.45–8, paralleled freely in Luke 6.32–6, is usually attributed to Q. Its fundamental meaning is that human love must strive to imitate God's love for mankind; it must be disinterested, seeking nothing in return, thus reflecting divine generosity, mercy and perfection. The extreme, hyperbolical opportunity for the demonstration of such unselfish, and as it were super-human, goodness presents itself in one to whom nothing is owed and from whom no kindness of any sort can be expected. Charitable behaviour towards an enemy is the recipe for a person seeking to become perfect as the heavenly Father is perfect.

Although 'hate your enemy' may be seen as a negative counterpart of 'love your neighbour' – the two, love of the sons of Light and hatred of the sons of Darkness, are instinctively coupled in the Qumran Community Rule (1QS 1.9–10) – the association is without biblical basis, and is more likely to come from Matthew than from Jesus. The view that it may have been borrowed from an otherwise lost Targum is pure specula-tion.[38] The nearest parallel to this much debated teaching of Jesus may be found in Josephus' undoubtedly less colourful statement that Moses inculcated *epieikeia* (generosity, con-sideration, gentleness) even towards avowed enemies (*C.Ap.* ii. 211).

In sum, it is to be concluded that while the six 'antitheses', despite the possibility of Matthean redactional changes, may be accepted as conveying the general sense, if not the actual word-ing, of the corresponding teaching of Jesus, in no way can they be identified as a frontal attack by him on the Law of Moses or on traditional Judaism.

4. Jesus' summaries of the Law

There was a tendency among Jewish religious teachers of the inter-testamental and Mishnaic-Talmudic eras to search for the central tenets, even the essence, of the Torah and to reduce the many commandments, the six hundred and thirteen positive

[38] Cf. M. Smith, 'Matt. V. 43: "Hate Thine Enemy"', *HTR* 45 (1952), 71–3. A more natural sequence of ideas is: love – do not hate. It is well attested in T.Gad 6.1: 'Now, my children, each of you love his brother. Drive hatred out of your hearts.'

and negative rules according to the reckoning of the rabbis, to a more manageable number, and, if possible, to unity.[39]

(a) The Decalogue (Mark 10.17–19; Matt. 19.16–19; Luke 18.18–20)

The first of the three attempts to uncover the kernel of the Torah, recorded in the Synoptic Gospels in the name of Jesus, is presented as an answer to someone (Mark 10.17), specified as a young man (Matt. 19.22) or a ruler (Luke 18.18), who asked how to gain access to 'eternal life'. The brief reply of Jesus is: observe the ethical and social commandments of the Decalogue. All three evangelists list those relating to murder, adultery, theft, false witness and filial piety, starting with the prohibitions and ending with the positive 'Honour your father, etc.' Mark inserts 'Do not defraud' (cf. Ecclus. 4.1) as the last negative precept, possibly replacing the various 'Do not covet' clauses, whereas Matthew ends the series with 'You shall love your neighbour' (Lev. 19.18). The spontaneity of the reply may be attributed to the fact that the recitation of the Ten Commandments was part of the daily prayers during the period of the Second Temple (mTam. 5.1; yBer. 3c). They stand out as supreme not only because they alone were proclaimed by God (Philo, *Decal.* 175; Josephus, *Ant.* iii.89), but also because 'they are *summaries* of the special laws recorded in the Holy Scriptures' (Philo, *Decal.* 154; *Spec. Leg.* i.1). Hence, although the formulation of the story as a whole with its introductory variations is no doubt the work of the evangelists, there is no reason why its substance should not be accepted as the authentic teaching of Jesus.[40]

(b) The Golden Rule (Matt. 7.12; Luke 6.31)

In two parallel sayings, presumably borrowed from Q,

[39]Cf. *JWJ*, 45, 160. The main sources quoted are Philo, *Spec. Leg.* i. 1; bShab. 31a; Philo, *Hypoth.* 7, 6; bMak. 24a. These and other passages will be discussed below.

[40]Despite his usual scepticism, Bultmann appears to have admitted something to this effect. 'It is in itself highly probable that Jesus was asked questions about the way to life, or about the greatest commandment, but it is quite another thing to ask whether the scenes which relate those questions to us are historical reports or not. They are such only in the sense that the Church formulated such scenes *entirely in the spirit of Jesus*' (my emphasis), *HST*, 54.

Matthew and Luke hand down Jesus' one-article code of ethics which since the sixteenth century is regularly alluded to as the 'Golden Rule'. The Lucan version (6.31), which immediately precedes the saying on love of one's enemies, is thought to be more original:

As you wish that men would do to you, do so to them.

Matthew (7.12) has inserted it into the Sermon on the Mount and expounded it by means of an appended gloss:

Whatever you wish that men would do to you, do so to them; for this is the Law and the Prophets.

The basic message conveys universal good-will towards fellow-humans. In putting it into practice, one's own likes and dislikes are to be used as easy, indeed instinctive, yardsticks. It is not to be regarded with Bultmann as a precept giving 'moral expression to a naif egoism' (*HST*, 103); neither should this 'positive' Golden Rule be declared a spiritually higher formulation than its negative (Jewish) counterpart, as Christian apologists are accustomed to do.[41] Both are simple and practical rules of thumb of universal morality, the motive for every do and don't.

As in the case of the Decalogue, there is no reason to doubt – on the contrary, we have a good case to postulate it – that Jesus was acquainted with, and actually employed, this method in simplifying the ethics detailed in the Torah. One hardly needs to reiterate that sayings similar to his are widely attested in post-exilic, intertestamental and rabbinic Judaism as well as in other Mediterranean cultures. Albrecht Dihle's pioneering monograph, *Die goldene Regel. Eine Einführung in die Geschichte der antiken und frühchristlichen Vulgärethik* (1962), furnishes all the necessary information in this regard. A few selected Jewish examples will suffice. They all represent the negative rule.

---

[41]'There is truth in Bultmann's description of the Golden Rule ... and in Tillich's description of it as "calculating justice" which needs love to be transformed into "creative justice" and thus to be truly "just". In the Gospels this sort of transformation of the Golden Rule has taken place' (V. P. Furnish, *The Love Command in the New Testament* (1973), 63–64). – 'An ethical programme which consists in not-doing ... can hardly be compared with one which calls for positive and unlimited benevolence', so writes G. B. Caird in his Pelican *Saint Luke* (1963), 104. Most scholars acknowledge today that this is a theologically biased outlook.

The earliest attestation belongs to one of the Apocrypha, Tobit 4.15: 'Do not do to anyone what you yourself would hate.' The author of Tobit may, in fact, have borrowed it from the maxims of Ahiqar: 'Son, what seems evil to you, do not do to your companion' (8.88 in Armenian).[42]

Closer to the age of Jesus, the same pattern figures in Philo's *Hypothetica* (7.6) – 'What someone would hate to suffer, he must not do to others' – and in rabbinic literature. The famous saying, attributed to Hillel in the Talmud (bShab. 31a), is regularly reproduced in every study of the Golden Rule. It occurs in a semi-ironical context, revealing the irascibility of Shammai and the lack of serious intent, or silliness, of his Gentile interlocutor.

> Make me a proselyte (he asked) on condition that you teach me the entire Torah while I stand on one foot.

The short-tempered Shammai threw him out. He then approached the tolerant and kind-hearted Hillel, who received him into the Jewish fold on his acceptance of the single-sentence teaching:

> *What is hateful to you, do not do to your fellow.*

To which Hillel added: 'This is the whole of the Torah. The rest is its interpretation. Go! Study!'

Divorced from the anecdotal setting, Hillel's counsel echoes the negative Golden Rule, accompanied by its explicit identification as the briefest possible recapitulation of the Mosaic doctrine regarding correct behaviour towards one's neighbour. In this respect it resembles Matthew's comment (7.12), 'For this is the Law and the Prophets', where the clause 'and the Prophets', is either a *quasi*-automatic Christian enlargement, or an echo of the ancient Jewish idea that the Prophets were transmitters and expositors of the Torah (mAb. 1.1).

The same doctrine is repeated in a non-sarcastic context in Abot de-R. Nathan (Recension B, ch. 26). Hillel is replaced by Akiba and the cheeky Gentile by an indefinite 'someone' who respectfully asks:

[42]Cf. J. M. Lindenberger in *OTP* II, 490. On Tobit and Ahiqar, cf. *HJP* III.1, 222–39.

Rabbi, teach me the whole of the Torah in one (sentence). He said to him, My son, our Master Moses, may peace be on him, spent forty days and forty nights on the mountain before learning it, and you say: Teach me the whole of the Torah in one (sentence)! But, my son, this is the principle of the Torah: What you yourself hate, do not do to your fellow.[43]

It should be noted that Judaism, before and after the first century AD, was aware, when summing up the Law, of both the positive and the negative aspects of its moral teaching. Jesus ben Sira in the early second century BC advised his readers (31 [34].15):

Be as friendly to your neighbour as to yourself, and (in his regard) be attentive to all that you hate.

In rabbinic writings, too, the negative Golden Rule is understood as the counterpart of the commandment of love towards one's neighbour. Thus the *lemma*, 'Loving mankind', introducing chapter 26 in Aboth de-R. Nathan B, the chapter which contains Akiba's teaching on the (negative) Golden Rule, is borrowed from the Hillel maxim in mAb. 1.12, 'Be of the disciples of Aaron, loving peace and pursuing peace, loving mankind . . . '. But the most striking expression of the bond between the two concepts occurs in Targum Pseudo-Jonathan's rendering of Leviticus 19.18:

And you shall love your neighbour: *whatever you yourself hate, do not do to him.*

To sum up, the broad familiarity of the Golden Rule in inter-testamental and rabbinic Jewish milieux can be interpreted both in favour and against the authenticity of the Gospel logion. However, the very fact that the distinctive positive wording is used rather than the common negative formulation, must — it would seem — count as a definite argument in favour of Jesus having actually framed it as an abbreviated statement of the commandments of the Torah governing the entire domain of human relations.

---

[43]See ed. S. Schechter, *Aboth de Rabbi Nathan* (1887, repr. 1967), 53. Cf. A. J. Saldarini, *The Fathers according to Rabbi Nathan* (1975), 155.

(c) The first or great commandment (Mark 12.29–31; Matt. 22.37–40; Luke 10.26–28)

The third doctrinal statement attributed to Jesus concerning the Torah in brief is the most comprehensive of them all. Reported by all the Synoptic Gospels, it is given as an answer to an inquiry. But whereas in Matthew and Luke the approach is devious, the intention being to 'test' the speaker, in Mark the questioner is portrayed as sincere, and at the end is assured by Jesus that he is 'not far from the Kingdom of God' (12.34). The Marcan setting has all the appearances of being the more primitive.[44]

Jesus' answer takes two main forms. Either the great commandment is subdivided into a first and second (Mark and Matt.), or the precept, combined though it is, is given singly (Luke). Bearing in mind that the purpose is to provide an all-inclusive doctrine, a chief commandment, the Lucan structure ought to be preferred, although Mark's wording, starting with the *Shema'*, 'Hear O Israel . . .' (Deut. 6.4) and followed by 'And you shall love the Lord . . . ' (Deut. 6.5), its continuation in the principal daily Jewish prayer, reflects a natural way of quoting by heart.[45]

The commandment to love God is followed by, 'You shall love your neighbour . . .' (Lev. 19.18) already discussed in connection with the 'antitheses' (cf. above). According to R. Akiba, this is 'the greatest principle in the Torah' (Sifra on Lev. 19.18; GR 24.7).[46]

The necessary association of man's basic duty towards God

[44]The pejorative overtone in Matthew and Luke represents the general tendency of 'trick-questioning' by Pharisees, Herodians and Sadducees in the neighbouring Gospel sections: cf. Mark 12.13–17; Matt. 22.15–22; Luke 20.20–26 (payment of imperial taxes); Mark 12.18–27; Matt. 22.23–33; Luke 20.27–40 (marital status after the resurrection); Mark 12.35–37; Matt. 22.41–46; Luke 20.41–44 (the Messiah as son or lord of David). It is most unlikely that the different presentation of Mark 12.28–34 results from a process of 'laundering'.

[45]On the *Shema'*, see *HJP* II, 454–5. In the Nash Papyrus, the *Shema'* follows the Decalogue. Cf. E. Würthwein, *The Text of the Old Testament* (1980), 33 and plate 6.

[46]It is noteworthy that Matthew concludes with 'On these two commandments depend all the Law and the Prophets' (22.40) as he did in 7.12 partly paralleling the words ascribed by the Talmud to Hillel in bShab. 3b.

and towards his fellows *quasi* automatically derives from that other summary of the Torah, the Decalogue, which itself preceded the liturgical recitation of Deut. 6.4–9 (cf. mTam. 5.1).

The fundamental link between the love of God and the love of mankind is clearly expressed in various inter-testamental writings, in particular the Testaments of the Twelve Patriarchs. Issachar, for example, exhorts his children to love the Lord and their neighbour (T.Iss. 5.2) and offers his own example for imitation:

> I acted in piety and truth in all my days.
> I loved the Lord with all my strength;
> Likewise, I loved every man like my children.
> You do likewise, my children . . . (T.Iss. 7.6)

Philo, in a more sophisticated style advances the same message. Discussing the transition in the Decalogue between duties to God and man, he comments:

> Now we have known some who associate themselves with one of the two sides and are seen to neglect the other. They have drunk of the unmixed wine of pious aspirations and turning their backs upon all other concerns devoted their personal life wholly to the service of God. Others conceiving the idea that there is no good outside doing justice to men have no heart for anything but companionship with men . . . These may be justly called lovers of men, the former sort lovers of God. Both come but halfway in virtue; they only have it whole who win honour in both departments (*Decal.* 108–10).

While the bond between the two loves is unquestionably present in inter-testamental and rabbinic thought, its simple expression by means of coupling Deut. 6.5 with Lev. 19.18 is characteristic of the New Testament, and probably of Jesus himself. In doing so, he succeeded in coining a single principle, incorporating all the theological and ethical contents of the Torah.[47]

[47]A parallel coupling of higher and lower duties appears in the second-century BC Letter of Aristeas (228) in connection with honouring God-parents-friends, and in Josephus' *Contra Apionem* II.206: 'Honour to parents the Law ranks second only to honour to God . . . It requires respect to be paid by the young to all their elders, because God is the most Ancient of all.'

IV   Ethicizing the Law

The Mishnah and the Talmud display, it is commonly taught, a legal approach to the Law. This is generally true when it comes to detail, but does not necessarily apply when radical understanding is at issue. Perhaps the most telling example figures in the third-century R. Simlai's attempt (bMak. 24a) at reducing, in successive stages and in exclusively non-halakhic terms, the many commandments of Moses to a single one.

> Six-hundred and thirteen commandments were given to Moses . . . David came and reduced them to eleven. For it is written: *A Psalm of David. O Lord, who shall sojourn in thy tent? Who shall dwell on thy holy hill?* (1) *He who walks blamelessly,* (2) *and does what is right,* (3) *and speaks truth from his heart;* (4) *who does not slander with his tongue,* (5) *and does no evil to his friend,* (6) *nor takes up a reproach against his neighbour;* (7) *in whose eyes a reprobate is despised,* (8) *but who honours those who fear the Lord;* (9) *who swears to his own hurt and does not change;* (10) *who does not lend his money at interest,* (11) *and does not take bribe against the innocent. He who does these things shall never be moved* (Ps. 15.1–5) . . . Isaiah came and reduced them to six, for it is written: (1) *He who walks righteously* (2) *and speaks uprightly;* (3) *he who despises the gain of oppressions,* (4) *who shakes his hands, lest they hold a bribe,* (5) *who stops his ears from hearing of bloodshed,* (6) *and shuts his eyes from looking upon evil* (Isa. 33.15) . . . Micah came and reduced them to three, for it is written: *He has showed you, O man, what is good; and what does the Lord require of you but* (1) *to do justice,* (2) *and to love kindness,* (3) *and to walk humbly with your God* (Micah 6.8) . . . Isaiah came again and reduced them to two, for it is written: *Thus says the Lord:* (1) *Keep justice* (2) *and do righteousness* (Isa. 56.1). Amos came and reduced them to one, for it is written: *For thus says the Lord to the house of Israel:* (1) *Seek me and live* (Amos 5.4).

Whereas the rabbinic sages are mostly portrayed as practical experts in the finer details of what is forbidden or permitted, that is to say, the correct way to implement the Torah, and only less frequently as moralists or theologians, the most outstanding feature in Jesus' attitude is an all-pervading concern with the ultimate purpose of the Law which he perceived, primarily and essentially and positively, not as a juridical, but as a religious-ethical reality, revealing what he thought to be the right and divinely ordained behaviour towards men and towards God.[48]

[48]Here again the Letter of Aristeas (234) furnishes a significant precedent when it proclaims that honour is paid to God ultimately by a pure heart and devout disposition rather than by gifts or sacrifices.

3

Jesus the Teacher:
Scriptural and Charismatic Authority

I   Jesus as Teacher

Whatever else he may have been, Jesus was unquestionably an influential teacher. He was a popular rather than a professional figure, an itinerant master who did not deliver his message in a fixed location such as a 'school' (*bet midrash*) or a particular synagogue. Instead, surrounded by a group of disciples, the nucleus of which was established, he travelled up and down the Lower Galilean countryside, proclaiming his gospel and healing. Later rabbinic writings mention 'wandering Galilean' Bible interpreters (bSanh. 70a; bHul. 27b), but the evidence is too meagre to permit us to speak of representatives of an institution and wonder whether Jesus was one of them.

He was also heard on at least one Passover, and according to the fourth evangelist, on several Jewish feasts in the course of two or three years, in Jerusalem and its sanctuary. As he was not a member of any recognized teaching group such as the 'scribes' (*soferim*) or even the less clearly defined 'preachers' (*darshanim*), who pronounced homilies on Bible readings in the synagogues, the nature of his mission was bound to be questioned in his own day and throughout the ages. The anecdote recorded in all three Synoptic Gospels, in which chief priests, scribes and elders enquire about Jesus' teaching authority may be fictional, but it echoes a genuine problem.[1]

In the Gospel story, Jesus refused to reply unless his interlocutors were prepared to declare their stand concerning the

[1] Luke 20.1f.; Mark 11.27f.; Matt. 21.23. On the scribes, forerunners of the rabbis or sages, and the preachers, cf. *HJP* II, 322–36, 453.

origin, divine or human, of the ministry of John the Baptist. As they apparently took refuge behind a convenient 'don't know', Jesus emerged as the winner of the polemical bout, which entitled him to evade the question. Nevertheless, the character of his teaching needs to be queried by all, including the critical student.

In the domain of religion, commonly held rules and doctrines count as axiomatic and require no proof. The issue of the validity of a teaching arises only if either the claim of the teacher or the purport of the teaching is unusual or conflicts with other generally accepted laws or beliefs. No justification is necessary to declare that murder is wrong, but is a man who in his own house, in the defence of his own property, kills a thief caught in the act, guilty of homicide? The doctrine of bodily resurrection is argued only if it is seen as a novelty, or if, although adhered to by the bulk of society, it is nonetheless denied by a significant group of unbelievers, *minim* (heretics) or 'Epicureans' (sceptics). Again, as has been explained in the previous chapter, the elasticity of Jesus in regard to a strict interpretation of the sabbatical rest must be envisaged from the point of view of a charismatic for whom the healing of the sick overrides all other constraints, however legitimate they may be in themselves.

As for doctrinal authority in Judaism, it depends on whether the period envisaged is biblical or post-biblical. In general terms, biblical teachings fall into two main categories. Those said to be of divine origin are either described as publicly proclaimed by God, like the Decalogue, announced from above and engraved on stone by heavenly fingers, or as revealed to an individual such as the laws and commandments dictated on Sinai to Moses, the earthly scribe of celestial and eternal precepts, and subsequently explained and applied by their appointed guardians, the levitical priests.

Likewise the prophets, prefacing their message with 'Thus said the Lord' or 'These are the words of the Lord', and concluding them with 'Oracle of the Lord', declare themselves to be bearers of a direct divine communication, conveyed through words uttered by the lips of the Almighty, or through supernatural visions. Sapiential teaching in scripture is presented, on the other hand, as the fruit of the sages', first and foremost Solomon's, discernment, itself a gift of God, and a reflection of his everlasting *Hokhmah* or Wisdom (Prov. 8). By the time of Jesus ben Sira, the author of Ecclesiasticus, in the opening decades of the second century BC, this divine *Hokhmah* and the Torah of Moses coalesced into a single conceptual entity (Ecclus. 24).

In the post-biblical age, new criteria of validity or authority appeared, finally superseding those at work during the creation of scripture. The earliest compositions are modelled on the Bible and pseudepigraphically ascribe new teachings to Enoch, Moses (Book of Jubilees and Assumption of Moses), Ezra, Baruch, Solomon etc.[2]

These pseudo-authors receive their messages, as in the biblical books, through revelations, apparitions and the gift of wisdom. Enoch sees visions. Moses and Ezra hear words, sometimes mediated by angels. Post-biblical psalms, like their scriptural predecessors, are attributed to David. Solomon, unnamed but hardly disguised in the apocryphal work ascribed to him (Wisd. 9.7f.), continues to inherit wisdom.

Once the canon, i.e. the recognized list of books constituting the Hebrew scriptures, was established in its essentials during the first half of the second century BC, the concept that ultimate authority in all religious matters lies in the *written* word of God began to impose itself. The Essenes of Qumran attempted to combine exegesis with prophetic knowledge and introduced the notion of an interpretation of the hidden true meaning of the Law and the Prophets revealed by God to the Teacher of Righteousness and other official masters, and passed on to the initiates within the community.

It is true that the development of common law continued as before, and much of the Mishnah, its first redacted form, is composed of precepts without biblical backing. However, an increasing amount of non-scriptural teaching, whether legal, ethical or theological, took the form of Midrash, i.e. an expansion of, or commentary on, the Bible. Conformity with scripture was the final condition of religious truth and no doctrinal formulation could be accepted unless supported by biblical proof-texts.[3] The process of amalgamation of the *mishnah* form

---

[2]Pseudepigraphy is not a post-biblical invention. No serious scholar would take it for granted today that all the words attributed in scripture to Daniel, Isaiah, Solomon or Moses are genuine. In many cases the authorship would be held to be largely, or even completely, fictional. Cf. *HJP* III, 241 and n. 1.

[3]For the case of the Dead Sea Scrolls, see my 'Biblical Proof-Texts in Qumran Literature', *JSS* 34 (1989), 493–508.

and *midrash* form can be observed in the halakhic midrashim, though another kind of sanction for the legal contents of the Mishnah and Talmud which are additional to the Bible was found in the idea of a supplementary revelation granted by God to Moses on Sinai. Transmitted orally by a chain of chosen witnesses, Joshua, the Judges, the Prophets, the sages and rabbis, the so-called oral Torah, completing that recorded by the Lawgiver and of equal standing with it, remained unwritten until the early centuries of the present era.[4]

The use of scripture in Jewish traditional teaching in the inter-testamental and rabbinic epochs is attested in a variety of shapes and styles. In the category described as the re-written Bible, represented by Josephus's *Antiquities*, Pseudo-Philo's *Book of Biblical Antiquities*, the Palestinian Targums, etc., the canonical text is mingled with exegetical glosses and supplements to offer a single, coherent enlarged narrative. Elsewhere, words and phrases borrowed from the sacred text are re-arranged and thus endowed with fresh meaning. Alternatively, a scriptural story is cited as an example to justify a newly proposed doctrine. Again, a biblical statement may be creatively emphasized or contrasted with another scriptural passage. Often in the Qumran writings, and less frequently in rabbinic literature, the significance of a prophetic prediction is indicated by pointing to its 'fulfilment'. Finally, we come to the *midrash* proper, entailing the linkage of Bible verses taken from separate contexts, or the association of such verses with theological or legal principles, resulting in a more developed formulation.[5]

To revert to our original question, it must be asked where and how Jesus' manner of teaching fits into this canvas and what was his personal attitude to the ancestral holy scriptures? A literary analysis of the Gospel passages which include Bible citations will, it is hoped, assist in the search for the genuine message of the Galilean master.

---

[4]Cf. G. Vermes, 'Bible and Midrash', *CHB* I (1970), 199–231 [= *PBJS*, 59–91]) Scripture and Tradition in Judaism: Written and Oral Torah', in G. Baumann (ed.), *The Written Word; Literacy in Transition* (1986), 79–95. See also David Weiss Halivni, *Midrash, Mishnah and Gemara* (1986) and the penetrating analysis offered in Sanders, *Jewish Law*, 97–130.

[5]For a classification of the Qumran evidence, se G. Vermes, 'Bible Interpretation at Qumran' in *Yigael Yadin Memorial Volume*, Eretz-Israel XX (1989), 184*–191*.

II   The Use of the Bible in the Teaching of Jesus

Jesus does not seem to fall into any of the biblical moulds in regard to the source of his doctrinal authority, nor is he the heir of a school of thought handed down from teacher to pupil.

Not that the Gospels and the rest of the New Testament are unfamiliar with revelations and visions: Zechariah and Mary see angels (Luke 1.8–23; 1.26–38); Joseph is instructed by heavenly messengers in dreams (Matt. 1.20f; 2.13; 2.19); Peter in an ecstatic state witnesses an apparition which prepares the entry of the Gentiles into the Christian community (Acts 10.9–16); Paul is blinded by a celestial manifestation when he approaches Damascus (Acts 9.3–9); and elsewhere he 'boasts' about 'visions and revelations', including one relating to his assumption to the 'third heaven' or 'paradise', and about hearing 'things that cannot be told, which man cannot utter' (II Cor. 12.2–4). As for the author of the Book of Revelation, he is continuously confronted with visual and verbal divine mysteries. But, strikingly, Jesus is never portrayed as the actual beneficiary of such spiritual gifts. Apparently, it is not on such charisms that his teaching authority rested.

We are nowhere told that his message on the Law and on ethics was issued in response to a supernatural command, and none of his quasi-prophetic announcements is introduced as ordered by God or coming from him. The only saying classifiable under the present heading is Matt. 11.27/Luke 10.22, 'All things have been delivered to me by my Father . . . ', implying a complete revelation of God's message and plans to Jesus. However, in its present form, few if any Gospel critics are prepared to recognize the passage as genuine.[6]

If Jesus did not invoke God as guarantor of his teaching, is he portrayed as a Bible interpreter or as a preacher customarily seeking confirmation in the written divine word? The Synoptic Gospels definitely convey this impression, and a survey and analysis of the relevant excerpts will help to understand the evangelists' purpose and determine the reliability or otherwise of the attributions.

Of the various scripture-related didactic forms which have

[6]Cf. *JJ*, 201; *HST*, 159 ('a Hellenistic revelation saying'); C. K. Barrett, *Jesus and the Gospel Tradition* (1967), 27.

been listed above (see p. 49), five figure in the Synoptic Gospels in the framework of Jesus' teaching: (1) the re-employment of biblical words or phrases; (2) the citation of scriptural precedents; (3) the derivation of a new meaning by emphasis or contrast; (4) the pesher-type fulfilment interpretation; and (5) the midrashic model entailing the combination of different Bible passages to support the proposed doctrine.

1. Re-employment of biblical words

Implicit Bible quotations commonly appear in Gospel narratives. They suggest, without clearly asserting it, that the event described follows a prediction, and that it has consequently been providentially foreordained. Characteristic examples may be found in the allusions to verses from Psalms 22 and 69 in the Synoptic Passion story. Thus Mark 15.24 (Matt. 27.35), 'They divided his garments among them, casting lots for them', echoes Ps. 22.18, 'They divide my garments among them, and for my raiment they cast lots'. Later on, Mark 15.29 (Matt. 27.39), referring to onlookers deriding Jesus on the cross, 'wagging their heads', re-uses Ps. 22.7, 'All who see me mock at me . . . , they wag their heads'. The last words of the crucified, *Eloi, Eloi, lama sabachtani*, 'My God, my God, why hast thou forsaken me?' correspond to the Aramaic rendering of Ps. 22.1 in Mark 15.34 (Matt. 27.46).[7] Finally, the episode recounting how one of the bystanders tried to relieve Jesus' thirst, 'One ran and, filling a sponge full of vinegar, put it on a reed and gave it to him to drink' (Mark 15.36; Matt. 27.48), is framed according to Ps. 69.21, 'For my thirst, they gave me vinegar to drink.'[8]

[7]Why the phrase is quoted in Aramaic and not in Hebrew is unexplained. Perhaps it was a proverbial exclamation by people in despair? – In Luke 23.46, Jesus expires with the words, 'Father into thy hands I commit my spirit', slightly paraphrasing Ps. 31.5, 'Into thy hand I commit my spirit; thou hast redeemed me, O Lord, faithful God.'

[8]The writer of the Fourth Gospel no longer needs allusive language. He formally presents the details referred to as the realization of prophecies. John 19.23f.: 'His tunic was without seam . . . so they (the soldiers) said to one another, "Let us not tear it, but cast lots for it to see whose it shall be." This was to fulfil the scripture, "They parted my garments among them, and for my clothing they cast lots"' (Ps. 22.18). John 19.28f.: 'After this Jesus . . . said (to fulfil the scripture), "I thirst". A bowl full of vinegar stood there; so they put a sponge full of vinegar on hyssop and held it to his mouth. (Ps. 69.21).'

A number of similar citations or re-wordings, without any hint that they derive from the Bible, appear in doctrinal passages or prayers placed on the lips of Jesus. Whether they are deliberately borrowed or subconsciously introduced, whether they are intended to inject particular holiness into the saying and thus endow it with supernatural dignity or simply represent a literary style, is impossible to decide in a general manner. The examples fall essentially into three categories: parables, apocalyptic sayings and prayers.

Three of the parables are given incidental biblical flavour. The description of the vineyard entrusted to wicked tenants opens with a recognizable allusion to Isa. 5.1–2 (Mark 12.1; Matt. 21.33, but not Luke 20.9). The parable of the mustard seed (Mark 4.30–32; Matt. 13.31f.; more briefly Luke 13.18f.) may possibly be inspired by the imagery of Dan 4.21 concerning a tree 'under which beasts of the field found shade, and in whose branches the birds of the air dwelt'. Finally, the parable of the secretly growing seed (Mark 4.26–29), symbolizing the Kingdom of God, ends with a phrase lifted from Joel 3.13.[9]

In the case of apocalyptic sayings, the utterances attributed to Jesus by the evangelists are frequently peppered with the eschatological similes of the prophets. The phenomenon is so richly attested in the Eschatological Discourse (Mark 13; Matt. 24; Luke 21) that a single illustration will be enough.

The day of judgment is said to be heralded by signs from the sky and the apparition of the 'son of man': 'After that tribulation, the sun will be darkened, and the moon will not give its light, and the stars will be falling from heaven . . . And then they will see the son of man coming in clouds . . . ' (Mark 13.24–26; Matt. 24.29f.). The picture is inspired by traits taken from Isa. 13.10, 'For the stars of the heavens and their constellations will not give their light; the sun will be dark at its rising and the moon will not shed its light' – combined with Isa. 34.4, 'All the host of heaven . . . shall fall', followed by a free re-wording of Dan. 7.13, 'And behold, with the clouds of heaven there came one like a son of man.'[10]

[9]Note, however, that the prophetic context differs and the Greek wording departs from the Septuagint. Matt. 13.41 in interpreting the parable of the weeds may allude to Zeph. 1.3, but the issue is too complicated to serve any useful purpose here.

[10]Somewhat similar examples may be seen in Matt. 10.34–36/Luke 12.51–53, alluding to Micah 7.6, or in Mark 9.47f. in which the notion of Gehenna is

A third class of implicit quotation is associated with prayer. The words of Jesus in Gethsemane, 'My soul is very sorrowful, even to death' (Mark 14.34; Matt. 26.38), faintly echoes Ps. 42.5f., and his instruction in the Sermon on the Mount, 'When you pray, go into your room and shut the door and pray to your Father who is in secret' (Matt. 6.6) re-employs, in a totally different setting, Isa. 26.20, 'Come, my people, enter your chambers, and shut your doors behind you; hide yourselves for a little while until the wrath is past.'

Informal rehearsal of scripture in actual teaching only seldom occurs. The next item (Matt. 18.15f.) shows how a biblical passage is woven into a church ruling. The passage deals with a conflict between two members of the community and issues instructions on how to settle the affair. Reconciliation must first be attempted in private by the wronged party, and if both agree, no further steps are required. If not, he has to take with him two or three other 'brothers' before delivering a second admonition that 'every word may be confirmed by the evidence of two or three witnesses' (Deut. 19.15). If still unrepentant, the 'sinner' may be reported to 'the church'.

The introduction of the Deuteronomy citation is tangential and justified merely by the reference to the number of external attendants. The purpose of the biblical legislation stipulating that a single witness in a lawsuit is worthless, is completely different from this rule relating to internal community discipline possibly leading to excommunication. Since the connection between quotation and doctrine is slight, no significant conclusion can be drawn from this example. Nor is there any need to investigate whether the section belongs among the

---

rendered vivid by a gloss consisting of a slightly re-written version of Isa. 66.24. Again, the future (eschatological) fate of Capernaum, brought down to Hades after having been exalted to heaven (Matt. 11.23; Luke 10.15), is depicted with the help of Isa. 14.13,15, where the words originally relate to Babylon. Dan. 7.13, joined to Ps. 110.1, is re-used freely in the reply which Jesus is supposed to have given to the High Priest in Mark 14.62/Matt. 26.64/Luke 22.69. Note that whereas Ps. 110 is introduced formally in Mark 12.36/Matt. 22.44/Luke 20.42f. (see p. 61,n.19), Dan. 7.13 is only indirectly referred to in the Gospels.

authentic teachings of Jesus, a point doubted by most scholars.[11]

In retrospect, the three main categories – parables, apocalyptic sayings and prayers – seem to represent a use of biblical texts either for literary or stylistic purposes or for the creation of an atmosphere appropriate for the message. Is it likely that the introduction of such unannounced citations can be credited to Jesus? While in principle adoption by a teacher of the inter-testamental era of biblical style is perfectly possible, on the whole the judgment should be negative. The extracts considered do not strike one as universally known among first-century Palestinian Jews, let alone in uneducated Galilean circles, and in consequence would have passed unnoticed by the large majority of Jesus' audience. So, even if it could be argued that he was so familiar with the scriptures that words of such inconspicuous prophets as Joel or Zephaniah instinctively issued from his lips – and this hypothesis is in no way borne out by the New Testament – the use of implicit quotations cannot be acknowledged as playing a real didactic role and validating in any manner the teachings in which they figure. In fact, there can be hardly any doubt that they owe their existence to the literary/editorial efforts of the evangelists.

2. Scriptural precedents

Among the doctrinal statements ascribed to Jesus, several take the form of an argument in which the proof merely consists in an example borrowed from biblical history. Such an interpretative procedure was, of course, not invented by him, but belongs to the literary tradition of inter-testamental and rabbinic Judaism.

Here is a fairly elaborate, but typical example, based on Ex. 14. The Israelites, hotly pursued by Pharaoh's horses and chariots, arrive at the sea. At that critical moment, God reproachfully asks Moses why he is 'crying' to him. He should rather 'lift up' his rod (Ex. 14.15f.). The late first-/early second-century rabbi, Yose the

[11]Cf. *HST*, 146 (saying created independently by the Church). On the passage see K. Stendahl, *The School of St Matthew* (1954), 138f. On rebuke, witnesses and excommunication in the Qumran sect, cf. *QIP*, 92f., 100f., 113f.; G. Forkman, *The Limits of the Religious Community: Expulsion from the Religious Community within the Qumran Sect, within Rabbinic Judaism and within Primitive Christianity* (1972); Lawrence H. Schiffman, *Sectarian Law in the Dead Sea Scrolls: Courts, Testimony and the Penal Code* (1983).

Galilean, brings out the dramatic significance of the scene by comparing the fate of the Jews at the time of the exodus from Egypt to that of Isaac bound on the altar and ready to be slaughtered by his father.

> When the Israelites were on the point of entering the sea, Mount Moriah had already been moved from its place with the altar for Isaac built on it and prepared (for the sacrifice), with Isaac as it were bound and laid on it and Abraham as it were stretching out his hand and holding the knife to slay his son.

The danger, the urgency and the implied imminence of the redeeming divine intervention are all brought home through the allusion to the Genesis 22 story. The tension is so great that, to relieve it, the preacher feels justified in injecting a slight irony into his account.

> God said to Moses: 'Moses, my children are in distress. The sea bars (their way). The enemy pursues them. And you just stand there and keep on praying!' Moses said before him: 'And what should I be doing?' He said [using a Hebrew pun]: 'Lift up [HaReM] your rod, etc. (Ex. 14.16): you should extol (MeRoMeM), praise and glorify, utter songs and glorification and magnification and praise and thanksgiving and exaltation to him to whom wars belong' (Mekh. II, 222f.).

In R. Yose's presentation, the reference to the binding of Isaac is merely a homiletic device employed to supply a fuller meaning to the Exodus story. The underlying theological doctrine, viz, that redemption at the sea was a consequence of the Akedah, may be guessed, but is not stated.[12]

Authentication of a teaching by means of a scriptural example or precedent figures in the Synoptic Gospels both in connection with practice and ideas.

In regard to practice, namely the permissibility to pluck heads of corn in a field on the Sabbath, the Gospel story has already been touched on in the previous chapter (pp. 23f.). Discussing Mark 2.23–26 (Matt. 12.1–7; Luke 6.1–4), it has been argued that hunger, the first stage of starvation, excuses the very light breach of the sabbatical rest for which the disciples are criticized

[12]Cf. *S & T*, 206–8.

by hostile observers. Jesus defends their action with the help of a precedent testified to in I Sam. 21. 1–7.

> 'Have you never read', Jesus retorts, 'what David did, when he was in need and was hungry, he and those who were with him: how he entered the house of God . . . and ate the bread of the Presence, which it is not lawful for any but the priests to eat, and also gave it to those who were with him?' (Mark 2.25f.)

The tacit reasoning built into this reply may be rendered explicit as follows. If hunger entitled David, God's elect, to disregard the rule prohibiting a layman from partaking in food so sacred that only Temple priests were allowed to eat it, the much slighter disregard of the Sabbath interpretation is hardly worth considering seriously. The same principle, namely that Temple legislation overrides the Sabbath laws is expressly stated in a Matthean supplement to Mark's account: 'Or have you not read in the Law how on the Sabbath the priests in the Temple profane the Sabbath (by performing "work" in the course of sacrificial worship), and are guiltless?' (Matt. 12.5)

Good parallels are extant for this kind of teaching from the inter-testamental and early rabbinic era in which, as in the Gospels, David's example is presented as final and decisive. When seeking to clarify the significance of Deut. 17.17, 'And he (the king) shall not multiply wives to himself', the Mishnah (Sanh 2.4), which understands the ban on 'multiplying' to mean that the ruler must not exaggerate as did Solomon with his seven hundred wives without mentioning his concubines, but be content with a reasonable number of women, i.e., a maximum of eighteen, inferred in a tongue-in-cheek manner from a rabbinic interpretation of David's story in II Samuel.[13]

On the other hand, when a Qumran writer claims that anything more than one is a 'multiple' and consequently the king must be monogamous, he in turn is compelled to explain away David's well-known polygamous habits. The king is excused on account of an invincible ignorance: in his time the Torah was a

---

[13]According to II Sam 3.2–5, David had six wives; in 12.8, the prophet Nathan, rebuking him after the Bathsheba episode and the murder of her husband, Uriah, remarks that if David found his harem 'too little', God might have enlarged it by, literally, 'as much and as much', that is, six plus six plus six!

'sealed book' the message of which was hidden and inaccessible (CD 5.2–5).[14]

Turning now from practice to religious ideas, we are faced with the problem of the charismatic teacher whose sceptical audience is clamouring for 'signs', a not unusual Jewish custom of the age if we are to believe Paul's stereotypical contrast between Jews who 'demand signs' and Greeks who 'seek wisdom' (I Cor. 1.22). All three Synoptics deal with the issue, Mark supplying a straight negative reply, 'No sign shall be given to this generation' (Mark 8.12), which in the Gospel context must mean that 'signs' are not available on request, an instinctive reaction by a 'miracle-worker', believable both from the historical and the psychological points of view.

By contrast, Luke and Matthew (or Q) reproduce a saying, which in the more straightforward and probably more original Lucan form is expressed with the help of a scriptural example.

> This generation is an evil generation; it seeks a sign, but no sign shall be given to it except the sign of Jonah. For as Jonah became a sign to the men of Nineveh, so will the son of man be a sign to this generation.[15]

The most likely meaning of this simile has nothing to do with the prophet's maritime adventure for which he is notorious, and about which, as will be shown, Matthew has something to say. It resides rather in the story recorded in Jonah 3, namely that his appeal for repentance addressed to the inhabitants of Nineveh carried such supernatural power that it was accepted as a sign from God and they all turned away from their wickedness. Jesus – the son of man in given contexts being a customary reference to the speaker himself – describes his own mission as the eschatological antitype of that of Jonah. Further developments on the same theme in Luke 11.31f./Matt. 12.41f. attests editorial emphasis on the superiority of Jesus: 'Behold, something greater than Jonah (or greater than Solomon) is here.'

A very different doctrinal twist is introduced by Matthew into his version of the saying. Far from being content with a vague hint at Jonah as a sign resulting in the Ninevites' conversion, here

---

[14]Cf. *PJBS*, 41, 54.

[15]Luke 11.29f. Cf. Matt. 16.4 where the sign of Jonah is mentioned without further explanation.

Jesus is represented as identifying the three days and nights spent by the prophet inside the 'big fish', to use the generic phrase of the Hebrew Bible (Jonah 1.17), with the period which Jesus is said to have spent in his tomb.

> For as Jonah was three days and three nights in the belly of the sea-monster (*kētos*), so will the son of man be three days and three nights in the heart of the earth (Matt. 12.40).

This interpretation of the Jonah passage requires some explanation as the figures given do not tally with the Gospel chronology according to which Jesus did not remain buried for three nights. Technical midrashic exegesis, though attested only from a later age (fourth/fifth century AD) in its definitive formulation, may help to grasp the Matthean expansion. This implies, on the one hand, that following a halakhic rule, part of a day or a night is reckoned as amounting to the full twelve-hour period (yShab 12a; bPes 4a), and on the other hand that 'the third day' is associated with the idea of revival and salvation.

The best rabbinic summary of the latter, assembling all the relevant Bible passages, is given in a midrashic commentary, Genesis Rabbah 56.1, on Gen. 22.4: 'On the third day Abraham lifted up his eyes and saw the place (of Isaac's sacrifice) afar off.'

> *On the third day, etc.* (Gen. 22.4). It is written: *After two days he will revive us, on the third day he will raise us up, that we may live before him* (Hos. 6.2).

> On the third day of the tribes: *On the third day Joseph said to them,* ['*Do this and you will live*'] (Gen. 42.18).

> On the third day of the gift of the Torah: *On the morning of the third day* (Ex. 19.16, with the implied teaching that the Torah is the source of life).

> On the third day of the spies: *Hide yourselves there three days* [*until the pursuers have returned*] (Josh. 2.11).

> *On the third day of Jonah*: *And Jonah was in the belly of the fish three days* (Jonah 2.1).

On the third day of those who returned from the exile: *And we remained there* (in Jerusalem) *three days* (Ezra 8.32).

On the third day of the resurrection of the dead: *After two days he will revive us, on the third day he will raise us up* (Hos. 6.2).

Although this learned and sophisticated theological speculation can scarcely be seen as the historical source of the Matthean logion, it can even less be said to derive from the latter. It may, however, be treated as a pre-existent didactic model from which the evangelist drew his inspiration.

While they supply no fresh information, a few further examples pertaining to this class deserve mention. In Luke 17.26f./Matt. 24.38, the unexpectedness of 'the days of the son of man' is compared to the situation prevailing immediately before the flood. Noah's generation is depicted as calm and relaxed: 'They ate, they drank, they married, they were given in marriage, until the day when Noah entered the ark, and the flood came and destroyed them all' (cf. Gen. 7.7). The saying, which has no visible link with the ideas familiar in Jewish writings of the period, viz. that Noah's contemporaries were a particularly wicked lot and that he was appointed to be a preacher of repentance to them (cf. even II Peter 2.5), is part of the eschatological discourse which in general is held to reflect the views of the primitive church more than those of Jesus. A similar comment applies also to Luke 17.28–30, illustrating the same doctrine from the story of the destruction of Sodom in 'the days of Lot' (Gen. 19).[16]

Yet another example occurs in the discourse against the Pharisees in Matt. 23.34f./Luke 11.49f., where the predicted persecution of Christian 'prophets and apostles' (Luke) or 'prophets, wise men and scribes' (Matt.), is presumed to be the culmination of a long series of murders of the just, starting with Abel and leading up to a Zechariah (son of Barachiah [Matt.]), killed in the Temple. The latter individual's identity remains obscure, but since the nature of the saying hardly leads one to believe in its authenticity – detailed anti-Pharisee polemics reflect

[16]For Jewish tradition, both the generation of the flood and the men of Sodom are quintessential sinners. Cf. CD 2.19f.; mSanh 10.3.

a situation prevailing in the post-AD 70 Palestinian church – no full discussion of the matter is called for.[17]

Did then Jesus have recourse to biblical precedent to support his teaching? There is no theoretical reason to deny this possibility. However, in investigating the question of the likely authenticity, a preliminary issue – additional to matters pertaining to Synoptic history – must be raised, viz. the relationship between the argument and the audience to which it is addressed.

It should be noted first that in the halakhic discussions of the rabbis, strict hermeneutical rules, the so-called *middot* (e.g. *a fortiori* or analogical reasoning), were followed.[18] An example could be used only as illustration with no real evidential value. But it is perfectly acceptable and effective in popular teaching and preaching as long as the story cited was known to all and sundry. Hence the example of David would not have convinced learned Pharisees that plucking corn in a field on the Sabbath was blameless, but it may have satisfied simple Galileans. Likewise, Jonah, the preacher in Nineveh, – i.e. the Lucan formulation of the saying concerning the sign of Jonah – could easily symbolize Jesus' function as one calling for repentance in preparation of the coming of the kingdom of God. But the argument presented by Matthew with the Jonah anecdote linked to the resurrection of Jesus entails too much scholastic presupposition to carry conviction without further ado.

In short, in the light of the Synoptic Gospels it can be taken for granted that Jesus could and did handle the homiletic device of the biblical precedent; that he did so in a very unsophisticated fashion and, if we can rely on the extant data, only occasionally and not as a regular means to endow his teaching with scriptural authority.

3. *Exegesis by means of emphasis or contrast*

It has been shown in the course of the previous chapter, in the sections devoted to 'The so-called antitheses' and to 'The

---

[17]Cf. T. W. Manson, *The Sayings of Jesus* [1937] (1979), 103–5; K. Stendahl, *The School of St Matthew* (1954), 92f. and S. H. Blank, 'The Death of Zechariah in Rabbinic Literature', *HUCA* 12–13 (1937–38), 327–46.

[18]On the *middot*, cf. *HJP* II, 344.

Decalogue', that Jesus developed his ethical teaching on subjects such as murder, adultery, divorce, oaths, retaliation and the love of one's enemies by stressing the meaning implied in certain biblical commandments or prohibitions, or by introducing an element of contrast in order to highlight his own approach to basic aspects of morality. Since all the relevant passages have been discussed there (pp. 30–38), further examination is superfluous.[19]

4. *Pesher-type exegesis or fulfilment interpretation*

One of the commonest forms of utilization of scripture in the Synoptic Gospels is what used to be called in former, less refined times, the prophetic argument. An Old Testament verse is cited to indicate that an event associated with the life of Jesus was foretold so that it can now be recognized as the realization of the saying by Isaiah, Daniel, or David, the psalmist, the fulfilment of a messianic prophecy. With the age of criticism, these prophecies were thought to be after the fact, *prophetiae ex eventu*, another simplistic way to treat an important cultural phenomenon. Nowadays, however, with the Dead Sea Scrolls to enlighten the horizon of inter-testamental Judaism, this category of Bible interpretation is easily pigeonholed as a New Testament *pesher*. Of course, this is yet another summary classification. The Qumran *pesher* is essentially a literary genre in which a biblical book which is, or is thought to be, prophetic, is subjected to a systematic exposition with the help of incidents belonging to the history of the Essene sect. The explanation of biblical verse 1 is event A, that of verse 2 is event B, and so on until the end of the chapter or the book. Needless to say, the Gospels do not correspond to this sort of exegetical literature. However, both at Qumran and in rabbinic writings, we encounter theological reasonings which employ either extracts from existing *peshers*, or manufacture an *ad hoc* demonstration. Such texts constitute appropriate material for a genuine understanding of the New Testament parallels.[20]

---

[19]Jesus' argument turning Ps. 110.1, 'The Lord said to my lord, sit at my right hand', into a polemical instrument by attributing special significance to the phrase 'my lord' could fall into the same category. Cf. Mark 12.35–37/Matt. 22.41–45/Luke 20.41–44.

[20]For the Qumran evidence, see my studies cited in notes 3 and 5 above.

Docrinal passages placed by the evangelists in Jesus' mouth contain ten or so cases where the significance or the predestined character of a happening is explained or demonstrated with the help of such a 'prophetic' quotation. They occur in all types of Gospel tradition, Marcan, Q, as well as sayings attested by Matthew or Luke alone, and fall into three main categories.

(*a*) The first of these, a fulfilment interpretation in a controversy story, figures in Mark 7.1–8/Matt. 15.1–9: Jesus qualifies as hypocritical the Jerusalem Pharisees' quibbling about the disciples' habit of eating with unwashed hands. The critics rate custom as high as, if not higher than, divine commandments, thus fulfilling Isaiah's words: 'This people honours me with their lips, but their heart is far from me; in vain do they worship me, teaching as doctrines the precepts of men' (Isa. 29.13). The biblical text is intended to underline that true religion springs from the heart and is impeded by too much concern with external observances, an attitude fully consonant with charismatic spirituality.

(*b*) The second class of *pesher*-type citation serves to derive a practical or doctrinal conclusion from the assumed fulfilment of a prophetic prediction. Mark 13.14, and even more explicitly Matt. 24.15f., exemplify the case. The installation of a sacrilegious object in the Temple (Dan. 9.27) will indicate the arrival of the final cataclysm and signal the moment when the faithful disciples must flee.

> So when you see the desolating sacrilege, spoken of by the prophet Daniel, standing in the holy place (let the reader understand), then let those who are in Judaea flee to the mountains (Matt. 24.15f.).

Again, in the garden of Gethsemane, Jesus announces that his apostles will relinquish him by virtue of the prophecy of Zechariah (13.7).

> You will all fall away; for it is written, 'I will strike the shepherd, and the sheep will be scattered' (Mark 14.27/Matt. 26.31).[21]

[21]The same verse is quoted in full in the Damascus Document (CD 19.5–9) foretelling the punishment of the wicked and the salvation of the humble ('I will stretch my hand over the little ones'), rather than the loss of 'the shepherd' as in the Gospels.

Elsewhere, Matthew (9.12f.), unlike the two other Synoptics, makes Jesus suggest that his unorthodox approach to the 'tax-collectors and sinners' is the realization of a saying of Hosea (6.6).

> Those who are well have no need of a physician, but those who are sick. Go and learn what this means, 'I desire mercy, and not sacrifice.'[22]

Finally, in an unusual and clumsy manner, and on a single occasion, the principal point of a parable is claimed to be the fulfilment of a Psalm. The story of the murderous tenants of a vineyard is followed by Jesus' comment in Mark 12.10f./Matt. 21.42/Luke 20.17.

> Have you not read this scripture: 'The very stone which the builders rejected has become the head of the corner . . . ' (Ps. 118.22).

The metaphors of the quotation have nothing to do with the story itself and the juxtaposition of the two appears to be purely artificial. The verse belongs to the apologetical arsenal of primitive Christianity (Acts 4.11; I Peter 2.6); hence its addition to the parable, if not the parable itself, may be presumed to be of ecclesiastical origin.

(c) The third category, the *pesher* exegesis proper, i.e. the portrayal of an event as fulfilment of a prophecy, may in turn be subdivided into citations which Jesus is said to have applied to circumstances or individuals other than himself, and those which he claims to have personally accomplished.

As regards the first variety, attested by Mark, Q and Matthew, there is the case of the merchants and money-changers whose presence in the Temple fulfils Isa. 56.7 with an echo of Jer. 7.11.

> And he taught and said to them, 'Is it not written, "My house shall be called a house of prayer for all the nations" (Isa.), but

---

[22]The appositeness of the quotation is somewhat questionable since only the first half of the Hosea verse, the notion of mercy, is relevant. The same extract seems to fit better another Matthean supplement (12.5–7 to Mark 2.23–26/Luke 6.1–4) in connection with plucking and eating corn on the sabbath where the argument runs as follows: Temple worship has priority over the sabbath, but an act of mercy is preferred by God to a sacrifice. It should be noted that the phrase, 'Go/come and learn/listen/see!' often occurs in Jewish exegetical terminology.

you have made it "a den of robbers" (Jer.)'? (Mark 11.17; Matt. 21.13; Luke 19.46).

Almost next to it, we find in Matthew (21.15f.) Jesus justifying, as though they needed justification despite the petty grumble by the Temple authorities, a group of children who greeted him with 'Hosanna to the son of David', by quoting to the chief priests and scribes the words of Ps. 8.2,

> Have you never read, 'Out of the mouth of babes and sucklings thou hast brought perfect praise'? (Matt. 21.16)

The most outstanding Gospel *pesher* is preserved in a Q passage in which Jesus identifies John the Baptist as the person foretold by the prophet Malachi (3.1), whose words are suitably modified with the help of Ex. 23.20.

> What did you go out to the wilderness to behold? ... To see a prophet? Yes, I tell you, and more than a prophet. This is he of whom it is written, 'Behold, I send my messenger before your face, who shall prepare your way before you' (Matt. 11.7–10).[23]

The second kind of fulfilment interpretation is peculiar to Luke. The Gentile evangelist, in passages without Synoptic parallels, twice presents Jesus as applying prophecy to his own person. The first instance is the episode of the public reading by Jesus of Isa. 61, 'The spirit of the Lord is upon me, because he has anointed me to preach good news to the poor ... ', followed by the momentous comment: 'Today this scripture has been fulfilled in your hearing' (Luke 4.16–21). Further, in the Lucan passage on the two swords (22.35–38), Jesus sees himself as realizing the oracle concerning the Suffering Servant:

> For I tell you that this scripture must be fulfilled in me, 'And he was reckoned with the transgressors' (Isa. 53.12); for what is written about me has its fulfilment (Luke 22.37).

In the light of these data, there can be no question concerning the familiarity of the *pesher*-type exegesis in the circles responsible

---

[23]The same argument appears, though not on the lips of Jesus, in Mark 1.2 where the Malachi *cum* Exodus compound is prefixed to Isa. 40.3.

for the creation of the Gospels. But are there any good reasons to link it to Jesus himself? That this is not necessarily so and that this type of proof is not indissolubly bound to Jesus is evident not only from the Qumran precedent – most of the Scrolls antedate the first century AD – but also from the frequency of its use by the evangelists, especially Matthew, without placing the words on Jesus' lips.

The preaching of John the Baptist in the Judaean desert is described in the triple tradition (Mark 1.2–4/Matt. 3.1–3/Luke 3.2–6) as the realization of Isa. 40.3 read as, 'The voice of one crying in the wilderness: Prepare the way of the Lord', instead of bringing forward the caesura to give, 'The voice of one crying: In the wilderness prepare the way of the Lord'.[24]

The remainder of the evidence comes from Matthew and relates to the virgin birth (Matt. 1.22f./Isa. 7.14); to Bethlehem as the Messiah's birthplace (Matt. 2.3–5/Micah 5.2); to the massacre of the boys up to two years old in the area (Matt. 2.16–18/Jer.31.15; Gen. 35.19); to the healing role of Jesus as fulfilling literally, and not spiritually, the mission of the Servant of Deutero-Isaiah (Matt. 8.18/Isa. 53.4; Matt. 12.18/Isa. 42.1–4); to his teaching in parables (Matt. 13.35/Ps. 78.2); to his riding into Jerusalem on a donkey (Matt. 21.5f./Zech. 9.9, edited and combined with Isa. 62.11);[25] and finally to the purchase of the Field of Blood with Judas's thirty shekels of silver (Matt. 27.7–10, claimed to be the fulfilment of a non-existent saying of Jeremiah. Matthew possibly mingles Jer. 32 here with Zech. 11.12f.).

Moreover, the Matthean and the Qumran *pesher* exegesis as well as similar relics in rabbinic writings – such as Yohanan ben Zakkai's prediction that Vespasian would become emperor as adumbrated in Isa. 10.34, or Rabbi Akiba's identification, in the light of Num. 24.17, of Simeon bar Kokhba as the royal Messiah (*S & T*, 34f.; 165f.) – indicate that the home ground of this kind of argument is apologetics rather than teaching, preaching or

[24]The latter division, consonant with the meaning of the Hebrew text, underlies the *pesher* proof of why the Qumran sect established itself in the wilderness (1QS 8.12–14).

[25]In order to make it appear more convincing, the evangelist has omitted those words of the Hebrew text which allude to the triumphal power of the Messiah, 'righteous and victorious', before describing his lowly condition, 'humble and mounted on an ass'.

exposition. Hence, whereas the hypothesis that Jesus turned from time to time to fulfilment interpretation cannot be absolutely excluded, its likelihood on an extensive scale is minimal. Nor is there any compelling reason why any of them should be considered genuine. In particular, *pesher* authentication of his own divinely predestined role is testified to only in Luke, whose sensitivity in Jewish matters is not particularly developed. Only someone with Alexander the Great's self-importance is likely to be depicted by a Jew (e.g. Josephus) as priding himself on the fulfilment in his person of what he believed to be an ancient prediction.

> And when the book of Daniel was shown to him [Alexander the Great] in which he [Daniel] had declared that one of the Greeks would destroy the empire of the Persians, he [Alexander] believed himself to be the one indicated (*Ant.* xi.337).

5. *The Gospel midrash*

The synoptic evangelists transmit a few examples of scriptural proof backing legal or doctrinal statements which can best be described as *midrash*, that is to say, either the interpretation of one biblical text with the help of another, or the exegesis of a passage in combination with a general principle. Both procedures commonly figure in rabbinic writings. The former is represented by the commandments concerning filial piety and divorce, contrasted with the *qorban* rule and the divine model of marriage, and the latter by the deduction of the doctrine of resurrection from the terminology of the Pentateuch.

The first item concerns a potential conflict between divine law and ancestral custom. In a controversial context Jesus opposes one of the commandments of the Decalogue, 'Honour your father and mother', to a contemporary interpretation of scriptural rules relating to a vow whereby money is devoted to Temple use, a practice known as *qorban* (offering).

In the Marcan version (7.9–13), Jesus' argument runs as follows:

> You have a fine way of rejecting the commandment of God, in order to keep your tradition! For Moses said, 'Honour your father and your mother' (Ex. 20.12; Deut. 5.16); and 'He who

speaks evil of father or mother, let him surely die' (Ex. 21.17; Lev. 20.9); but you say, 'If a man tells his father or his mother, What you would have gained from me is *Qorban* (that is, given to God) – then you no longer permit him to do anything for his father or mother, thus making void the word of God through your tradition which you hand on.'

The parallel in Matthew (15.3–6) curiously omits the Hebrew/Aramaic technical term and reads:

If anyone tells his father or mother, What you would have gained from me is given to God, he need not honour his father (Matt. 15.5).

The implication of this contradiction is that for Jesus the divine precept ensuring care for parents in need supersedes an ultra-rigoristic understanding of Temple legislation. It would seem that neither rabbinic Judaism, nor even the strict school of Qumran Essenism went as far as the evangelists' Pharisees.[26] It is worth observing that whereas the biblical text, taken from the Ten Commandments, must have been familiar to all, the ritual law of *qorban* belongs to a very different category. Nevertheless, the point made by this fairly advanced exegetical reasoning is wholly congruous with the basic religious outlook of Jesus.

The second New Testament *midrash*, accredited to Jesus by Mark 10.2–9 (and Matt. 19.3–8), re-interprets the divorce legislation of Deut. 24 by setting it against Gen. 1.27, 2.24.

And Pharisees came up and in order to test him asked, 'Is it lawful for a man to divorce his wife?' He answered them, 'What did Moses command you?' They said, 'Moses allowed a man to write a certificate of divorce, and to put her away.' But Jesus said to them, 'For your hardness of heart he wrote you this commandment. But from the beginning of creation, God

[26]For *qorban*, see *JWJ*, 78f. The most relevant Mishnah passage is Ned. 3.2: 'If someone [from a distance] saw people eating figs and said, "Behold these are *qorban* for you", if they turned out to be his father and brothers, according to the School of Shammai, if there were others [non-relations] with them, they were bound [by the vow], but they [the members of the family] were exempted, but according to the School of Hillel both were exempted.' At Qumran, in turn, it is simply forbidden to consecrate to the Temple the food required for the well-being of one's family (CD 16.14f.).

"made them male and female" (Gen. 1.27). "For this reason a
man shall leave his father and mother and be joined to his wife,
and the two shall become one flesh" (Gen. 2.24). So they are no
longer two but one flesh. What therefore God has joined
together, let no man put asunder.'

The permission to issue a document whereby a marriage is
terminated – the rabbinic *get* – results from a divine (or Mosaic)
tolerance, which would and should be unnecessary if the Jews
heeded the blueprint laid down in Genesis 1 where God is said to
have created, and united for life with no hint at an eventual
separation, one man and one woman. The subject and its relation
to the Damascus Document have already been treated in the
previous chapter (cf. pp. 33f.). Needless to say, it represents an
elaborate exegetical argument.

The last remaining item pertaining to this class seeks to
demonstrate the doctrine of the resurrection from the dead with
the help of a Torah citation expounded by means of a theological
principle, namely that God is not the God of the dead but of the
living. In an alleged controversy with Sadducees who rejected the
belief in after-life, Jesus is purported to have declared:

And as for the dead being raised, have you not read in the book
of Moses, in the passage about the bush, how God said to him,
'I am the God of Abraham, and the God of Isaac and the God of
Jacob'? He is not the God of the dead but of the living' (Ex.
3.6). You are quite wrong (Mark 12.26f.; Matt. 22.31f.; Luke
20.37f.).

A paraphrase clarifying the logic of this statement could run as
follows. It is an axiom that God is the God of the living, and not of
the dead. But Abraham, Isaac and Jacob, buried in a cave at
Hebron, are no longer alive. If nevertheless he calls himself the
God of Abraham, Isaac and Jacob, this is because at the end they
will all be raised again. Hence the Torah, the 'book of Moses',
conveys the doctrine of resurrection.

The style of the reasoning is typically rabbinic, although this
particular verse has not been employed, as far as is known, in
Talmud or Midrash with such an end in view. It should be
recalled, however, that the Babylonian Talmud in the tractate
Sanhedrin (90b) assembles a number of attempts to prove the

resurrection doctrine from the Bible, and primarily from the Pentateuch, by means of inferences not unlike that underlying the Gospel passage. Again, the examples come from a later age, but are obviously unrelated to, and independent of the New Testament. The first is attributed to Rabbi Yohanan, a third-century Palestinian teacher, who sought to deduce the resurrection of the dead from Num. 18.28 (bSanh 90b):

> It is written, 'And from it (the tithe offering) you shall give the Lord's offering to Aaron the priest'. But does Aaron live for ever – in fact, he did not even enter the land of Israel – that they should give him an offering? But this teaches that he will live again and Israel will give him an offering. Hence the resurrection of the dead can be inferred from the Torah.

As in the Gospels, the internal logic of the text is thought to demand an interpretation leading far beyond the literal meaning of Numbers.

Another instance, attributed to Rabbi Simai who flourished *circa* AD 200, is even more apposite since it uses Abraham, Isaac and Jacob in arriving at the conclusion that the Pentateuch refers to the resurrection.

> 'I also established my covenant with them (the three patriarchs) to give *them* the land of Canaan' (Ex. 6.4). It is not written, 'you' but 'them'. Hence the resurrection of the dead can be inferred from the Torah (bSanh 90b).

Again the implication is that the divine promise to Abraham, Isaac and Jacob concerning the possession of the land demands belief in the resurrection since the conquest of Palestine did not occur during their lifetime. The technique is characteristic of rabbinic exegesis intent on discovering in the Torah ideas which are alien to it, a technique ill-suited to teaching the unlearned.[27]

---

[27]Another peculiarity, grammatical this time, which the rabbis saw as a pointer to the doctrine of resurrection consists in the use of the imperfect (or the future) tense of verbs instead of the past tense. 'It is taught: R. Meir said, Whence do we know that the resurrection of the dead is from the Torah? It is written, "Then Moses and the people of Israel *yashir* (literally, will sing) this song to the Lord" (Ex. 15.1). It is not said, "sang" but "will sing": hence the resurrection of the dead can be inferred from the Torah' (bSanh 91b). The same principle is applied also to Josh. 8.30, 1 Kings 11.7; Ps. 84.5; Isa. 5.8 (bSanh ibid.).

All in all, the main impression emerging from this survey of five classes of didactic form employing scriptural proof-texts is that in general they figure only on a small scale in Jesus' teaching as presented by the evangelists and that most of the examples lack the force necessary for a strong hypothesis, let alone a demonstration, of authenticity. *Pesher* and midrash almost always presuppose a polemical framework with Pharisees or Sadducees and, whereas such a reality is easily admissible in the case of controversies between the Jewish groups in question and first-century representatives of Judaeo-Christianity, it is very questionable in the context of Jesus' mostly Galilean ministry. As I have outlined in *Jesus the Jew*, prior to AD 70 there was little Pharisee presence outside Judaea, and the same applies to the Sadducees. By contrast, as is patent from the Acts of the Apostles, from the early years of the Jesus movement a well-defined community existed in Jerusalem with members knowledgable in mainstream Jewish matters and providing a suitable setting for debates with the other Palestinian schools.

This notwithstanding, it would be unreasonable to doubt that Jesus ever had recourse to biblical arguments, and of these, as has been suggested, the adoption of biblical idiom, the use of scriptural precedents and the emphatic or hyperbolical interpretation of commandments with which all his contemporaries were familiar, enjoy the strongest claims for genuineness. But they seem to be few and far between and in no way form a sufficiently solid corpus to endow the preaching of Jesus with exceptional power. Yet from the outset, from the very first reference to his teaching in the synagogue of Capernaum, all three synoptists portray him as a man speaking with *exousia*, i.e. authority. This remarkable claim necessitates some further investigation.

III   The Charismatic Authority of Jesus

Max Weber, the most prominent twentieth-century exponent of the idea of charismatic authority, envisaging the issue in general terms, describes the person wielding such a power as follows:

> The charismatic hero does not deduce his authority from codes and statutes, as is the case with the jurisdiction of office; nor

does he deduce his authority from traditional custom or feudal vows of faith, as is the case with patrimonial power.

The charismatic leader gains and maintains authority solely by proving his strength in life. If he wants to be a prophet, he must perform miracles; if he wants to be a war lord, he must perform heroic deeds.[28]

The principal evidence regarding Jesus' personal power and particular doctrinal authority appears at the very beginning of the Gospel, in the account of his first public pronouncement in Galilee. The episode is described in two of the Synoptics (Mark 1.21f./Luke 4.31f.), with a supplementary comment placed after the story of the healing of a man possessed by an 'evil spirit' (Mark 1.27/Luke 4.36). The Matthean parallel to Mark 1.21f. figures as the conclusion of the Sermon on the Mount (Matt. 7.28f.) with a minor, but significant variant. This changed location of the passage, which is clearly secondary, results in the absence of the supplementary reference. The Marcan narrative, which is unquestionably the original version, will serve as basis for our analysis, but the other Synoptic variants will also be borne in mind.

And they went into Capernaum; and immediately on the sabbath he entered the synagogue and taught. *And they were astonished at his teaching, for he taught them as one who had*

---

[28]*From Max Weber: Essays in Sociology*, ed. by H. H. Gerth and C. Wright Mills (1979), 248f.

The charismatic concept is expressly applied to Jesus by Rudolf Otto in the final section of *The Kingdom of God and the Son of Man* (1938), 333–76, entitled 'The Kingdom of God and the Charisma'. He examines, in particular, the questions of the gift of healing and exorcism and of the charismatic preaching. They are all highly relevant in an investigation of the mode of teaching of the historical Jesus and its relation to scriptural authority.

Healing and exorcism practised by Jesus on persons who appear to have been suffering from hysterical conditions are discussed in *JJ*, 22–25, and a whole chapter of that book is devoted to 'Jesus and charismatic Judaism' (pp. 58–82, 239–43). Martin Hengel has many pertinent comments to make on this topic in *The Charismatic Leader and his Followers* (1981), 63–66, and more recently Irving M. Zeitlin has adopted the concept of *charisma* as the guiding principle of his analysis in *Jesus and the Judaism of his Time* (1988), vii. E.P. Sanders also concurs in defining Jesus as a 'charismatic' or 'charismatic prophet' (*Jewish Law*, 3).

authority (hōs exousian echōn), *and not as the scribes*. (Mark 1.21f.) [Here follows the pericope relative to an exorcism.]

And they were all *amazed*, so that they questioned among themselves, saying, 'What is this? *A new teaching with authority* (kat' exousian). He commands even the unclean spirits, and they obey him' (Mark 1.27).[29]

That Jesus' method of instruction did not consist of supporting scriptural quotations are manifest (*a*) from its being contrasted with the scribal style; (*b*) from the positive assertion that it was a 'new' kind of teaching; (*c*) from the repeated emphasis that it revealed 'authority', and (*d*) that, as a result, his audience was 'astonished' and 'amazed'.

The distinctive mark of the 'scribes' (*soferim/grammateis*) as teachers consisted, as is well known, in their expertise as Bible interpreters (*HJP* II, 322–5), and it is no doubt in this regard that Jesus differed from them. Such appears to be the clear implication of Mark 1.22. If Matt. 7.28 attempts to soften the opposition and suggests that Jesus' way of communicating his message merely diverged from the didactic techniques of the run-of-the-mill scribes, this is because, as has been noted, the statement is placed at the end of the Sermon on the Mount, which incorporates a good many biblical interpretations, and because Matthew himself holds the scribal office in high esteem as long as the scribe has received the correct 'eschatological' education. This transpires from the words he places on the lips of Jesus in Matt. 13.52, 'Therefore every scribe who has been trained for the kingdom of heaven is like a householder who brings out of his treasure what is new and what is old.' In the eyes of the first evangelist, Jesus was a

---

[29]The principal variants concern the omission of the reference to 'the scribes' in Luke 4.32 which reads, 'for his word was with authority (*en exousia*)', and the specification in Matthew 7.29 that the scribes belonged to the synagogue congregation, literally, that they were '*their* scribes. Luke (4.36) re-edits the final comment too, and associates 'authority and power', not with Jesus' teaching, but his miraculous acts: 'What is this word? For with authority and power (*en exousia kai dunamei*) he commands the unclean spirits, and they come out'. This appears to be a simplification of the Marcan wording and should be classified as secondary. Some early manuscript witnesses of Mark also delete the mention of the scribes, whereas others harmonize the Marcan reading with Matthew's 'their scribes'.

novel type of 'traditional master' who taught in a manner other than the common Galilean scribe. In fact, Matthew himself is seen by more than one New Testament scholar as a former 'rabbi', who introduced a new sort of scribal office into his church.[30]

Compared to the preaching to which the members of the Capernaum synagogue were accustomed, that of Jesus is defined as 'new' (*didachē kainē*), and its novelty is assigned to its being delivered 'with authority'. Since this '*exousia*' is parallel to the 'authority and power' (*en exousia kai dunamei*) with which Jesus is depicted in Luke 4.36 as an exorcist, it is logical to conclude that both as teacher and as miracle-worker, he was primarily perceived as a charismatic, that is as a person whose paramount authority was spiritual in nature. Also, acts of healing and exorcism were seen as tangible confirmation of the validity and compelling character of his teaching. Hence both provoked astonishment (Mark 1.22/Luke 4.32) and amazement (Mark 1.27/Luke 4.36), the natural reaction to unexpected, unusual, enigmatic phenomena. In Rudolf Otto's words, 'Preaching and power over the demons are regarded . . . as on the same level, i.e. the level of supernatural charismatic power.'[31] The same two subjects are coupled in Mark 6.2/Matt. 13.54, and thus point to an early standard Galilean portrayal of Jesus.

> And on the sabbath he began to teach in the synagogue (at Nazareth); and many who heard him were astonished (*exeplēssonto*), saying, 'Where did this man get all this? What is the wisdom (*sophia*) given to him? What mighty works (*dunameis*) are wrought by his hand!'

In Palestinian Jewish parlance – *charisma* being a Greek concept, absent from the Gospels and used only by Paul in the New Testament – a person wielding such authority is known as a prophet, a term appearing a little further on in the same passage (Mark 6.4/Matt. 13.57) relating to Jesus. Such a divine messenger had no need to verify his utterances by suitable biblical proof-

[30]Cf. G. D. Kilpatrick, *The Origins of the Gospel according to St Matthew* (1946), 136f; K. Stendahl, *The School of St Matthew* (1954), 30–35.
[31]*The Kingdom of God and the Son of Man: A Study in the History of Religion* (1938), 351.

texts. His personality, his presence, the power of his voice, his awe-inspiring reputation as a wonder-worker, ensured that his words were accepted.[32]

To strengthen this conclusion, it may be useful to recall that the other outstanding charismatic preacher in the Gospels, John the Baptist, is equally depicted as proclaiming his message without seeking biblical support, although it would have been easy to supply a number of suitable scriptural arguments. Without the evangelists actually saying so, they picture John, too, as one speaking with authority.

> You brood of vipers! Who warned you to flee from the wrath to come? Bear fruit that befits repentance . . . Even now the axe is laid to the root of the trees; every tree therefore that does not bear good fruit is cut down and thrown into the fire . . . I baptize you with water for repentance, but he who is coming after me is mightier than I, whose sandals I am not worthy to carry; he will baptize you with the holy spirit and with water . . . (Matt. 3.7–11/Luke 3.7–9,16/Mark 1.7–8; cf. Luke 3.10–14; Matt. 3.12/Luke 3.17).

Even on the famous occasion of the rebuke administered to the tetrarch of Galilee, Herod Antipas, on account of his irregular marital status, when it would have been both easy and appropriate to quote chapter and verse, viz. Lev. 18.16 or 20.21, the evangelists simply make John assert with fearless candour: 'It is not lawful for you to have your brother's wife' (Mark 6.18/Matt. 14.4).

In short, it was the people's belief in the heavenly origin of Jesus' and John's teaching, reinforced in the case of the former by his apparent mastery over corporal and mental sickness, that dispensed them both from the need to demonstrate the truth of their doctrine. Their words were endowed with authority not because they were confirmed by scripture, but because both men were revered as prophets, inspired by the spirit of God. To use once again the language of Rudolf Otto, it was the constant experience by Jesus' disciples of the holy and the numinous, springing from his words and deeds, that rendered superfluous any traditional form of biblical argument or proof.

[32]On Jesus as prophet, see *JJ*, 86–99. Cf. also ibid., 27f.

Certain of the slighter touches of the Synoptic portrait of Jesus confirm the fact expressly [viz. a real or presumed experience of veritable holiness] in particular cases . . . Especially apt in this connexion is the passage in Mark x.32 [following a long doctrinal section]: 'And Jesus went before them: and they were amazed; and as they followed, they were afraid'. This passage renders with supreme simplicity and force the immediate impression of the numinous that issued from the man Jesus, and no artistry of characterization could do it so powerfully as these few masterly and pregnant words.[33]

[33]*The Idea of the Holy* (1959), 175f. – It may be worth remarking also that in the Testimonium Flavianum, i.e. Josephus' brief paragraph on Jesus (*Ant.* xviii.63), he is sketched as a master of wisdom, a *sophos anēr*, who was a performer of astonishing deeds (*paradoxōn ergōn poiētēs*) and a teacher (*didaskalos*), the two functions going hand in hand. See G. Vermes, 'The Jesus Notice of Josephus re-examined', *JJS* 38 (1987), 1–10; cf. also 'Josephus' Portrait of Jesus Reconsidered', in *Orient and Occident: A Tribute to the Memory of A. Scheiber* (1988), 373–82.

4

Proverbs and Parables

The examination of the role – relatively restricted, as has been seen – of the Hebrew Bible in the shaping of the teaching of Jesus almost automatically leads to a further analysis of his didactic function. Any attentive reader of the Synoptic Gospels is bound to wonder about the style of his preaching, and the place and circumstances of its delivery. The traditional forms of Jewish instruction – Bible interpretation (Targum, Midrash, homily) and exposition of laws and customs (Mishnah, halakhah) – had the school (*bet ha-midrash*), the academy (*yeshivah*) and the synagogue (*bet ha-keneset*) as their normal venue. To these may be added, prior to AD 70, the Temple court in Jerusalem where, according to rabbinic tradition, Judaism's supreme doctrinal and judicial body, the Great Sanhedrin, convened in the so-called Hall of the Hewn Stone (*lishkat ha-gazzit*). The same courtyard seems to have served also as a kind of open forum, if not a specific 'Speaker's Corner', for Jewish preachers and teachers wishing to convey a religious message.[1]

Jesus is associated in the Gospels with two of the customary places of religious instruction: the synagogue and the Temple. He 'taught' (*didaskein*), 'preached' (*kērussein*) or, in Luke's terminology, 'proclaimed the gospel' (*euangelizesthai*) in anonymous Galilean synagogues (Luke 6.6; Matt. 9.35/Luke 4.15; Matt. 4.23/Luke 4.43f.; 13.10) as well as in those of Nazareth (Mark

---

[1]For the seat of the Sanhedrin, cf. mSanh. 11.2: mMid. 5.4. see *HJP* II, 224f. According to tSanh. 7.1 and tHag. 2.9 on sabbaths and feast days, the members of the Sanhedrin examined doctrinal questions in the 'Bet Midrash' on the Temple Mount. It was in the Temple that Jesus son of Ananias uttered apocalyptic woes (Josephus, *War* vi.300), and Yohanan ben Zakkai is said to have taught 'in the shadow of the Temple' (yAZ 43b; bPes. 26a). In the New Testament, not only Jesus, but also Peter and the apostles taught bystanders within the precincts of the Sanctuary (Acts 3.12–26; 5.20f., 42).

6.2/Matt. 13.54) and Capernaum (Mark 1.21/Luke 4.31). He also 'taught', but not 'preached', in the Temple (Mark 11.17/Matt. 21.13; Luke 19.46 – Matt. 11.23/Luke 20.1; Mark 12.35 – Luke 19.47; 21.37 – Mark 14.49/Matt. 26.55/Luke 22.53). He is furthermore depicted as giving instruction in the open air: in the streets of towns and villages (Mark 1.38/Luke 4.43; 8.1 – Mark 6.6; 10.1), on a Galilean mountain-side (Matt. 5.2/Luke 6.20), and as addressing from a boat crowds gathered on the shore of the lake of Gennesaret (Mark 4.1/Matt. 13.2 –Luke 5.3).

In most of the passages listed, the teaching topics are not specified. In the synagogue events which follow, the argument usually turns on the problem of healing on the sabbath, already discussed in chapter 2. In Capernaum, Jesus' message is hailed simply as a 'new teaching' (cf. pp. 72f.), and from the boat he issued parables (Mark 4.2/Matt. 13.3; Luke 8.4). His 'daily' teaching in the Temple (Luke 19.47; 21.37; Mark 14.49/Matt. 26.55/Luke 22.53) is not detailed either. It is alluded to in general terms, though occasionally scriptural exegesis is entailed (Mark 11.17; 12.35). Subsequently, the evangelists record that in the sanctuary Jesus was engaged in polemics with the officialdom of Jerusalem. Nevertheless, as has already been repeatedly surmised, the authenticity of these is doubtful and according to common scholarly opinion they are more likely to reflect controversies between representatives of the Judaeo-Christian church and rabbinic masters in the final decades of the first century than actual conflicts between Jesus and the Temple authorities. Only the Sermon on the Mount includes a substantial amount of didactic material, a good deal of which may belong to the genuine message of Jesus, even though, as most experts agree, the arrangement of the 'sermon' is Matthean.

The subject of the *kerygma*, i.e. the preaching, is better defined. First and foremost, it contains a call for repentance as is obvious from the Gospel examples concerning the prophet Jonah (3.2), at whose 'preaching' the Ninevites 'repented' (Matt. 12.41/Luke 11.32), and John the Baptist. The latter is reported by all three Synoptics as proclaiming a 'baptism of repentance for the forgiveness of sins' (Mark 1.4/Luke 3.3), the reason for it being the imminent arrival of the Kingdom of God.[2]

[2]The eschatological overtones are conspicuous in Matt. 3.7–10, 12/Luke 3.7–9,17 and the phrase itself appears in Matt. 3.2.

The same two motives characterize Jesus' proclamation referred to as his 'gospel of God':

> The time is fulfilled, and the Kingdom of God is at hand; repent and believe in the gospel! (Mark 1.14).

In turn, Matt. 4.17 simply reiterates the wording of the Baptist's exclamation:

> Repent, for the Kingdom of heaven is at hand! (Matt. 3.2)[3]

It is generally agreed that an appeal for *teshuvah* or repentance, and a heralding of the impending arrival of the divine Kingdom (on which see chapters 5 and 8) form the central themes of the message of Jesus. Yet neither is developed anywhere in any detail. The most likely explanation is that he taught not systematically, but at random, in an *ad hoc* manner, and that his explanations and descriptions resulted from questions addressed to him by occasional listeners or by one of his regular disciples. This is why the bulk of the doctrines attributed to him has been preserved in the form of incidental sayings (*logia*) and similes, or as the title of the chapter has it, proverbs and parables.

Both these rhetorical devices are common in Jewish writings outside the Gospels and constitute the substance of biblical and post-biblical wisdom literature and the rabbinic *mashal* (cf. below pp. 92–7). In fact, many Gospel sayings or images coincide wholly or partly with examples attested in cognate sources. However, even when they are materially more or less the same, the careful reader will often notice an individual twist in the New Testament formulation, as has been remarked earlier in connection with the positive or negative formulation of the Golden Rule (cf. p. 41). In our study of Jesus' proverbs and parables particular attention will be paid to such peculiarities.

I   Teaching in Proverbs

Proverbs and axioms are universally used in conveying wisdom

---

[3]Luke has his own phraseology: 'to announce the gospel of the Kingdom of God' (4.43; 8.1). In Mark 1.14, there is substantial manuscript evidence for both 'gospel of God' and 'gospel of the Kingdom of God'. Judging from Matthew 21.23, Jesus 'taught', but did not *evangelize*, in the Temple of Jerusalem. Mark (11.27f.) avoids both terms. (For further discussion, see pp. 139f. below.)

teaching. Since as a rule, they are characterized by brevity and pithiness, they possess a twofold didactic role: they either offer an impressive starting-point or a forceful conclusion. Without introductory or subsequent explanatory comments, they are ill-suited for instruction. A series of loosely connected or independent wisdom sayings, proclaimed orally, is unlikely to engross the listeners' attention. Any attempt at an oratorical delivery of the Sermon on the Mount will unwittingly supply tangible proof of the artificiality of Matthew's composition.

Bearing this in mind, one realizes that despite the substantial amount of proverbial *logia* surviving in the Gospels, the genre in itself is not very congenial for determining the genuine message of Jesus. Since many such sayings derive from popular wisdom, they may be seen simply as literary clichés, possibly introduced or developed by the early church, and pseudonymously attributed to Jesus.[4]

Nevertheless, the very choice of a proverb testifies to the teaching style of Jesus. Indeed, re-worded Jewish sayings and/or explanations appended to them are even more likely to furnish authentic insights into the mind of the master. A representative sample follows, arranged under eight headings (*a*)-(*h*).

(*a*) The narrow gate

To start with unrevised fomulae, the metaphor of the narrow gate and the difficult access leading to 'life' and salvation (Matt. 7.13f./Luke 13.24) is employed also in IV Ezra 7.6–8:

There is a city built and set on a plain, and it is full of good things, but the entrance to it is narrow and set in a precipitous place so that there is fire on the right and deep water on the left, and there is only one path lying between them.

The Matthean version, 'For the gate is narrow and the way is hard, that leads to life' is terser and rhetorically more powerful.

[4]R. Bultmann, *HST* 69–108 contains much valuable information. G. Dalman, *Jesus-Jeshua: Studies in the Gospels* (1929), 223–32, includes two lists of Gospel proverbs, the first with, the second without, rabbinic parallels. For a recent study, see Alan P. Winton, *The Proverbs of Jesus: Issues of History and Rhetoric* (1990).

(*b*) Exaltation – Humiliation

Again, the wording of the proverb, 'Whoever exalts himself will be humbled and whoever humbles himself will be exalted' (Matt. 23.12/Luke 14.18; 18.14), reflects the customary avoidance of mentioning God. The surviving Hebrew examples similarly use verbs in the third person plural with no subject, a common form of indirect reference to the Deity:

> Whoever exalts himself above the words of the Torah, at the end he will be humbled [literally, they will humble him], but whoever humbles himself for the sake of the words of the Torah, at the end he will be exalted [= they will exalt him] (ARN A, 11 and B, 22, ed. Schechter, p. 46).

But the Talmud is less scrupulous in naming God: 'Whoever humiliates himself, the Holy One blessed be he will exalt him, and whoever exalts himself, the Holy One . . . will humiliate him' (bEr. 13b).

(*c*) Speck and beam

Often the imagery remains the same, but the purpose is altered. Thus the Talmud repeatedly remarks on people's unwillingness to accept the mildest criticism. If someone is told, 'Take the chip out of your eye!', he retorts, 'Take the beam out of yours!' (bArakh. 16b; bBB 15b). The corresponding Gospel logion presents a moral message.

> Why do you see the speck that is in your brother's eye, but do not notice the beam that is in your own eye?, etc. (Matt. 7.3–5/Luke 6.41f.).

Jesus requires objectivity and truthfulness in judging failures in the self and in others. The personal touch seems to be the hallmark characterizing his approach.

(*d*) Physician – Prophet

Two maxims quoted in the context of Jesus' clash with his fellow-citizens of Nazareth provides a good starting-point for the study of reshaped proverbs. The first, 'Physician heal yourself'

(Luke 4.23), was current in one form or another both in the Jewish and in the Hellenistic world. The second, 'A prophet is not without honour except in his own country' (Mark 6.4; Matt. 13.57; Luke 4.24), has familiar echoes, but no clear equivalents in Jewish literature.

'Physician, heal yourself' and its parallels in Genesis Rabbah 23.4 – 'Physician, physician, heal your lameness' – and in a Euripides fragment (1086) – 'A physician for others, but himself full of sores', is a sarcastic warning: a sick doctor does not inspire trust in his prospective patients. But in the Lucan context, the proverb is totally inapposite. Jesus places the saying on the lips of the people of his home town jealous of the miraculous cures achieved by him in Capernaum. But the proverb does not apply to the case. For it to be meaningful, it would require an equivocal formulation in which 'yourself' is replaced by something like 'your own', i.e. the people of your town. Such a deliberate slant which would favour the logion's authenticity, is no longer detectable in the Greek translation of the Aramaic sentence. However, the inadequacy of Luke's phrase did not escape notice, as will be shown presently, in the reformulation of the verse in an Oxyrhinchus papyrus.

The main Gospel tradition, represented by all the Synoptics (Mark 6.4 and par.), employs another proverb-like statement to explain Jesus' unpopularity in Nazareth: prophets are never honoured at home. At that time, openness to charismatic healing power presupposed a kind of reverence and awe which did not come easily to members of the extended family or to close acquaintances and the required submissive trust is found more easily away from home.[5]

[5]The talmudic parallels quoted by Strack-Billerbeck are ill-chosen and unconvincing. The honorific clothing worn by Babylonian sages was not meant to distinguish them locally, but among foreigners (bShab. 145b). Again, Yehudah ha-Nasi's unwillingness to ordain as rabbi a man from Sepphoris who has been criticized by fellow-citizens (yTaan 68a) is not tantamount to declaring all Sepphoritans unsuitable for religious leadership in their own city. In the biblical context, it is not at home, but abroad that the prophet is without authority. The proclamation by the Judaean Amos of an unpopular message in the northern sanctuary of Bethel results in the local high-priest ordering him to 'go home and prophesy there' (Amos 7.10–12). Similarly, a Qumran fragment (4Q375) envisages the case of a person recognized as a 'just and faithful prophet' within his own tribe, but rejected as a preacher of apostasy by the rest of the Israelites (J. Strugnell, 'Moses Pseudepigrapha at Qumran' in L. H. Schiffman,

There is furthermore a double saying, attested in Greek in P. Oxyrhinchus 1, logion 6, and in the Coptic Gospel of Thomas, logion 31, which artfully combines Luke's allusions both to the physician and to the prophet:

> Jesus says: A prophet is not acceptable in his own country [village: GTh], neither does a physician work cures in those who know him.

This formulation can be interpreted as a clever rationalization of the clumsy Lucan redaction rather than an original dictum of Jesus.

(e) Lamp – Salt

The proverbs relating to the lamp and the salt, when analysed in their synoptic variations and compared with their occurrences in Jewish literature outside the New Testament, afford an interesting insight into the evolution of their significance.

Two similes of Jesus are connected with the lamp. The first, Matt. 6.22f./Luke 11.34, likens it to the eye which is 'the lamp of the body'. If the eye is sound, it fills the body with light, otherwise darkness reigns. The eye/lamp is depicted, therefore, as the chief source of spiritual perception, and in this respect the Gospel is echoed by a saying of Eliezer ben Hyrcanus for whom the 'good eye' is synonymous with the 'good way' (mAb. 2.9), i.e. proper religious behaviour. The teacher focusses on the individual and no doubt implies that the good or sound eye is a divine gift, as is also the light reflected by it.[6]

In the second simile (Mark 4.21; Matt. 5.15; Luke 8.16), the point of the message is that the lamp must not be hidden but placed on a stand. In Mark, the logion takes the form of a terse, unanswered question, 'Is a lamp brought in to be put under a

---

Archaeology and History in the Dead Sea Scrolls (1990), 226, 228). Seen against the fact that Jesus was acknowledged, and very likely identified himself, as a prophet (*JJ*, 87–90), the maxim under consideration is directly attributable to him.

[6]According to the 'horoscopes' from Qumran (4Q186), people consist of a variable nine-part mixture of light and darkness, the proportions in the two examples being 6:3 and 8:1, with the light mentioned first. Cf. *DSSE*, 306; *HJP* III, 364f., 464f.

bushel, or under a bed, and not on a stand?', whereas the Q tradition spells out the consequence: 'that those who enter may see light' (Luke); 'and it gives light to all the house' (Matt.). The implicit teaching is that illumination is the aim of the lamp, and the beneficiaries are people in dark places. The Matthean context, opening with, 'You are the light of the earth' (Matt. 5.14), patently envisages the propagators of the Christian gospel. This provides a striking contrast with the use of the imagery in a rabbinic source where the emphasis is laid on the futility of a lamp in sunlight or even in moonlight. When Moses begs Jethro not to depart, he replies: 'Is a lamp of any use except in a dark place? Of what use could a lamp be with the sun and the moon? You are the sun and Aaron is the moon.' (Mekh. on Ex. 18.27 [II, 185f.]).

The proverb regarding salt appears also in diverse formulations. In Mark 9.50, the saying runs, 'Salt is good; but if the salt has lost its saltness, how will you season it? Have salt in yourselves, and be at peace with one another.' The saying seems to contain a warning. Look out that the spiritual value symbolized as salt does not deteriorate because the process is irreversible. The internal quality of the effect produced and preserved by 'salt' is manifest from the final sentence proclaiming that those who have been 'salted' will be of a common mind. The Q explanatory gloss (Matt. 5.13/Luke 14.35) develops, unnecessarily it would appear, the uselessness of the 'unsalty' salt, and Matthew, as in the case of the lamp simile, applies the metaphor to the ministers of the church. Again, the Marcan individual formula appears as original. In fact, the corresponding Jewish proverb is a picturesque description of an impossibility. Thus a talmudic story speaks of a mule, sterile by nature, producing young, and follows it up with the question, 'If salt rots, with what will they salt?' The joking answer is, 'With the after-birth of a mule'. The inventive originality of Jesus' use of the maxim consists in envisaging the corruption of the salt as both possible and irreparable, and consequently something that must absolutely be prevented.

(f) Harvest – Labourers

The saying, 'The harvest is plentiful, but the labourers are few' (Matt. 9.37/Luke 10.2) is also given a special slant by Q, and no doubt by Jesus, in linking it to the eschatological ingathering where workers are in short supply. 'Pray therefore', he adds, 'the Lord of the harvest to send out labourers into his harvest'. By contrast, the saying attributed to Rabbi Tarfon (mAb. 2.15) envisages limited time, lazy labourers and an impatient master. 'The day is short. The task is great. The labourers are idle. The wage is abundant. The master is pressing.'

(g) Millstone

The proverb concerning the huge millstone[7] tied to a neck is viewed from different angles in the Gospels and in the Talmud. The New Testament logion figures in two versions and heads a collection of sayings related to temptation. In Mark 9.42/Matt. 18.6 the sin envisaged is the seduction of 'little ones'; in Luke 17.1f. (cf. also Matt. 18.7), it is more generic: 'Temptations to sin are sure to come, but woe to him by whom they come.' This statement is followed by the allusion to the proverb, 'It would be better for him if a great millstone were hung round his neck and he were thrown into the sea.' The threat is solemn and the atmosphere eschatological.[8]

By comparison, the rabbinic citation is sarcastic: 'A father must teach Torah to his son and provide him with a wife . . . Samuel says. According to the halakhah, he is first to provide him with a wife and then send him to study. R. Yohanan says, With such a millstone round his neck will he occupy himself with the Torah?' (bKid 29b).

The eschatological context of the Synoptic wording and the specific intention to protect the 'little ones' called to the Kingdom are fully consistent with an attribution of the passage to Jesus himself.

---

[7]Literally donkey-stone, i.e., one turned round by a donkey, as opposed to the smaller 'man-stone' of a hand-mill (cf. mOhol. 8.3).

[8]The eschatological overtone is manifest in the subsequent saying (Mark 9.43–48/Matt. 18.8f.) where explicit reference is made to the 'Kingdom of God' or 'life' and 'gehenna' or 'gehenna of fire'. The 'woe' in Luke 17.1/Matt. 18.7 has the same implication in Mark 13.17/Matt. 24.19/Luke 21.23 (Woe to those who are pregnant . . . in those days!); cf. further Matt. 11.21/Luke 10.13 (Woe to you Chorazin!) and the fourfold Lucan 'woe' (Luke 6.24–26) contrasted with the beatitudes. The apocalyptic cries of Jesus son of Ananias furnish additional proof: 'Woe to Jerusalem' (*War* vi.304, 306) and 'Woe again to the city and to the people and to the Temple . . . and woe also to me!' (vi.309).

(h) Birds and beasts and flowers

A final group of New Testament maxims is centred on fauna and flora. The nature of their imagery points to a countryman rather than a town-dweller and the particular slant disclosed in them is important in judging the teacher who uses them. Such similes are common both in the Bible and in rabbinic literature, hence their significance can only be established on a comparative basis.

To begin with, the metaphorical association of a very large animal – a camel in the Gospel, an elephant in the Talmud – with the eye of a needle, conveys the idea of a quasi-impossibility. The ancient rabbis, innocent of Freudian psychoanalysis, claimed that dreams were entirely built on rational thought (*hirhūre lev*) and never contained references to unrealities such as a golden palm tree or an elephant passing through the eye of a needle (bBer 55b). Only the pernickety rabbis from Pumbeditha, renowned for their hair-splitting cleverness, are ironically credited with such flights of fancy (bBM 38b).

In Jesus' teaching, by contrast, the saying is moral and eschatological, rather than psychological and satirical. The narrow gate (cf. Matt. 7.13f./Luke 13.24), reduced here by exaggeration to a scarcely visible hole in a needle, is said to keep the wealthy out of the new world.

> It is easier for a camel to go through the eye of a needle than for a rich man to enter the Kingdom of God (Mark 10.25; Matt. 19.24; Luke 18.25).

The grave urgency of the end-time, excluding even the thought of light-heartedness, – Jesus is never described as laughing – again argues in favour of the authenticity of the logion.[9]

A proverbial *a fortiori* reasoning, apparently current among Jews, runs as follows: birds and plants feed and 'clothe' themselves without producing the wherewithal, or more exactly, are providentially looked after, how much more should human beings trust God? An early rabbinic example, attributed to Simeon ben Eleazar (second half of the second century AD), appears in mKid. 4.14.

[9]Both this saying and that concerning the narrow gate figure among the 'very few cases' which, according to Bultmann, 'can be ascribed to Jesus with any measure of confidence' (*HST*, 105).

Have you ever seen a wild beast or a bird practising a craft? Yet they are catered for without trouble although they have been created only to serve me. And I have been created to serve my Master, should I not all the more be catered for without trouble? But I have done evil and have forfeited my sustenance.

The underlying argument assumes that whereas the conditions prevailing in the garden of Eden – availability of food without labour to produce it – have continued in some way below the level of man, humans find themselves, despite their superiority in the divine plan, in an inferior position.

The same imagery, and some of the pertinent presuppositions, characterize also several Gospel logia. Jesus counsels his rural Galilean followers that they should cease worrying over food, drink and clothing.

Look at the birds of the air: they neither sow nor reap nor gather into barns, and yet your heavenly Father feeds them. Are you not of more value than they? (Matt. 6.26).

The emphasis differs from that in the Mishnah where man's sinfulness accounts for his unfavourable situation in spite of his superiority to other creatures. The Matthean formulation with its appended question, assumes the same anthropocentric outlook, but the lesson is that anxiety over essential earthly needs should be overcome by trust which, by implication, leaves one free to devote oneself wholly to the affairs of the Kingdom.

A rather dissimilar idea inspired the Q logion about sparrows. Although two such birds can be bought for one *assarion* (Matt. 10.29), or five for two 'assaria' (Luke 12.6), 'not one of them will fall to the ground without your Father's will' (Matt.) or 'is overlooked by God' (Luke). 'Fear not, therefore; you are of more value than many sparrows' (Matt. 10.31/Luke 12.7). The message seems to be that if divine providence is concerned with the fate of such insignificant creatures, human beings should surely feel safe.

Yet, compared to the previous saying, this one sounds a false note. It does not fit either the eschatological context or the general thrust of Jesus' teaching. A rabbinic presentation of the bird story is more apposite because it ends on a note of encouragement. Having spent thirteen years in hiding during the Hadrianic persecution in the second century A D, Simeon ben Yohai came to the entrance of his cave and saw a fowler trying to catch birds. A *bat qol* or heavenly voice cried out: *Dimissio* (Release), and the bird escaped. 'Not even a bird perishes without the will of heaven,' – Simeon remarked – 'how much less the son of man!' (ySheb. 38d). Read against this story, the Gospel logion, in Matthew's formulation at least, seems to have been distorted in the process of transmission. No one can derive much comfort from the knowledge that God is aware of the death of every young bird.[10]

To the same category of logia belong two Q sayings, the first on wild flowers (Matt. 6.28f./Luke 12.27) and the second on foxes and birds (Matt. 8.20/Luke 9.58). The former is a mere extension of Matt. 6.25/Luke 12.24. Just as birds find food without labour, so the lilies of the field surpass the proverbial pomp and glory of Solomon[11] although they 'neither toil nor spin'. The conclusion is even more colourful and emphatic than in the case of food. If God provides so lavishly for quickly fading 'grass', 'will he not much more clothe you, O men of little faith' (Matt. 6.30/Luke 12.28)?

Matt. 8.20/Luke 9.58, seen against the previous maxims, is manifestly an overstatement: in this simile, wild animals and birds are better treated than 'the son of man'.

> Foxes have holes, and birds of the air have nests; but the son of man has nowhere to lay his head.

The lesson imparted concerns the complete trust in God necessary for all wishing to embark on an itinerant ministry for the Kingdom. More exposed than foxes and birds which have their 'homes', they must be prepared to face the pangs of the last days. In short, the entire group of nature proverbs developed in the Gospels perfectly fits the context of eschatological enthusiasm and self-surrender. There is no reason whatsoever to question their authenticity.

[10]A parallel account of the Simeon ben Yohai story figures in GR 79.6 (Th-A 942) where, in addition to the heavenly 'Dimissio', we hear also the decree *Specula* (Execution), resulting in the bird's capture. Yet Simeon's comment is the same: 'Not even a bird is caught without the will of heaven; how much less the soul of the son of man (or: my soul)!' For the interpretation of the phrase 'son of man', see *PBJS*, 162f. and n. 39.

[11]Cf. e.g. the allusion in mBM 7.1 to a banquet 'like Solomon's in his time'. See also Josephus, Ant. viii.40, based on I Kings 5.2f. (4.22f.ET).

A final group of similes deals either with disliked or despised animals (dogs, swine), or contrasts friendly creatures with dangerous and feared ones (sheep, dove – wolf, snake). Both classes address the problem of the servants of the Kingdom in a hostile world.

> (*a*) Do not give dogs what is holy
> (*b*) and do not throw your pearls before swine,
>   lest they trample them underfoot
>   and turn to attack you (Matt. 7.6).

Various attempts have been made to reconstruct an Aramaic proverb underlying the logion. Gustaf Dalman (*Jesus-Jeshua*, 232) lists the part designated (*b*) among proverbs and maxims used by Jesus but not found in Jewish literature. Matthew Black, in turn, in the footsteps of A. Meyer and F. Perles, presents for both (*a*) and (*b*), and more recently J. A. Fitzmyer just for (*a*), an Aramaic original presumed to have been 'mistranslated' in the Greek Gospel. So Black (after Perles) would have:

> Hang not (precious) rings on dogs,
> and adorn not the snout of swine with your pearls.

Whereas Fitzmyer suggests merely the substitution of 'a ring' for 'what is holy'.[12]

The animal imagery belongs to the common language of rabbinic literature. The proverb, 'Nothing is poorer than a dog and richer than a pig' (bShab. 155b), mentions the two in the one breath. The derogatory associations of 'swine' require no explanation and it is also well-known that dogs were not as popular in the ancient Jewish world as they are in Britain today. The story of the young Tobit's four-legged friend is an exception (Tob. 5.16; 11.4). They symbolized the detested Samaritans (BR 81.3) and more generally, the Gentiles (Midr. on Psalms 4.11, ed. Buber 47f.). But although in Matt. 15.26f. dogs definitely depict

---

[12]M. Black, *Aramaic Approach*, 200f., quoting A. Meyer, *Jesu Muttersprache* (1896), 80f. and F. Perles, 'Zur Erklärung von Mt 7.6', ZNW 25 (1926), 163f. Cf. also J. A. Fitzmyer, *Wandering Aramean* (1979), 14f. and G. Vermes, *JWJ* 80. To solve the riddle created by the apparently unsuitable parallelism between 'the holy' and 'pearls', it is proposed that the Aramaic *qdsh*' should be read as *qedasha*' (= ring) instead of *qudsha*' (= holy). The saying is believed to be modelled on Prov. 11.22.

non-Jews, such an association is by no means absolute. In fact, the dog metaphor is explicitly applied in mSot. 9.15 to Jews living in the messianic age; 'Young men shall put elders to shame and elders shall rise before young men, *for the son dishonours his father and the daughter rises up against her mother, and the daughter-in-law against her mother-in-law: a man's enemies are the men of his own house* (Micah 7.6). The face of the generation is like the face of a dog.'

The latter parallel helps to set the logion firmly in an eschatological context. The purpose of the dual saying is to prohibit the divulgation of the secrets of the Kingdom to the unrepentant. In brief, we are once more in the centre of the basic message of Jesus. In the circumstances, it appears to be advisable to take the Greek version, 'what is holy', as a true reflection of his words; that is to say, if an Aramaic proverb existed associating the concepts of 'dog' and 'ring', it is no less easy, and more meaningful, to imagine that Jesus was making a pun (ring/holy) than to postulate a mistranslation on the part of the compiler of the Greek Gospel.

The twofold contrasting proverbial simile is attested in a Q passage (Matt. 10.16/Luke 10.3), reinforced by an additional logion in Matthew alone in the same verse.

> Behold I send you as sheep in the midst of wolves (Q).
> So be wise as serpents and innocent as doves (Matt.).

Both metaphors were, it would seem, common currency in Jewish literature. It is often pointed out that in I Enoch 90.6–17, the chosen Israelites (the Hasidim) are portrayed as lambs attacked by predatory birds. In rabbinic literature, on the other hand, the opposition 'sheep – wolves' appears in a fictional conversation between the emperor Hadrian and Rabbi Joshua, in which the former exclaims, 'Great are the sheep (the Israelites) which endure among seventy wolves (the nations)'; to which Joshua replies, 'Great is the shepherd who saves and preserves the sheep and destroys the wolves in their presence' (Tanh. Toledot 5). Again the Gospel formulation displays an exaggerating twist characteristic of Jesus: the sheep are sent among the wolves, and no doubt only those filled with limitless trust have the courage to obey.

The Matthean supplement about serpent-like wisdom (Gen.

3.1) and innocence of doves (the silly pigeon of Hos. 7.11 is turned into a simple dove in rabbinic exegesis) reveals no specific bias. The adjectives used in Matthew figure also in a saying attributed to the Palestinian Amora, R. Judah bar Simon, commenting on Song of Songs 2.14 (in SSR in loc.):

> God spoke thus concerning the Israelites: Towards me they are innocent like doves, but among the nations of the world they are as clever as serpents.

Since the logion adds nothing peculiar to our information about Jesus, the question of genuineness – for which the odds seem to be even – is of slight importance.

Proverbs are built on simple images. They naturally lead to the second and more elaborate rhetorical device adopted by Jesus, and characteristic of the Gospels, the parable.

II   Teaching in Parables

1. From the Bible to Qumran

In Jewish thinking, biblical and post-biblical, proverb and parable belong to the same category and are covered by the single concept of *mashal*, denoting a whole variety of ideas based on comparison: by-word, proverb proper, sapiential utterance, similitude and the so-called story-parable, whether in prose or in poetry. With a notion as broad as this, akin to the genres of the biblical fable, riddle, prophetic allegories, as well as the occasional scriptural parables in the narrower sense, a few words of clarification may not be superfluous despite the considerable amount of literature on the subject.[13]

Since practically every study of the parables of Jesus includes a

[13]For fable, see Judg. 9.7–15 on the trees seeking a king, or II Kings 14.9 on the thistle intending to marry the cedar's daughter. For riddle, see Judg. 14.12–18 and I Kings 10.1. Josephus alludes to a large sum of money won by Solomon in a riddle competition with Hiram, king of Tyre (*Ant.* viii.148f.). For prophetic allegory, see Ezek. 17.3–10 on the great eagles, the cedar and the vine. For scriptural parable, see II Sam. 12.1–4 – Nathan's story about the little ewe lamb and the song of the vineyard in Isa. 5.1–7. On parables in general, cf. diverse dictionary articles (*TDNT* V, 747–51 [F. Hauck]; *IDB* III, 649–54 [L. Mowry]; *IDBS* 641f. [C. E. Carlston]; *Enc. Jud.* 72–77 [L. I. Rabinowitz and R. B. Y.

claim of some sort to the effect that, despite all the changes that occurred in the course of their transmission and redaction, they represent 'a fragment of the original rock of tradition' and thus 'a particularly firm historical foundation' (Jeremias, *Parables* (11), or possess a 'ring of authenticity' (Dodd, *Parables* 13), it is essential to discover whether these parables fit within an evolutionary process in Jewish literature or are so different that they constitute a complete novelty and serve as source and model for the rabbinic parables as a narrative form. The latter is the odd view advanced by Joachim Jeremias (*Parables*, 12), the former is the majority opinion among scholars.

It goes without saying that developed forms of metaphorical teaching (parable, similitude, allegory) can be noted at all the stages of the literary history of Judaism, from the Bible to the rabbis and beyond.[14] So in a general sense the New Testament phenomenon is simply a part of a larger whole, a phase in an unbroken evolution. On the other hand, in order to enable the individual features of the Gospels to stand in greater relief, they must be set against their pre-rabbinic and rabbinic parallels. What we need to determine are the common traits, the formal and structural relationships between the parables. The aims motivating the narrators are very variable and indicate their

---

Scott]. Among monographs, see in particular A. Jülicher, *Die Gleichnisreden Jesu* I–II (1886–1910); J. Ziegler, *Die Königgleichnisse des Midrasch* (1903); P. Fiebig, *Altjüdische Gleichnisse und die Gleichnisse Jesu* (1904); *Die Gleichnisreden Jesu im Lichte der rabbinischen Gleichnisse des neutestamentlichen Zeitalters* (1912); A. Feldmann, *The Parables and Similes of the Rabbis, Agricultural and Pastoral* (1927); C. H. Dodd, *The Parables of the Kingdom* (1935, 1961); J. Jeremias, *The Parables of Jesus* (1954, 1963, 1972); D. Flusser, *Die rabbinischen Gleichnisse und der Gleichniserzähler Jesus* (1981); B. H. Young, *Jesus and his Jewish Parables: Reconsidering the Roots of Jesus' Teaching* (1989); and most recently D. Stern, *Parables in Midrash: Narrative and Exegesis in Rabbinic Literature* (1991), in particular pp. 188–206 ('The Parables in the Synoptic Gospels'). For a review of the status quaestionis, see C. L. Blumberg, 'Interpreting the Parables of Jesus: Where are we and where do we go from here?' *CBQ* 53 (1991), 50–78.

[14]Jerome, in his *Commentary on Matthew* (18.23), stresses the popularity of parables among Jews. 'Familiare est Syris et maxime Palaestinis ad omnem sermonem suum parabolas iungere: ut quod per simplex praeceptum teneri ab auditoribus non potest, per similitudinem exemplaque teneatur' (PL xxvi, 132C). (Syrians and especially Palestinians are accustomed to add parables to all their discourses so that whatever cannot be fully grasped by the listeners by means of a simple statement should be understood through similitudes and examples.)

peculiar stances. In fact, even in connection with the same Gospel parable, contemporary redaction criticism identifies distinct purposes in the accounts of the various evangelists.

The literary genre of the parable, at least in the broader sense, is attested not only in the Bible, but also in the Pseudepigrapha and Qumran. The scriptural specimens have no formal requirements but are usually accompanied by an interpretation. The prophet Nathan's tale concerning a rich man who took and slaughtered a poor man's only pet lamb, though transparently clear, is followed by his dramatic, 'Thou art the man!' addressed to David (II Sam. 12.7). The Song of the Vineyard, equally limpid, still contains a statement that it relates to Israel (Isa. 5.7), while the more complex historico-prophetic parable of Ezek. 17.2–10 is furnished with a direct prose commentary in verses 11–18, identifying the eagle as the king of Babylon. Likewise the parable of the forest and the sea in IV Ezra 4.13–18, a writing contemporaneous with the Gospels, is to some extent clarified in 4.20f. By contrast, the three highly elaborate eschatological parables in I Enoch 37–71, apparently also of the same age, are meant to be and remain, visions of mystery, and as such are 'very different from . . . the NT parables' (*TDNT* V, 750).

Parable-like poetry figures in the Qumran Community Rule and Thanksgiving Hymns, describing the Community as a fortified city built round a spring (1QH 8). Nevertheless the difference of the genres is too great to call for closer comparison.

2. Rabbinic parables

Formal characteristics are regularly, though not universally, displayed in the parables of the rabbis. They usually begin with the heading *mashal* (parable) or *'emshol lekha mashal* (let me tell you a parable), often accompanied by the question, *lemah hadavar dōmeh* (To what can this be compared?). Then follows the story: this is like a king, etc. A number of literary units in the Gospels also display one or several of these elements. No less than eight passages begin with the term 'parable' and in nine instances, three of which overlap with the first series, the narrator uses the phrase 'it is like' or something similar. Mark 4.30f. reads:

And he [Jesus] said, 'With what can we compare the kingdom of God, or what parable shall we use for it? It is like a grain of mustard seed . . .'[15]

Turning now to the structure of the rabbinic parables, the majority seem to occur in an exegetical context and either serve as an illustration of the meaning of a scriptural citation, or introduce in the form of a story some biblical teaching. For example, in the Mekhilta de-Rabbi Ishmael, a parable attributed to the late first-century AD Rabbi Eleazar ben Azariah serves to explain Jer. 23.7–8 where the prophet announces that in the future the form of oath mentioning Israel's deliverance from Egypt will be replaced by another alluding to the return of the exiles.

It can be explained by a parable. To what can this be compared? To a man who wanted children. He had a daughter and he made a vow by the life of the daughter. Afterwards he had a son. So he relinquished the daughter and made a vow by the name of the son (on Ex. 13.2; ed. Lauterbach I, 132f.).

The structural order may be reversed. Thus to the clever reasoning presented by the Emperor Antoninus claiming it to be possible for both the body and the soul to escape punishment after death for sins committed, Rabbi Judah the Prince first advances a parable and later confirms its message by means of a Bible citation and its exegesis.

Antoninus said to Rabbi: The body and the soul can free themselves from the judgment. How? The body says: It is the soul that sinned, for since it has separated from me, I am lying in the grave like a stone. But the soul says: It is the body that sinned, for since I separated from it, I am flying in the air like a bird. He [Rabbi] said to him [Antoninus]. I will tell you a parable. To what does this resemble? To a king of flesh and blood who had a beautiful orchard. In it there were beautiful figs. He placed in it two guards, one lame and one blind. The

[15]The parallels in Matt. 13.31 and Luke 13.18f. abbreviate the rabbinic style. The word 'parable' figures further in Mark 4.2 par.; 12.1 par.; 13.28 par.; Matt. 13.33; 22.1; 13.24; Luke 19.11. For the expression 'it is like' or 'it resembles', see Matt. 7.24 par.; 11.16 par.; 13.24; 13.51; 18.23; 20.1; 22.2; 25.1. The parables reported only by the Gentile Luke include neither formula!

lame man said to the blind man: I see beautiful figs in the orchard. Come and let me ride on you and we shall collect them and eat them. The lame man rode on the blind man and they collected them and ate them. After a time the owner of the orchard came. He said to them: Where are the beautiful figs? The lame man said to him: I have no legs to walk. The blind man said to him: I have no eyes to see. What did he [the owner] do? He made the lame man ride on the blind man and judged them as one.

The Holy One blessed be he will also bring the soul and cast it into the body and judge them as one as it is written, *He calls to the heavens above and to the earth to judge his people* (Ps. 50.4).

'He calls to the heavens above' – this is the soul. 'And the earth to judge his people' – this is the body. (bSanh. 91ab; for a short version, cf. Mekh. on Ex. 15.1; ed. Lauterbach II,21).

Such a simple mixture of Bible text and parabolic interpretation stands at one end of the literary evolution. At the other end, in the highly formalized homiletic midrash, we find a whole tissue of quotations woven together in the exposition of a parable. It is illustrated in an extract from a sermon preached by the famous haggadist, Rabbi Levi, in Pesiqta de Rav Kahana 3.1 on the pericope, 'Remember' (Deut. 25.17).

Rabbi Levi said: To what are the children of Israel like? To a man who had a son. He let him ride on his shoulder, and carried him to the market. The son saw an object he wanted and said to his father, Get this for me. He bought it for him once, twice, three times. Then the son saw another man and said to him, Have you seen my father? The father said to him, You silly boy, you're riding on my shoulder and all that you request, I get it for you, yet you ask this man, Have you seen my father? What did his father do? He threw his son off his shoulder and a dog came and bit him.

So when Israel came out of Egypt, the Holy One blessed be he wrapped them in seven clouds of glory as it is written, *He encircled him, he cared for him* (Deut. 32.10). They asked for manna and he gave it to them, quails and he gave them to them. When he had given them all that they needed, they began to

meditate and say, *Is the Lord among us or not?* (Ex. 17.7) The
Holy One blessed be he said to them, You have meditated
against me. By your life, I will make you know [that I am in
your midst]. Here comes a dog and will bite you. What is this?
This is Amalek for it is written, *And Amalek came and fought
with Israel* (Ex. 17.8). Therefore it is written, *Remember what
Amalek did to you* (Deut. 25.17).

We may take it for granted that the parable in its interpretative
function was an integral part of the synagogue sermon which as a
rule began with an appropriate passage from scripture. In one
famous example which will be discussed later, it provides the
substance of the funeral oration pronounced by Rabbi Zeira at
the burial of Rabbi Bun (yBer. 2.8, 5c). Ability to handle parables
seems therefore to have been a prerequisite for any successful
preacher or teacher. Jerome, as has been shown, confirms the
extant rabbinic evidence (cf. n. 14 above). Nevertheless, not
surprisingly some were more skilled than others. Tradition has it
that the Tannaitic master, Rabbi Meir (mid-second century AD)
was the practitioner par excellence of the genre. His discourses
are said to have consisted of halakhah, haggadah and *mashal* –
parable in equal proportions (bSanh 38b), and with rhetorical
exaggeration it was claimed that his demise marked the end of
parabolic teaching:

Since the death of R. Meir the parable-tellers (*mōshele
meshalim*) ceased (mSot. 9.15).

Legend credits him with three hundred fox similitudes, which
have not survived, but extant rabbinic sources have preserved a
smaller number of parables in his name.[16] Of the two examples
which follow, the first is exegetical, the second is without
reference to the Bible.

R. Meir said, What does Scripture mean by *For a hanged man
is a curse of God* (Deut. 21.23). It is like twin brothers who
resembled one another. One of them was the king of the whole
universe; the other set out to practice robbery. After some time,

[16]W. Bacher (*Die Agada der Tannaiten* II (1890), 57–60) lists over a dozen
items. The validity of the attributions can neither be demonstrated nor refuted.
The illustrations are chosen from Tannaitic attestations.

the one who had set out to practice robbery was caught and was crucified on a cross. And every passer-by said, It seems that the king has been crucified. Therefore it is written, *For a hanged man is a curse of God.*[17]

Compared to this symmetrically construed parable exegesis, with the same opening and closing Bible quotation, the second example is simple and non-technical. It is also laced with humour.

> R. Meir said: As people's attitudes to food differ, so too their attitudes to women.
>
> Take this man. A fly flies over his cup. He empties it without even touching its contents. He is a bad sort as far as women are concerned for his eyes are fixed on his wife with a view to divorcing her.
>
> Take this other man. A fly falls into his cup. He leaves it there and does not taste the contents. He is like Pappos ben Judah who locks the door on his wife before he goes out.
>
> Take this [third] man. A fly falls into his cup. He throws out the fly and drinks [the contents]. This is the behaviour of the average man. He permits his wife to speak to her male relatives and neighbours.
>
> Take this [fourth] man. A fly falls on to his plate. He picks it out, sucks it, and then eats what is on the plate. He is a wicked man. He allows his wife to go out with her head uncovered, to be familiar with her male servants and neighbours, and to bathe with men (tSot. 5.9).

In this story, Rabbi Meir exemplifies the multiple potentialities of a parable, supplying as does also Jesus occasionally in the Gospels, a full explanation for each variety.[18]

----

[17]tSanh. 9.7. The Deuteronomy quotation has been translated to suit the argument. It is so understood already in mSanh. 6.4. No interpretation of the parable is supplied, but a clue is given by the underlying idea that man is made in God's image. Cf. M. Wilcox, 'Upon the Tree – Deut. 21.22–23 in the New Testament', *JBL* 96 (1977), 85–99.

[18]Meir's exegetical parable concerning the grain of corn, akin to John 12.24, is worth recalling too. 'Queen Cleopatra asked R. Meir, saying, I know that those who sleep will live, as it is written, *May they [men] blossom forth from the city like the grass of the field* (Ps. 72.16). But when they rise, will they rise naked or with their clothes? He said to her, [You may reason] *a fortiori* from the grain of corn which is buried naked but comes out with many clothes. How much more will the righteous do so who are buried with their clothes?' (bSanh. 90b).

The purpose of these preliminaries is to bring home in a concrete fashion the role of parables in rabbinic, primarily Tannaitic, mode of thinking. It should be noted that in rabbinic parables an explanation of the imagery is common, a fact which is to be borne in mind in the study of the Gospels where the appended allegorical exposition is regularly understood to be secondary. As one might expect, the majority of the examples post-date the New Testament, let alone Jesus, but so does everything in the corpus of Talmud and Midrash. To conclude with Jacob Neusner that the parable is a post-70 AD didactic technique,[19] and what is worse, to suggest as Joachim Jeremias does, that the adoption of the parable form by the rabbis was seriously influenced by 'Jesus' model', amounts to a misreading of the evidence.[20] Jeremias's theory would hold water only if he could prove that Jesus made a positive and lasting impact on Jewish teachers of his, or any other, age, and this is patently not the case. As for Neusner's contention, it depends on the validity of certain attributions and on whether Yohanan ben Zakkai's example is seen as pre- or post-70 AD. In any case, an appendix on 'Parables among the Pharisees and Early Rabbis', compiled by Robert M. Johnston, has been inserted into one of Neusner's volumes, thus tacitly envisaging a first-century AD date as possible.[21] His pertinent general conclusion, namely that 'the Christian and rabbinic tradents around the time of the destruction of Jerusalem exhibit much the same literary and formal tendencies' (art. cit. in n. 19, 390), should be applied to the parable genre as well. This is why Jesus' parables must be viewed in such a setting.[22]

[19]See J. Neusner, 'Types and Forms in Ancient Jewish Literature: Some Comparisons', *History of Religions* 11 (1972), 354–90, esp. 360f., 368.

[20]J. Jeremias, *The Parables of Jesus* (1972), 12.

[21]*A History of the Mishnaic Law of Purities. Part XIII* (1976), 224–6. The first-century AD authorities listed are Hillel (Lev.R. 34: and ARNa 15.3); the Schools of Hillel and Shammai (Gen.R. 1.14); Yohanan ben Zakkai (bShab. 153a); Eliezer ben Hyrcanus (Mekh. on Ex. 15.1; ed. Lauterbach II, 22f.); Eleazar ben Azariah (Mekh. on Ex. 13.2; ibid. I, 132f.); Gamaliel (Mekh. on Ex. 20.5; ibid. II, 245f.).

[22]The familiarity of the parable form in first-century AD Palestine may also be inferred from Josephus' allusion to a haggadah of Solomon's fabulous literary output. 'Solomon also composed 1005 books of odes and songs and 3000 books of parables and similitudes: for he spoke a parable about every kind of tree from the hyssop to the cedar, and in like manner about birds and all kinds of terrestrial creatures and those that swim and those that fly' (*Ant*. viii.44).

III   The Parables of Jesus

The Synoptic Gospels include, if my reckoning is correct, thirty-nine parables assigned to Jesus. Mark contains six. Nine derive from the source common to Matthew and Luke. Another ten are peculiar to Matthew and a further fourteen to Luke. A detailed list follows as an appendix to this chapter. While the substance of Jesus' message, the religion preached by him, will be discussed separately in chapter 7, the aim of the present bird's eye view is to grasp the style and general tendency of his teaching in parables, and point to traits common to their message which are also the central tenets of the doctrine attributable to Jesus.

According to their leading themes, the Synoptic parables easily fall into five groups: (*a*) countrymen's parables; (*b*) parables based on episodes of daily life; (*c*) social parables; (*d*) parables relating to judges and lawcourts; and (*e*) parables of the wedding feast.

(*a*) Countrymen's parables

The first class develops images familiar to rural and lakeside Galileans among whom Jesus was most at home.

1. The *Parable of the Sower* (Mark 4.3–8; Matt. 13.3–8; Luke 8.5–8) opens the series in all the Gospels. There is nothing peculiar to the imagery. IV Ezra 8.41, describing the fate of mankind, furnishes a close parallel.

> For just as the farmer sows many seeds on the ground and plants a multitude of plants, yet not all that have been sown will sprout in due season, neither do all that have been planted take root, so not all those who have been sown in the world shall be saved.

However, despite the customary title, the protagonist of the New Testament parable is not the sower. He is rather an anti-hero, not very competent at his job, and carelessly wastes a great deal of the seed. The attention of the story-teller is centred, instead, on the various parts of the ground: the path, the rocky surface, the thorny corner of the field and the fertile soil.[23]

[23]In Ezra, by contrast, the chief character is the farmer, i.e. God. The fate of the seed depends on his action: viz. on the distribution by him of the right amount of water at the correct time. Cf. IV Ezra 8.42–45.

The success of the sowing is determined by the response of the ground, that of the listener. The explanation given in Mark 4.13–20 – the seed represents the word, the good soil those who accept the teaching, etc. – is a straight and genuine echo of Jesus' story. If, as is often suggested, the interpretation in its present Greek wording is the product of the primitive church, the possibility of an earlier non-ecclesiastical formulation in the light of rabbinic parallels remains undeniable.[24]

2. The first Kingdom parable, that of the *Secretly Growing Seed* (Mark 4.26–29), contrasts the actions of the farmer and the corn. Once sown, and having germinated, the seed progresses without his intervention until the corn is ripe for the harvest. The message seems to stress that even in the work preparatory to the coming of the Kingdom, i.e. the essence of Jesus' mission, the minister, once he has completed his task, must allow matters to take their mysterious, God-directed course. Such an understanding of the invisible growth of the seed suits the text and the parallels better than the historical exegesis, still repeated by J. Jeremias (*Parables*, 152), according to which Jesus is opposed here to political Zealotry.

3. An almost opposite point of view is revealed in the story of the *Fig Tree*. Its leafy branches mark the onset of summer. Whether the pun summer/*qaiz* = end/*qez* is intended here, as it is in Amos 8.2, cannot be taken for granted. Nevertheless, the summer obviously alludes to the nearness of the harvest, symbolizing the imminent arrival of the Kingdom (Luke 21.31) or of the Messiah (Mark 13.29; Matt. 24.33). Thus we are faced in this parable with a search for signs foreshadowing the *eschaton*, a phenomenon disapproved of by Jesus which scarcely favours the authenticity of the parable.[25]

[24]The use of the verb 'to explain' (*diasaphein*) apropos of the parable of the Weeds (Matt. 13.36) associates this exegetical phenomenon not only with dream interpretation in Gen. 40.8 (*diasaphēsis = pitrōn*), but also with the type of Qumran Bible commentary called *pesher* which is intended to reveal the hidden meaning of a text (cf. above p. 61). In the esoterical framework of the Essene sect, such an exposition was considered indispensable if scripture was to be understood correctly.

[25]For Jesus' dislike of 'signs', cf. Mark 8.12; Luke 17.20. See also *JWJ* 38. The associated saying concerning the fig tree which, despite being covered with leaves, bore no fruit and was unable to satisfy the hungry Jesus, makes sense in the Matthean version (21.18f.), but not in Mark 11.12–14, where it is incorrectly claimed that it was not the season for figs. The latter story with its curse of the

4. The astonishing growth of the proverbially tiny *Mustard Seed* into a substantial shrub on which birds can nest, provides an excellent basis for a Kingdom parable (Mark 4.30–32; Matt. 13.30–32; Luke 13.18f.). The story is construed on familiar metaphors. The mustard seed exemplifies the smallest quantity of blood (yBer. 5,8d; bBer. 31a), and the Galilean Rabbi Simeon ben Halafta (late second-century AD) asserts that he climbed a mustard bush which was as tall as a fig tree (yPe'ah 7, 20b).

5. The last agricultural parable, that of the *Weeds*, (Matt. 13.24–30), is a revision of that of the sower of good seed whose cornfield, while his men slept, was sown with weeds by an enemy. The destruction of the weeds must wait until the time of the harvest. The servants are not blamed for their failure to prevent the crime. Their task at the end will be to distinguish between the good and the worthless, and to burn the weeds. The message is patience, abstention from untimely action, because ultimately all will be sorted out. A wholly apocalyptic interpretation with an allegorical rendering is furnished by Matthew 13.36–43: sower = the son of man; enemy = devil; good seed = sons of the Kingdom; weeds = sons of Satan; harvest = end-time; reapers = angels. Since the parable itself is primarily an exposition of the co-existence of good and evil and an encouragement to leave the resolution of the problem to God, the interpretation appended by the first evangelist with its essentially eschatological stance and the incoherent use in the same passage of 'sons of the Kingdom', 'Kingdom of the son of man' and 'Kingdom of the Father', seem to be additions clumsily inserted by the ecclesiastical editors of the parable.

6. Besides agriculture, Galilean country life furnishes imagery connected with the work of shepherds and fishermen. The former constitutes the background of the *Parable of the Lost Sheep* (Matt. 18.12–14; Luke 15.3–7) in which the shepherd leaves his flock of ninety-nine on a mountain (Matt.) or in the wilderness (Luke) in order to look for a single stray sheep. Its discovery fills him with delight.

---

tree, should be contrasted with a haggadah from bTaan. 24a. A certain Rabbi Yose failed to bring food to his labourers, so his son commanded a fig tree to produce fruits for the hungry workers. When the father, who had been delayed by some charitable activity, discovered what his son had done, he cursed him saying,'My son, you have importuned your Maker to cause the fig tree to produce fruits prematurely. May you be gathered in before your time!'

The idea that a person in charge of a number of animals should abandon those which are grouped together to go to the rescue of one in danger is attested also in an Amoraic parable in Genesis Rabbah 86.4 concerning a wine-merchant, driving twelve beasts of burden. One of these wanders into the property of a Gentile, thus exposing the wine to possible ritual defilement. So the Jew leaves his eleven animals in a public square, where no one can interfere with their load unobserved, and hurries to find the twelfth. In the midrash, the story is given as a figurative pragmatic exegesis of Gen. 39.2, 'And the Lord was with him (Joseph)', namely that being young and alone, he needed divine protection while his eleven older brothers were safe in the house of Jacob.

The Gospel parable is more dramatic, yet the two evangelists derive different lessons from it. Luke's Jesus claims that a single repentant sinner causes more joy in heaven than ninety-nine just men, whereas Matthew's Jesus stresses God's paternal solicitude which ensures 'that none of these little ones should perish'. Luke's conclusion, though typical of Jesus' thought, hangs in the air: there is no question in the story of the lost, or more exactly the stray, sheep's return to the fold. Matthew's message issues naturally from the parable and is consequently the more authentic of the two.[26]

7. The final Galilean country parable is borrowed from the experience of fishermen. In the formulation of Matt. 13.47–50, the *Net* cast into the sea catches all kinds of fish which need to be sorted out and the inedible thrown away. The lesson drawn from it is eschatological: at the actual establishment of the Kingdom of God, i.e. at the Judgment, the angels will separate the just and consign the wicked 'into the furnace of fire'. Here again the conclusion creates a mixed metaphor no doubt through contamination by the parable of the Weeds (Matt. 13.30,41f.). But if the purpose of the story is to inculcate a religious attitude demanded at the present time, the true intention of Jesus in recruiting workers for the Kingdom is to encourage them to cast the net and gather in the good fish. The

[26]Primary, even exclusive, concern for the 'lost sheep of Israel' by Jesus and the twelve apostles is presented emphatically in Judaeo-Christian preaching (Matt. 10.6; 15.24). The total unsuitability of the teaching for the needs of the primitive Gentile church is a strong argument in favour of its authenticity.

eternal fate of the just and the unjust, entrusted to angels, is superimposed on this imagery and must be considered secondary.[27]

(b) Parables based on episodes of daily life

The raw material of the second group of parables is furnished by diverse aspects of daily existence in first-century Palestine.

8. To begin with traditions common to Matthew and Luke, there is the *Similitude of the Wise and Foolish Builders* (Matt. 7.24–27; Luke 6.47–49), the former laying the foundation of his house on rock, the latter on sand (Matt.) or on the ground without any foundation at all (Luke). The first construction withstands storm and flood, the second collapses. The two builders represent the devoted and the superficially committed disciples: those who learn and act accordingly, and those who merely listen. The architectural imagery is familiar. Qumran Thanksgiving Hymns speak of a 'foundation' set 'on the rock' (1QH 6.26) or of an edifice 'established . . . upon the rock' (7.8f.). Furthermore, Elisha ben Abuyah, the early second-century Tannaitic rabbi turned heretic, is accredited with a parable akin to that of Jesus:

> A man of good deeds who has studied much Torah, to what may he be likened? To someone who first lays stones and then bricks. Even when much water rises and lies against them, it does not dislodge them . . . (ARN A, 24, p. 77).

There is no reason to doubt the possibility of Jesus adopting such a cliché. His emphasis on the paramount importance of the religious deed can hardly be questioned.[28]

---

[27]The phrases 'fishers of men' (Mark 1.17; Matt. 4.19) and 'catchers of men' attributed to Jesus in a fishing context (Luke 5.10) reflect the same positive imagery. By contrast, the aim of the fishermen and the hunters alluded to in a Qumran Thanksgiving Hymn (1QH 5.7f.), like that of their biblical models in Jer. 16.16, is to capture 'the sons of iniquity'.

[28]The same metaphorical teaching, replacing the image of a house built on rock with that of a tree with strong roots which bears the brunt of the storm, is handed down in the name of the late first-century AD R. Eleazar ben Azariah. He cites Jer. 17.6,8 in support. The opening paragraph reads: 'A man whose works exceed his wisdom, to what is he like?' Cf. mAb. 3.18. The same doctrine was propounded also by Hanina ben Dosa: 'Any man whose deeds exceed his wisdom, his wisdom will endure' (mAb. 3.9; ARN B 32 (p. 35)).

9. The *Parable of Children* in the public square, intent on spoiling their friends' games, depicts the unresponsiveness of Jesus' contemporaries to either the harsh or the gentle appeal to seek entry into the Kingdom (Matt. 11.16–19; Luke 7.31–35). The historical application to the preaching of John the Baptist and Jesus is clearly stated:

> For John came neither eating nor drinking, and they say, He has a demon! The son of man came eating and drinking, and they say, Behold a glutton and a drunkard, a friend of tax-collectors and sinners! (Matt. 11.18f.).[29]

10. The *Return of an expelled Demon* from the desert to its former abode, an idea that no doubt haunted exorcists like Jesus, employs the image of a house thoroughly cleansed after an unclean (satanic) occupant, which becomes very attractive to him now residing in uncomfortable quarters (Matt. 12.43–45; Luke 11.24–26). The implied lesson addressed to the exorcized person is always to keep the door tightly shut.[30]

11. Moving to the kitchen, the leaven in the *Parable of the Leaven* symbolizes the hidden transformation when work for the establishment of the Kingdom of heaven/God is set in motion (Matt. 13.33; Luke 13.20f.). Its message recalls the parables of the growing seed (Mark 4.26–29) and of the mustard seed (Mark 4.30–32; Matt. 13.31f.; Luke 13.18f.) Such a quiet arrival of the Kingdom is to be contrasted to its violent irruption in Matt. 11.12; Luke 16.16.[31]

[29]J. Jeremias (*Parables*, 161.f.) seems to have discovered a completely different message. For him the children who 'piped' and 'wailed' and urged their playmates to join in the game are 'domineering and disagreeable'. Such an interpretation misses the point and ruins the logic of the parable.

[30]The wilderness is the home of evil spirits. Sarah's demon fled to the desert area of Upper Egypt (Tob. 8.3); Azazel is cast out into the desert in Dudael (I Enoch 10.4). By pacifying two men living under the same roof whom the devil caused continuously to quarrel, R. Meir expelled the latter from 'his house' (bGit. 52a). Josephus alludes to incantations composed by Solomon enjoining the devil 'never to return' (*Ant.* viii.45).

[31]The metaphor of the leaven may also designate a deep-seated tendency towards error or wickedness. In Mark 8.15; Matt. 16.6; Luke 12.1, Jesus' disciples are warned against the 'leaven' of the Pharisees and Herodians (Mark), Pharisees and Sadducees (Matt.) or Pharisees (Luke). According to yAZ 2, 41a, the 'leaven' that remained in a converted Gentile barber-astrologer led him back to his original paganism. In I Cor. 5.7, Paul's Christians are said to be 'unleavened', i.e. freed from 'the old leaven of corruption'.

12. The domestic version of the search for the lost sheep is the *Parable of the Lost Drachma* in which a housewife lights a lamp and spring-cleans her house to find her missing coin (Luke 15.8–10). The lesson arising from the story is that even a single coin is very precious and has to be retrieved. As in the case of the lost sheep, Luke misses the point and speaks of the joy felt by angels over one repentant sinner.

(c) Social parables

A good many of the Gospel parables mirror Palestinian social life between landowners and labourers, masters and servants, fathers and sons, rich and poor. Others allude to a discovery of hidden treasure, to theft, or to the necessary alertness of a door-keeper at night. Further parables focus on groups such as Samaritans, Pharisees and publicans.

13. The *Parable of the Rich but Foolish Farmer*, intent on enlarging his barns to cope with a particularly abundant harvest, and contemplating a safe future, foretells sudden apocalyptic doom in the form of death (Luke 12.13–21). The evangelist prefaces the story with a condemnation of greed (v. 15), and concludes it with a contrast between great wealth and religious generosity. However, the underlying lesson, typical of Jesus' thought, concerns the fundamental impropriety of forward planning in the eschatological age.[32]

14. The *Parable of the Wicked Tenants* (Mark 12.1–12; Matt. 21.33–46; Luke 20.9–19), one of the three stories dealing with the vineyard and its workers, is peculiar from two points of view. The vineyard is described with the help of phrases borrowed from Isa. 5.2, and concludes, as do most rabbinic parables, with a direct Bible quotation: Ps. 118.22f. The latter, a standard 'anti-Jewish' proof-text (cf. Acts 4.11; I Peter 2.7), is totally alien and unsuited to the story. In what seems to be a Gentile-Christian allegory, the tenants of the vineyard (the leaders of Israel), instead

[32]Cf. Matt. 6.34: 'Do not be anxious about tomorrow!' and Luke 17.20: 'The Kingdom of God is not coming with signs to be observed.' See also *JWJ*, 38, 50. A non-eschatological rabbinic saying echoes the same ideas: 'Do not worry about tomorrow's trouble, for you do not even know what the day itself will bring. Tomorrow you may no longer be there, so why worry about a day which is not yours' (bSanh. 100b).

of fulfilling their legal obligations of paying the rent to the absentee landlord (God), ill-treat or kill the messengers (the prophets), despatched to them to collect their dues, and, finally, murder the landlord's son (Jesus). But in the end they themselves are put to death and their tenancy passes to new lessees (the Gentile church). In short, the composition in its present form is of ecclesiastical origin and cannot be ascribed to Jesus.[33]

15. The *Parable of the Two Sons*, sent by their father to work in the vineyard (Matt. 21.28–32) extols the virtue of repentance. The one who first refuses to obey but subsequently complies is preferable to the other who agrees, but fails to put his words into practice. The application of the doctrine to the penitent tax-collectors and harlots who accepted John's invitation to baptism, and to the self-righteous (Pharisees and lawyers according to Luke 7.29–30) who did not, contradicts the elements of the parable and is patently superimposed on it.

16. The *Parable of the Workers in the Vineyard* (Matt. 20.1–16) stresses the equality of the reward, one denarius, granted by the Master to all those who labour for the Kingdom. He pays the agreed wage to them all, to the men who were hired first, but also to the late-comers. The primary message is one of encouragement: it is never too late to join in the work. Inversely, a warning is issued against jealousy on the part of disciples of long standing to whom the parable seems to be addressed.[34]

The parallel story from the Palestinian Talmud, yBer 2, 5c, is often quoted (cf. Jeremias, *Parables*, 138f.). Rabbi Zeira opened the funeral oration of Rabbi Bun bar Hiyya with, 'Sweet is the sleep of the labourer' (Eccles. 5.11) and developed the quotation with the help of a parable about a king who employed many workers. One of them was exceedingly fast and industrious, and noticing this, the king kept him in his company for the rest of the day and paid him the same wages as to the others, although he worked for only two hours. When the other workmen com-

---

[33]The theme of such a bloody dénouement is introduced into Matthew's (but not Luke's) version of the royal wedding feast (Matt. 22.7). The parable of a king leasing a field to unworthy tenants, and their even less worthy children, before getting rid of them all in favour of his son (Sifre on Deut. 32.9, 312), uses the same ingredients as the Gospel story but for a very different purpose.

[34]See e.g. the ambitious demand of the apostles James and John concerning the best seats at the eschatological feast (Mark 10.35–37, 40f. Cf. also Luke 14.7–11 on p. 114).

plained, the king told them that no injustice had been done because their colleague had achieved more in two hours than they had during the whole day. Similarly, concluded Rabbi Zeira, Rabbi Bun put more Torah into practice during his short life-span of twenty-eight years than hard-working students manage to learn even if they reach the age of a hundred. Comparison discloses the specific bias in each version: divine generosity, in Jesus' teaching, and whole-hearted devotion to the performance of the Torah in the talmudic account.

17. The composite *Parable of the Cruel Servant* (Matt. 18.23–35), removed from Jesus' familiar country surroundings, is set in a royal court, probably a Gentile capital city, since the treatment inflicted by the king on his subjects is largely alien to Jewish customs, as J. Jeremias has correctly remarked (*Parables*, 211). The main theme is the remission of debt: a royal official (tax-farmer, provincial governor?), unable to pay his lord an enormous sum – ten thousand talents or six million denarii – due to him, begs for more time to collect the money. The harsh king unexpectedly turns merciful and cancels the debt altogether. But the 'servant' does not learn from this, and refuses to be patient with one of his own inferiors who owes him one hundred denarii. The central theme of forgiveness belongs to the kernel of Jesus' preaching, though the details of the story are foreign to his known mentality.[35]

18. The same message is expressed in the *Parable of the Creditor* who annuls two debts, one of five-hundred and the other of fifty denarii. Here the accent is laid on the gratitude of the debtor, symbolizing the town harlot who is said to have annointed Jesus' feet (Luke 7.36–50).

19. The *Parable of the Talents*, preserved in two recensions, is another topic, distant from the customary thought world of Jesus. Before setting out on a journey, a rich man entrusts his money to his servants and instructs them to increase it by successful trading. In Matt. 25.14–28, they are given varying sums, 'each according to his ability'; in Luke 19.12–26, they all receive one *mina*. The clever servants increase the capital, but both cases include an unadventurous person who hides the

---

[35]The Lord's Prayer in Matthew 6.12 asks for and promises remission of debt (*opheilēmata*), whereas the Lucan form requests God's pardon of sins and offers forgiveness to our debtors (Luke 11.4). Cf. also Mark 11.25f.; Matt. 6.14f.

money. The former are highly praised, the latter is condemned. In what appears to be the original meaning of the parable, the lesson conveyed is that in the work for the establishment of the Kingdom, fearless, unreserved and uncalculating effort is needed. Emphasis on risk is contained also in the similitudes of the hidden treasure and the precious pearl.

20. The *Parable of the Unjust Steward* (Luke 16.1–9), gives a negative echo to this instruction: the immoral wisdom of the 'sons of this age' is presented as an inverse model for the 'sons of light'.[36]

21. The *Parable of the Landowner and of the King* is similarly inspired by worldly wisdom: the first has to calculate whether he can afford to build a tower, no doubt in his vineyard, and the second whether he is able to face the eventuality of a battle against a more powerful opponent (Luke 14.28–32). Both cases fit an organized, settled and sedate situation in the primitive church rather than Jesus' age of eschatological turmoil.

22. The *Parable of the Servant's Reward*, again seemingly alien to the ideas of Jesus, represents a farmer (God?) keen on maintaining class distinctions (Luke 17.7–10). His only servant, simultaneously agricultural labourer, shepherd and cook, returning from a long day's work, is obliged first to prepare the master's supper (for which he is not thanked) before he himself is allowed to eat. The purpose of the story is apparently to remind the disciples of their lowly status. The parable may be a negative reworking of a similitude of Jesus, showing the master's appreciation of his faithful servants by serving at table (Luke 12.37).

Two unusual events belonging to life in first-century Palestine supply the imagery for a doctrine characteristic of Jesus.

23. In the *Parable of the Hidden Treasure* (Matt. 13.44), Jesus compares the Kingdom of God to a cache concealed in a field which its discoverer sets out to acquire with the price of all his possessions (Matt. 13.44), no doubt by insisting on a contract which specifies the sale of the land 'with all that is in it' (mBB 4.9).

24. Likewise the *Parable of the search for fine Pearls* (Matt. 13.45f.) portrays a merchant selling all his property to buy a specimen of great value. The lesson of both similitudes is total, unreserved self-surrender to the affairs of the Kingdom. The main

---

[36]The latter phrase and an earlier reference to 'unrighteous mammon' evoke Qumran associations with the idioms 'son of light' (passim) and 'wealth of wickedness' (CD 6.15; 8.5; 19.17).

difference between the two stories is that in the first, the find is accidental, whereas in the second the search is deliberate.[37]

25. The brief *Simile of the Clever Householder*, capable of making use of both the old and the new objects in his treasure, mirrors the typically Matthean scribe, 'trained for the Kingdom of heaven', i.e. one no doubt fully versed in traditional Bible interpretation of all the ages (Matt. 13.51f.). As has been noted in the previous chapter (cf. p. 72), the saying is unlikely to belong to Jesus.

26. The *Simile of the Thief* threatening to break into a house at an unforeseeable moment and the incessant vigilance that it imposes on the owner (Matt. 24.43; Luke 12.39), furnishes a negative but apposite parallel. The original meaning of the saying, before it was reinterpreted by the primitive church in the context of the return or *parousia* of Christ, points to the sudden coming of the Kingdom.

27. In the *Parable of the Unexpected Guest* arriving late at night when there is no refreshment in the house, the host, desperate to borrow food, makes such a nuisance of himself to a friend that he is obliged to rise from his bed and to lend him three loaves of bread (Luke 11.5–8). The teaching conveyed here in the form of a hyperbole is that childlike determination, persuades even God to give the suppliant all that he really needs.

Such an attitude, commended by Jesus to all his disciples, was tolerated by the rabbis only in the case of renowned holy men like the first-century BC charismatic Honi, who 'threatened' God that he would remain inside a circle which he drew in the dust until the rain for which he was praying was granted. He is portrayed therefore as a son importuning his father until he obtains his wish (mTaan. 3.8). Hence the later talmudic dictum, 'Impertinence (*huzpa*) works even vis-à-vis heaven!' (bSanh. 105a).[38]

Four further story-parables, reflecting aspects or caricatures of Jewish religious and social life, survive in Luke alone.

---

[37]The folk-loric theme of hidden treasure may be illustrated by the Qumran Copper Scroll (3Q15) with its sixty-four hiding-places. Cf. *DSSE* 308–10; *HJP* 467–9.

[38]The description of the protagonist of the parable as an 'immoral' individual, similar to the unjust steward in Luke 16.1–9, (cf. E. P. Sanders and Margaret Davies, *Studying the Synoptic Gospels* (1989), 289f.) is not borne out by my reading of the story.

28. The *Parable of the Pharisee and the Publican* (Luke 18.9–14) hammers home the contrast of two religious attitudes, one in line with Jesus' piety, the other representing its opposite. Whether the first of the two types, Pharisee – tax-collector, belongs to the original nucleus of the story is almost irrelevant. The Pharisee could, on the one hand, be a later substitute for a self-satisfied, vain, ostentatious person, while, on the other, pejorative stereotypes may have reached Galilee even before any substantial Pharisee presence could be presumed there. As for the tax-collector, he is frequently a central figure in Jesus' thought. The two characters are portrayed in Jerusalem, praying in the Temple. The Pharisee displays advanced vainglory, not only in congratulating himself on his supererogatory virtues, but in actually comparing himself to 'this tax-collector', and giving thanks for not being rapacious, adulterous and unjust like him and other men. His boasting is set against the contrite publican's prayer: 'God, be merciful to me a sinner.' The parable, implicitly extolling repentance, serves as a fitting illustration of the familiar logion, 'Whoever exalts himself will be humbled, but he who humbles himself will be exalted' (cf. Matt. 18.4; 23.12; Luke 14.11).[39]

29. The *Parable of the Good Samaritan* (Luke 10.29–37) is introduced in its present context as an interpretative explanation of the concept, 'neighbour', appended to Jesus' teaching on the first or great commandment (Mark 12.28–31; Matt. 22.34–40; Luke 10.25—38. Cf. *Jesus and the Law*, 42). In fact, the link is totally artificial. If 'You shall love your neighbour as yourself' refers only to those who have been kind to us, Jesus' emphasis on disinterested generosity (cf. ibid., 37) is nullified. Neither does the modern view, most recently voiced by E. P. Sanders and Margaret Davies (*Studying*, 181f.), that the story is an attack on priests and Levites, suit the tale any better. The Gospels offer no serious evidence to suggest that Jesus was particularly hostile to

[39]J. Jeremias remark (*Parables*, 142f.) that the prayer of the Lucan Pharisee is 'taken from life' and is provided with a commentary in a contemporaneous parallel from the Talmud, cannot be left unchallenged. For whereas the words of Luke 18.11f. exude conceit, those attributed to R. Nehunya ben Haqanah in bBer. 28b are inspired by humility and gratitude. The same comment applies also to the Qumran Thanksgiving Hymn (1QH 7.34) quoted by Jeremias. The dichotomy of the blessedness of the righteous and the disgrace of the wicked is traceable to biblical poetry, starting with Ps. 1.

the priesthood, with which he had little or no contact, nor was
he specially attracted to Samaritans (Matt. 10.5). By contrast,
Luke seems to find them of particular interest, as they
can be represented as 'foreigners' associated with Jesus (Luke
17.11–19).

Taking the parable in itself, its basic lesson appears to be that
charity and compassion towards the traveller left for dead by
robbers came, not from the religious leaders – who for apparently
good, but in fact mistaken, reasons kept their distance from him
– but from a most unexpected quarter, a Samaritan.[40] Normally
presumed to be hostile, he was the author of an act of loving-
kindness, one of the three pillars on which the world was believed
to stand (mAb. 1.2). On the whole, the structure of the parable
differs greatly from those examined so far, and doubts concerning its authenticity are justified. In fact, we may be faced here
with a Christian midrash in reverse on Jesus' command to love
one's enemies.

30. The *Parable of the Prodigal Son* is a very familiar
repentance-forgiveness story consisting of two acts (Luke
15.11–32). The first and essential part deals with the adventure of
an irresponsible younger son who, having obtained his share of
inheritance during his father's lifetime, wastes it all abroad on
harlots. Penniless and starving, he is struck by deep remorse and
seeks his father's pardon, which is granted with great kindness.
The second half of the parable is concerned with the complaints
of the first-born son who resents the father's generosity towards
his erring brother, and probably also the prompt paternal
forgiveness. He is reassured that his own inheritance is not under
threat, but that rejoicing is in order when a lost child is found. In
short, all the moral elements in the story echo the teaching of
Jesus, with repentance-*teshuvah* being the leading motive; nevertheless, the parable as a whole, supporting conventional morality

[40]The notion of the good Samaritan may have been borrowed from II Chron.
28.15. Judaean prisoners of war taken to Samaria under the king of Israel, Pekah
son of Remaliah, were released after the intervention of the prophet Oded and
entrusted to selected Samaritans to care for them. 'The men . . . rose and took the
captives, and with the spoil they clothed all that were naked among them; they
clothed them, gave them sandals, provided them with food and drink, and
anointed them, and carrying all the feeble among them on asses, they brought
them to their kinsfolk at Jericho, the city of the palm trees. Then they returned to
Samaria.' The reason why the priest and the Levite, heading for Jerusalem,

and not criticizing the elder brother's attitude, does not bear the hall-mark of his style.[41]

31. The *Anecdote of the Rich Man and the Poor Lazarus* (Luke 19.19–31) is more of a story than a parable. It has a double message: the wicked rich man's sufferings in hell cannot be relieved by a visit from his erstwhile client, Lazarus, now enjoying eternal bliss in 'Abraham's bosom'; nor can Lazarus be used as a miraculous messenger from beyond the grave to persuade the rich man's living brothers to repent. 'If they do not hear Moses and the prophets, neither will they be convinced if someone should rise from the dead' (v. 31). It would seem that we are faced here with the adaptation of a Jewish legend by the Jewish-Christian church which contains nothing that would link it directly with Jesus.[42]

(d) Parables relating to judges and law courts

The penultimate general topic of Gospel parables has to do with the judicial function, both historical and eschatological. The three examples have one interesting peculiarity in common: they all envisage a single judge. Rabbinic legislation, from the Mishnah onwards, knows only of three, twenty-three or seventy-two judges handling, the first civil cases, the second capital cases. The third is the supreme Sanhedrin, which appears also in the New Testament as a judicial college. However, in pre-70 AD Galilee, single magistrates seem to have dealt with property

---

avoided contact with what they believed to be a dead body was that it would have disqualified them from performing their duties in the Temple.

[41]A similar parable is handed down in the name of the mid-second century AD R. Meir in Deut.R. 2.3 on Deut. 4.30, 'When you are in tribulation, . . . you will return to the Lord, your God' [another *teshuvah* motive]. To what can this be compared? To a king's son who set out on a wicked path. The king despatched his tutor to ask him to come home. The son replied that unworthy and filled with embarrassment, he could not return. The father sent the pedagogue with the message, My son, can a *son* be ashamed of returning to his father? And if you return, is it not to your *father* that you return? The main difference between the two recensions of the parable is that here the initiative comes from the father, the son feeling too guilty to make the move. In the Lucan version the roles are reversed. Cf. *JWJ*, 82.

[42]Cf. Bultmann, *HST*, 203. The underlying lesson may be summarized as the story of the missed repentance. A partial rabbinic parallel may be found in ySanh. 6, 23c; yHag. 2, 77d; see below, p. 113.

matters (*dīnē mamōnōt*). To this disregard of Jewish law, as the rabbis understood it, was attributed the subsequent desolation of the district.[43]

32. In the fragmentary *Similitude of Litigation before a Judge* (Matt. 5.25f.; Luke 12.58f.), the doctrine of instant reconciliation among quarrelling brothers (in the age of eschatological urgency and approaching judgment?) is inculcated with the help of the story of two men arguing over a debt. The lesson is that they must settle out of court so that the judge does not send the guilty party to prison. Forgiveness is not explicitly mentioned, but neither is it excluded. There is therefore a possible link with previous parables referring to remission of debts (cf. Matt. 18.23–35 and Luke 7.36–50 on p. 106 above).

33. The *Parable of the Unjust City Judge*, negatively mirroring God, underlines the significance of boundless and persistent trust (Luke 18.2–5). When a poor widow continues to entreat him, the judge, to rid himself of her, in the end finds in her favour. The basic theme is that of the story of the importuning friend in Luke 11.5–8 (p. 108 above). Such seems to be the teaching attributable to Jesus, although Luke turns it into a prayer to expedite the *parousia* and the final judgment (18.6–8).

34. The *Parable of the Last Judgment*, prior to its recasting by Matthew so that it applies to the *parousia* of Christ (Matt. 25.31–46), envisages less surprisingly a single divine Judge (*the King*) as presiding over the eschatological tribunal and rewarding or punishing humankind.

The teaching, though not its universalist context (cf. p. 114 below) with no mention of Jews, and no doubt deriving from ecclesiastical manipulation, pertains to the nucleus of Jesus' doctrine of true piety.[44]

(e) Parables of the wedding feast

The last of the social occasions to serve as material for several

[43]Cf. tBQ 8.14. See M. D. Goodman, *State and Society in Roman Galilee* (1983), 126f. On the rabbinic judiciary, cf. *HJP* II, 186–88. bSanh. 4b–5a also alludes to the custom of rabbis dealing with civil cases single-handedly as long as they were recognized as experts in the relevant field of law.

[44]For the implied doctrine of *imitatio Dei*, see *JWJ*, 83f., and 200–206 below.

parables is a royal marriage (so in Matthew, but downgraded in Luke) and its accompanying customs.

35. The *Parable of the Wedding Feast of a Prince* has as its subject the revision of the list of guests in Matt. 22.2–10. In the Lucan version (Luke 14.16–24) this becomes a grand dinner-party organized by 'a man' (v. 16) or 'a property owner' (v. 21). All those invited send apologies, so the unworthy, the homeless, 'the poor and maimed and blind and lame', are brought in to fill the banquet hall.

The substance of the parable figures in a story recounted in the Palestinian Talmud (ySanh. 6, 23c; yHag. 2, 77d), where a tax-collector, by the name of Bar Maʿyan, prepares a great feast for the leading citizens. When these fail to turn up, he invites the poor, and on his death, is rewarded for this one good deed in his life-time. The New Testament version, without the Matthean twist (22.6,11–14),[45] corresponds to the basic teaching of Jesus about the reversal of earthly priorities at the approach of the Kingdom, and includes an indirect insistence on constant preparedness.

36. The *Parable of the Ten Virgins* (Matt. 25.1–13) is also developed around the theme of a wedding-feast. A retinue of ten girls awaits the bridegroom who is expected to arrive at the marriage feast after nightfall: hence the lamps. The foolish run out of oil, but the wise, or rather selfish, virgins refuse to help them and enter the banquet hall, whereas the others are locked out, and although they knock, the door does not open.

In its present shape, the parable is obviously a late church formulation stressing the necessary watchfulness and readiness while the parousia is delayed. Both the calculating self-centredness of the 'wise' virgins, and the heartless refusal of the 'bridegroom' to admit those who failed to be properly prepared, flatly contradict the piety taught by Jesus. The only possible understanding of the story compatible with his basic religious outlook would underscore the need for self-reliance during the great upheaval preceding the end. The heroines of the parable are

[45]The murder of the servants bringing the invitation is alien to this story and results from a conflation with the parable of the wicked tenants of the vineyard (Mark 12.1–12, etc., cf. above, pp. 104f.). The Matthean appendix concerning the guest arriving improperly dressed again does not fit the story. How could layabouts and passers-by be expected to be wearing 'wedding garments'?

the 'foolish virgins', and the message addressed to them is that, in the circumstances, they must not trust their 'wise' sisters.

37–38. The fragmentary *Parable of the Door-keeper* (Mark 13.33–37; cf. Matt. 24.45–51; Luke 12.42–46) whom the master must find awake at the moment of his unexpected return is characterized by the same theme of alertness. So is also the *Parable of the Closed Door* (Luke 13.25f.), which in its present Gentile-Christian version envisages the rejections of the Jews (the 'sons of the Kingdom' in Matt. 8.12) and their replacement by men 'from east and west and from north and south' (Luke 13.27–29).

39. The last of the wedding-feast parables concerns the *Choice of a Seat* (Luke 14.7–11). Those who modestly occupy the lowest places are likely to be directed towards higher positions and vice versa. The story is a re-working of Prov. 25.6f., which is divested of its royal setting. The lesson taught is humility, on which, it would seem, emphasis has to be laid, not only in normal circumstances – the scribes seek 'the best seats in the synagogues and the places of honour at feasts' (Mark 12.38f.; Luke 20.46) – but even in the context of the eschatological banquet. The sons of Zebedee, the apostles James and John, are purported to have asked Jesus to be allowed to sit at his right hand and at his left in his glory (Mark 10.37).[46]

IV   The Purpose and Teaching of the Parables of Jesus

Following this outline of the content and lessons of the Gospel parables, it remains now to attempt to sketch their import in the gospel of Jesus. Here, to begin with, two negative remarks have to be noted. First, unlike the majority of the rabbinic parables, those surveyed in the foregoing pages are not exegetical by nature; that is to say, they are not meant to interpret or introduce a passage from the Bible. The two instances falling under such a heading,

[46]The same moral instruction is conveyed in the form of an interpretation of Prov. 25.7 in rabbinic literature, in the name of the Tanna R. Simeon ben Azzai: 'Descend from your place two or three steps and sit there. It is better for you to be told to go up than come down, as it is written, "For it is better to be told, Come up here, than to be set lower in the presence of the prince".' Cf. Ex.R. 45.5; Lev.R. 1.5.

namely the *Parable of the Wicked Tenants of the Vineyard* (Mark 12.1–12, etc.), implicitly quoting Isa. 5.2 and concluding explicitly with Ps. 118.22f., and the *Parables of the Good Samaritan* (Luke 10.29–37), connected with Lev. 19.18, cited in Luke 10.27, have been shown to be secondary phenomena, inexpertly bound to the story itself (cf. pp. 104f. and 109). Again, with the exception of the parables of the *Sower*, of the *Weeds* and of the *Net*, none of the subsequent literary units is enriched with expository details. This is another feature distinguishing the teaching style of Jesus from that of the rabbis. These two negative traits intimate that, in their original form at least, the Gospel parables had an autonomous, rather than an auxiliary, existence, and were endowed with a significance that was immediately discernible.

This brings us to the question of the aim of the parables because, if it is true that they convey a message quasi automatically, without need of regular explanation, it follows that they themselves must be accepted as self-contained communication. Such a view, however, directly contradicts an explicit New Testament statement relating to the choice of the parabolic genre by Jesus.

Between the parable of the Sower (Mark 4.1–9, etc.) and the interpretation attributed to it by Jesus (Mark 4.13–20, etc.), the three Synoptists insert what appears to be a general statement (Mark 4.10–12) on the purpose of this didactic form. The inner circle is granted knowledge of the 'secret (or secrets) of the Kingdom of God or Heaven', but the less favoured outsiders receive the gospel only 'in parables'. By contrasting the concealed inner sense (i.e. 'mystery' or *raz*) of a doctrine with teaching 'in parables', the latter is given a definite pejorative sense in Greek which its Hebrew equivalent (*mashal*) does not possess. The semantic hint is positively confirmed by the concluding phrase:

> So that they may indeed see but not perceive, and may indeed hear but not understand; lest they should turn again and be forgiven (Mark 4.12).[47]

[47]The text is a free and abridged reproduction of Isa. 6.9f. In turn, Luke 8.10 is an abbreviation of Mark: 'so that seeing they may not see, and hearing they may not understand'. Mark concludes by adopting the targumic paraphrase 'be forgiven' for the Hebrew 'be healed'. For the whole problem, see Craig A. Evans, *To See and not Perceive: Isaiah 6.9–10 in Early Jewish and Christian Interpretation* (1989).

Matthew, in turn, enlarges on Mark's text, turns it into first-person speech, and confirms it with a direct full citation of Isaiah 6.9–10.

> This is why I speak to them in parables, because seeing they do not see, and hearing they do not hear, nor do they understand. With them indeed is fulfilled the prophecy of Isaiah which says: 'You shall indeed hear but never understand, and you shall indeed see but never perceive. For this people's heart has grown dull, and their ears are heavy of hearing, and their eyes they have closed, lest they should perceive with their eyes, and hear with their ears, and understand with their heart, and turn for me to heal them.'

The intended meaning is clearly that by embracing the parabolic style, Jesus deliberately kept the crowds of listeners at arm's length, and reserved his message to the initiates only. The term 'parable' is taken in the sense of 'riddle' or 'enigma'.[48] Such an attitude would make sense only if Jesus had been an esoteric teacher like the Essene or Gnostic masters, but neither the Gospel tradition in general, nor analysis of the parables, furnishes any supporting evidence of this.[49]

A more likely explanation of Mark 4.10–12 par., with its use of Isa. 6.9f. is that the synoptic tradition, anticipating Jewish unbelief from the outset of the Gospel story, portrays Jesus as foreseeing the unwillingness of most of his compatriots to listen to the good news of the Kingdom, and refuses to allow them easy access to it. Later layers of the New Testament, viz. Acts 28.23–28 and John 12.37–41, testify to the use of Isa. 6 as the proof-text demonstrating Jewish obduracy. The presentation of the parables as an obstacle to understanding pertains to church apologetics rather than to an historical approach to the teaching of Jesus. Besides, if the parable = enigma theory were seriously meant to

---

[48]The equivocal use of the noun is attested in the Greek Ben Sira. In 3.29 *parabolē* renders *mashal*, but in 47.17 it corresponds to *hīdah*. Similarly, in Num. 21.27 *mōshel* is translated as *ainigmatistēs*, whereas in Num. 12.8 *ainigma* equals *hīdah*.

[49]Cf. D. Stern, *Parables in Midrash* (1991), 200–1. According to Josephus (*War* ii.141), every Essene swore an oath 'to reveal nothing to outsiders', and the Master of the Qumran Community Rule was to 'conceal the teaching of the Law from the men of falsehood' (ix.16) and conduct himself towards them in a 'spirit of secrecy' (9.21).

apply to all the metaphorical instruction delivered by him, one would expect to find every parable, and not just those of the *Sower*, the *Weeds* and the *Net*, accompanied by a key to the riddle!

But if, as is generally accepted, the purpose of the parables was not to restrict, but to facilitate the comprehension of Jesus' preaching, how is this purpose achieved? Our survey of the whole corpus indicates, that possibly with the single exception of the *Wicked Tenants* of the Vineyard, which consists of an allegorical exposition, they all urge a single religious/ethical message, and most of them presuppose an eschatological atmosphere and context. The aim of the parable is, in consequence, to impress on the listener, in a lively and colourful manner, the obligation to adopt an attitude, or perform an act, of fundamental importance.

The central message of the parables may be reduced to three radical points which will be further developed in chapter 7. These are, in logical order, *teshuvah* (repentance/forgiveness), *emunah* (trust in God) and the superlative form of this trust, entailing the taking of high risks for the sake of the Kingdom. They all reflect, as may be expected, the simple and profound eschatological piety of Jesus the Jew.

To conclude on a polemical note, it has been claimed by an internationally known New Testament scholar, Eduard Schweizer, in his book entitled *Jesus* (1971) – already pilloried in the chapter on 'Jesus and the Law' (p. 26,n.20) – that the parables explain why Jesus was put to death. His paragraph on the story of the Prodigal Son deserves to be quoted in full.

With an assurance that must have struck his hearers as unexampled, he equates God's merciful conduct with his own conduct towards the tax collectors. Who but Jesus could venture to describe such incredible and absolutely unexpected conduct on the part of the father towards his windbag of a son? Who but Jesus would have the authority to assume the role of God himself in his parable and proclaim a celebration on behalf of the sinner who has been restored to fellowship with God? *Those who nailed him to the cross because they found blasphemy in his parables – which proclaimed such scandalous conduct on the part of God – understood his parables better than those who saw in them nothing but the obvious message,*

> which should be self-evident to all, of the fatherhood and
> kindness of God, meant to replace superstitious belief in a God
> of wrath [my italics] (pp. 28f.; p. 32 in German).

This magisterial misrepresentation of Judaism's doctrine of
imitatio Dei (to be discussed in Chapter 7) is coupled here with a
fundamental misunderstanding of the frame of mind of Jesus the
Hasid and the nature and truth of his Jewish parables.

Appendix: The Distribution of the Parables in the Synoptics

Mark-Matthew-Luke

The sower [1]	Mark 4.3–8	Matt. 13.3–8	Luke 8.5–8
The mustard seed [4]	Mark 4.30–32	Matt. 13.31–32	Luke 13.18–19
The wicked tenants [14]	Mark 12.1–4	Matt. 21.33–44	Luke 20.9–18
The fig tree [3]	Mark 13.28–29	Matt. 24.32–33	Luke 21.19–31

Mark-Luke

The door-keeper [36]	Mark 13.33–37		Luke 12.35–38

Mark

The growing seed [2]	Mark 4.26–29

Matthew-Luke

Litigation before a judge [3]	Matt. 5.25–26	Luke 12.58–59
The two builders [8]	Matt. 7.24–27	Luke 6.48–49
Children in the market [9]	Matt. 11.16–19	Luke 7.31–35
The return of a demon [10]	Matt. 12.43–45	Luke 11.24–26
The leaven [11]	Matt. 13.33	Luke 13.20–21
The lost sheep [6]	Matt. 18.12–14	Luke 15.4–7
The wedding feast [34]	Matt. 22.1–14	Luke 14.16–24
The thief [26]	Matt. 24.43–44	Luke 12.39–40
The talents [19]	Matt. 25.14–30	Luke 19.11–27

Matthew

The weeds [5]	Matt. 13.24–30
The treasure [23]	Matt. 13.44
The pearl [24]	Matt. 13.45–46
The net [7]	Matt. 13.47–48
The clever householder [25]	Matt. 13.51–52
The cruel servant [17]	Matt. 18.23–35

The vineyard [16]	Matt. 20.1–16
The two sons [15]	Matt. 21.28–37
The ten virgins [36]	Matt. 25.1–13
The last judgment [34]	Matt. 25.31–36

Luke

The creditor [18]	Luke 7.41–43
The good Samaritan [29]	Luke 10.29–37
The unexpected guest [27]	Luke 11.5–8
The rich farmer [13]	Luke 12.16–21
The closed door [38]	Luke 13.25–26
The choice of a seat [39]	Luke 14.7–11
The landowner and the king [21]	Luke 14.28–32
The lost drachma [12]	Luke 15.8–10
The prodigal son [30]	Luke 15.11–21
The unjust steward [20]	Luke 16.1–8
The rich man and Lazarus [31]	Luke 16.19–31
The servant's reward [22]	Luke 17.7–10
The unjust city judge [33]	Luke 18.1–8
The Pharisee and the publican [28]	Luke 18.9–14

5

Jesus and the Kingdom of God

From the mere frequency of the phrases, 'Kingdom of God' and 'Kingdom of Heaven' – they figure no less than a hundred times in the Synoptic Gospels – it is reasonable to infer that the concepts which they reflect played an important part in the teaching of Jesus. This plain statement represents the common ground of contemporary New Testament scholarship.

Thus the very first sentence of the opening chapter of Rudolf Bultmann's *Theologie des Neuen Testaments* (p. 3) introduces the 'Kingdom of God' as the dominant concept ('der beherrschende Begriff') of the preaching of Jesus. Christopher Rowland sees in it 'a central pillar' (*Christian Origins*, 133) and Norman Perrin, 'the central aspect' of the teaching of Jesus (*Rediscovering*, 54). For E. P. Sanders, it is one of the 'most discussed' New Testament topics (*Jesus and Judaism*, 123). In turn, Anthony Harvey (*Constraints*, 86) echoing Joachim Jeremias (*NT Theology*, 32–34), emphasizes the unparalleled nature of the idioms referring to it.

This consensus is, however, purely superficial and vanishes as soon as scholars seriously confront such basic questions as 'what?', 'how?' and especially 'when?'. To grasp the true sense of the kernel of the religion of Jesus, we shall not shirk these but seek to answer them with the help of a full analysis of the Gospel evidence compared to the doctrine of the Kingdom of God preserved in parallel Jewish sources.[1]

[1]The literature on the subject has grown enormously since the pioneering works of Johannes Weiss (*Die Predigt Jesu vom Reiche Gottes*, 1900) and Albert Schweitzer (*Von Reimarus zu Wrede*, 1906, better known as *The Quest of the Historical Jesus*, 3rd ed. 1954). Fortunately, Norman Perrin's book, *The Kingdom of God in the Teaching of Jesus* offers a most useful critical survey and discussion of the theories up to its publication in 1963. See also Martin Buber, *Kingship of God* (1967); N. Perrin, *Jesus and the Language of the Kingdom*

I   The Kingdom of God outside the New Testament

By the time Jesus first meditated on it, the idea of the Kingdom of God had already a lengthy history in the Hebrew Bible and in early post-biblical or inter-testamental literature. It continued to flourish at the beginning of the Christian era in the works of the rabbis of the first two centuries (the Tannaim), and in the early layers of the synagogal liturgy.

'Kingdom' being essentially a political notion, it is not surprising that its metaphorical association with God first retains an element of the original significance, i.e. a nation and territory ruled over by a (divine) king, before turning into a more abstract notion of the universal sovereignty and limitless power of the Deity.

1. *The biblical Kingdom of God*

During the existence of an independent Israelite monarchy, from David down to the fall of Jerusalem under Nebuchadnezzar in the early sixth century BC, the Kingdom of God as primarily conceived of as the reverse side, or celestial counterpart, of the earthly kingship. The Jewish people, regulated by, and living according to, a divinely granted Law, constituted the *de facto* province over which God ruled vicariously through a human monarch installed as the Lord's deputy on the day of his accession (Ps. 2.7). Needless to say, the bond between the heavenly and terrestrial Kingship was not forged instantaneously. In fact it would seem, if the testimony of I Samuel (8.7 and 12.12) is to be believed, that at the time of the birth of the Hebrew monarchy the anti-royalist faction identified the request for an Israelite king as an automatic repudiation of divine sovereignty. For such is the obvious meaning of the words addressed by God to Samuel according to I Sam. 8.7.

(1976); J. Schlosser, *Le règne de Dieu dans les dits de Jésus* I–II (1980); O. Camponovo, *Königtum, Königsherrschaft und Reich Gottes in den frühjüdischen Schriften* (1984). A full discussion may be found in the article, *basileus*, etc., in *TDNT* I, 564–93 by G. von Rad, K. -G. Kuhn and K. -L. Schmidt. For a more recent presentation of the subject by a leading New Testament specialist, cf. E. P. Sanders, *Jesus and Judaism* (1985), 123–241.

Hearken to the voice of the people . . . for they have not rejected you, but they have rejected me from being King over them.[2]

If God alone was recognized as the *de facto* ruler of Israel, his *de jure* Kingdom *qua* Creator of mankind was believed to be universal, and the hope was entertained that one day, a Jewish monarch would rule over the nations and lead them to acknowledge and worship the true Master of the universe. In the same Psalm (2.8), the king of Israel is instructed:

> Ask of me, and I will make the nations your heritage,
> And the ends of the earth your possession.

A little later in the same poem (Ps. 2.11), the Gentile rulers are admonished to 'serve the Lord with fear'. In another Psalm (99.1), the divine King is depicted as the object of dread and awe among foreigners.

The general perspective underwent a substantial change with the overthrow of the Kingdom of Judah by the Babylonians in 586 BC and the consequent loss of Jewish political autonomy. In the absence of national rulers, biblical Messianism was born, looking forward to the coming of a king to re-establish God's visible and institutional dominion over all the Jews liberated from alien empires. Some of the royal Psalms (Ps. 2, 110, etc.) were reinterpreted in this sense, and Ezekiel (34.24) explicitly foretells a new David who is to shepherd Israel:

> And I, the Lord, will be their God,
> and my servant David will be prince among them.

Yet the same Ezekiel also envisages God himself, without an earthly viceroy, as the great conqueror at the end of time, who will annihilate the hosts of Gog of the land of Magog, the final foe of Israel.

> I will strike your bow from your left hand,
> and will make your arrows drop out of your right hand.

---

[2]This anti-monarchist stand is expressly excluded by the post-exilic Chronicler who attributes to David the following quotation, '(God) has chosen Solomon, my son, to sit upon the throne of the Kingship of the Lord over Israel' (I Chron. 28.5; cf. 17.14).

> You shall fall upon the mountains of Israel,
> you and all your hordes and the peoples that are
>   with you.
> I will give you to birds of prey of every sort
> and to the wild beasts to be devoured.
> You shall fall in the open field (Ezek. 39.3–5).[3]

With or without a messianic intermediary, that is to say, the establishment of the divine Kingdom was indissolubly connected with the expectation of a battle which would culminate in God's, and at least indirectly Israel's, victory.

Exilic and post-exilic prophecy, the work of Deutero- and Trito-Isaiah (Isa. 40–66) dating to the second half of the sixth century BC, was the source of the concept of a non-bellicose inauguration of the universal Kingdom. In the context of the unforeseen and unforeseeable liberation of the Jews from Babylonian captivity, their former pagan masters, having discovered in the God of Israel the true Deliverer, submit themselves to him and testify to his saving power. In Deutero-Isaiah's words,

> They shall follow you;
> they shall come over in chains and bow down to you.
> They will make supplication to you, saying:
> 'God is with you only, and there is no other,
> no god beside him' (Isa. 45.14).

This recognition of the God of Israel by the Gentiles was expected to be accompanied by a simultaneous submission to the Jews – 'they shall bow down to you and lick the dust of your feet' (Isa. 49.23), and worship in the Temple of Jerusalem.

> And the nations shall come to your light . . .
> They shall bring gold and frankincense,
> and shall proclaim the praise of the Lord . . .
> they shall come up with acceptance on my altar . . .
>   (Isa. 60.3, 6f.).

[3]Tradition turns the single character of Gog, king of Magog (Ezek. 38.2) into the pair, Gog *and* Magog. Cf. *Enc. Jud.* 7, 691–3. The antiquity of the duplication is proved by their mention in the form of an easily understandable interpretative gloss in Rev. 20.8: 'And when the thousand years are ended, Satan will be loosed from his prison and will come out to deceive the nations . . ., that is, Gog and Magog, to gather them for battle.'

Here the coming of the Kingdom entails an element of mystery: the salvation of Israel is presented as a magnet attracting the rest of mankind to God.

An odd negative feature is shared by all the evidence considered so far, with the exception of the two chronologically late references to I Chronicles 17.14 and 28.5 (p. 122,n.2), namely that all the royal imagery is based on the noun 'King' and the verb 'to be King/to reign', while the word 'Kingdom', all-pervasive in the terminology of the Gospels, is still to make its first appearance.

If the Aramaic passages from the Book of Daniel are discarded – they will be more appropriately discussed along with other second- and first-century BC examples in the next section (cf. p. 126) – the biblical Hebrew 'Kingdom (*malkhūt* or *melūkhah*) of God', delineating the final state of mankind, echoes both the forceful imposition of the divine rule over the nations, and one brought about by peaceful means.[4]

Further emphasis is laid on universal power and eternal sovereignty: God's *malkhūt* 'rules over all' (Ps. 103.19) and 'Thy *malkhūt* is an everlasting *malkhūt*, and Thy dominion endures throughout all generations' (Ps. 145.13). However, the paucity of the use of the abstract concept compared to the concrete Hebrew imagery is remarkable, let alone to the frequency of the Greek *basileia* in the Gospel examples. For even if the two occurrences of the word in I Chronicles are included, there are only six instances of the use of *malkhūt* and *melūkhah* in the whole Hebrew Bible!

2. *The inter-testamental Kingdom of God*

During the highly creative period of Jewish literature, starting with the Maccabaean era in the first half of the second century BC, and terminating with the life-time of Jesus and the writing of the Gospels, the Kingdom ideology partly develops along the lines of the earlier biblical thought, but also partly opens fresh vistas. The Pseudepigrapha of the Old Testament and the Dead Sea Scrolls provide the evidence, but the canonical Book of Daniel, which received its final redaction in the 160s BC, also

---

[4]According to Obadiah 21, Edom will be judged by warriors from Zion and as a result the *melūkhah* will be the Lord's. Again in Ps. 22.29 [ET 22.28], God will be the master of the converted Gentiles and the *melūkhah* will be his.

belongs to this stage of doctrinal evolution. It is hardly necessary to underscore their significance for the student investigating the teachings of the Gospels: Jesus and the authors of the other works discussed in this section were children of the same age.

All the Jewish sources in question reveal, in one way or another, an atmosphere of eschatological and apocalyptic excitement. The political element of the original Kingdom concept still survives, but an increasing tendency towards the transcendental becomes apparent.

To begin with, royal Messianism, first developed by post-exilic prophets and psalmists, found its most potent expression in the first-century BC poems known as the Psalms of Solomon. In particular, Psalm 17 portrays a victorious Jewish saviour-king establishing divine rule over the Gentiles.

> Behold, O Lord, and raise up for them their king,
>   the son of David . . .
> And gird him with strength,
>   that he may shatter unrighteous rulers;
> And purify Jerusalem of the nations
>   which trample her down in destruction . . .
> And he shall have the peoples of the Gentiles
>   to serve him under his yoke (17.21f., 30).[5]

This framework of restoration at the end of time by the new David has as its climax the proclamation of perpetual divine rule (17.46). Royal Messianism and divine Kingship, in consequence, can go hand in hand in hand, but not necessarily. In fact, at the beginning of the same Psalm (verse 3), the subjection of the nations to the divine *basileia* is envisaged *without* human mediation. Likewise, in Psalms of Solomon 2, it is God, and not a Jewish prince, who is the victor over the conceited pagan invader (Pompey), mythically described as the dragon (2.25).

> He said, 'I will be lord of land and sea';
>   and he did not recognize that God is great,
>   mighty in his great strength.
> He is king in the heavens,
>   and judges kings and dominions (2.29f.).[6]

---

[5]Trans. S. P. Brock in H. F. D. Sparks (ed.), *The Apocryphal Old Testament* [*AOT*] (1984), 678f. On the Psalms of Solomon, see *HJP* III, 192–97.
[6]Cf. *AOT*, 657.

A similar cryptic historical canvas, alluding to the Roman rule of Egypt, filled with royal Messianism represented by a holy prince and with the apocalyptic eschatology of a deluge of fire, is used for the revelation of the Kingdom of God in a famous passage of the Jewish Sibylline Oracles (3.46–54).

> Then indeed the greatest Kingdom
> of the immortal King will become manifest over men.
> For a holy prince will come to gain sway
> over the sceptres of the earth
> forever as time presses on . . .
> All men will perish in their own dwellings
> when the fiery cataract flows from heaven.[7]

Two biblical notions, the acknowledgment of the God of Israel by Gentiles and the unending glory of his rule, appear in an accentuated form in the Aramaic Daniel. There, the kings of Babylon and Persia, personified by Nebuchadnezzar and Darius, extol the greatness of Daniel's God and proclaim the eternity of his Kingdom (Dan. 3.33; 4.31; 6.27).

The dream-vision of Daniel 7 also deserves a brief mention. Although the words King or Kingdom are missing, the figure designated as 'the Ancient of days', sitting on a heavenly throne and judging the four world empires, is obviously the divine Lord. It must be noted, however, that the kingdom granted by him to 'one like a son of man' is not described as God's Kingdom, but that of 'the saints of the Most High' (Dan. 7.18, 22) or 'the people of the saints of the Most High' (7.27).[8] While this chapter of Daniel contributes only indirectly to the understanding of the Kingdom of God ideology, it had to be introduced here because of the significant role it was to play in the creation of the doctrine of the Second Coming or Parousia in the Gospels, one which, as will be argued, is in total contrast to the authentic teaching of Jesus.

---

[7]Trans. J. J. Collins in J. H. Charlesworth, *OTP* I, 363. On the Sibylline Oracles, see *HJP* III, 618–54. A parallel imagery figures in IV Ezra 12.31–34, where the Davidic king Messiah, symbolized as a lion, condemns in judgment 'the eagle' (the Romans) before annihilating them.

[8]Cf. L. Dequeker, 'The "Saints of the Most High" in Qumran and Daniel', *Oudtestamentische Studien* 18 (1973), 108–87. A very similar idea to Dan. 7 is attested in the so-called 'Son of God' fragment (4Q246) from Qumran, mentioning the Kingdom of 'the people of God'. Cf. G. Vermes, 'Qumran Forum Miscellanea I', *JJS* 43 (1992), 301–3.

Furthermore, from Daniel onwards, in particular in the Assumption of Moses and some of the Qumran manuscripts, the concept of the Kingdom is increasingly enriched with other worldly features. In the War Scroll (1QM), the final victory over the forces of darkness and the concomitant establishment of the divine Kingdom are the outcome of the eschatological battle fought by the allied armies of the angelic and human 'sons of light' under the captaincy of the heavenly Prince Michael against the coalition of the demonic and human 'sons of darkness' (1QM 17.6f.).[9]

The symbolical annihilation of the enemy on the battle-field by 'the sword of God' is more colourfully depicted in this document (1QM 12.11f.; 19.4, 11) than probably anywhere else in ancient Jewish literature. The following are but two characteristic extracts.

The *melūkhah* shall be to the God of Israel and he shall accomplish mighty deeds by the saints of his people (1QM 6.6).

For Thou art [terrible], O God, in the glory of Thy *malkhūt*, and the congregation of Thy holy ones is among us for everlasting succour . . . For our Lord is holy, and the King of glory is with us . . . Valiant [warriors] of the angelic host are among our numbered men, and the Hero of war is with our congregation; the host of his spirits is with our foot-soldiers and horsemen (1QM 12.7–9).

Likewise, in chapter 10 of the Assumption or Testament of Moses, probably a pre-Maccabaean work revised at the turn of

[9]Michael's role as heavenly protector of Israel is also traceable to Daniel 10.21; 12.1. His identity as the 'Prince of Light', antagonist of the 'Angel of Darkness' (1QS 3.20–22) is generally recognized (cf. Y. Yadin, *The Scroll of the War of the Sons of Light against the Sons of Darkness* (1962), 235f.). He and the Kittim also figure in the Qumran fragments of a Rule of War. Cf. G. Vermes, 'The Oxford Forum for Qumran Research: Seminar on the Rule of War (4Q285)', *JJS* 43 (1992), 85–90. Michael's leadership of the celestial host against that of the devil is magnificently depicted in Rev. 12.7–10: 'Now war arose in heaven, Michael and his angels fighting against the dragon; and the dragon and his angels fought, but they were defeated . . . And I heard a loud voice in heaven, saying, "Now the salvation and the power and the kingdom of our God have come" . . .' A further parallel of interest may be found in II (Greek) Baruch 11.2 where Michael is described as the holder of the keys of the kingdom of heaven.

the era, the coming of God's Kingdom is presented as the sequel of the apocalyptic judgment of the Devil by God himself in the midst of earthquakes and disturbances among the heavenly bodies, and the simultaneous destruction of the pagans and all their abominations.

> And then shall his Kingdom appear in all his creation;
> and then shall the Devil meet his end . . .
> For the Heavenly One will arise from his royal throne . . .
> And the earth will tremble . . .
> And the sun will not give its light;
> and the horns of the moon will be turned into darkness . . .
> For the Most High will . . . appear to punish the Gentiles,
> And he will destroy all their idols (10.1, 3–7).[10]

The transcendental theme in the portrayal of the Kingdom culminates in the so-called Angelic Liturgy, or Songs of the (heavenly) Sabbath Sacrifice from Qumran (4QShirShab, *HJP* III, 462f.). This document includes some twenty-five examples of the term *malkhūt* representing, often in a fragmentary setting, the glory of the celestial court of the divine King. The poems reflect mystical visions and, as such, unlike the examples previously discussed, have no link with real space, but claim that Sabbaths above and below are celebrated at one and the same time. In heavily repetitive language, the psalmist praises the splendour of heaven.

> These are the Princes of those marvellously clothed for service, the Princes of the Kingdoms (*mamlakhōt*), the Kingdom of the holy ones of the King of holiness in all the heights of the sanctuaries of his glorious Kingdom (*malkhūt*).

While this mystical propensity is not without New Testament repercussions, especially in the Book of Revelation, and even, perhaps surprisingly, in St Paul (I Cor. 15.25–28), it remains to be seen how, if at all, it is reconcilable with the mentality of Jesus. There are, however, further aspects of the inter-testamental Kingdom theology which need to be defined with a view to their potential relevance to the Gospel teaching.

---

[10]Trans. J. P. M. Sweet in Sparks, *AOT*, 612f. On the Assumption of Moses, see *HJP* III, 282f.

To begin with, the mid-second-century BC Book of Jubilees 50.9–11 (*HJP* III, 308–18) describes the Sabbath as 'a day of the holy Kingdom for ever'. In other words, sabbatical abstinence from 'all work of the occupations of the children of men', and a total devotion to worship by means of offering incense, gifts and sacrifice in the sanctuary, symbolize and mystically achieve God's reign on earth.

A similar idea is expressed in another second-century BC text, I Enoch (91.11–17). In the eighth week of a world-history divided into ten weeks, the righteous will execute judgment over the wicked and at the end, 'a house will be built for the great King in glory for ever' (91.13). In the context of the Ethiopic version, this house is a new, restored Temple. However, if correctly reconstructed, the fragmentary Aramaic original surviving in 4Q introduces a definite eschatological overtone in the form of the 'Temple of the [King]dom of the Great One.'[11]

Still in the liturgical frame of reference, and as a terrestrial counterpart of heavenly worship, the Qumran priests are described in the Blessings from Cave I (1QSb; cf. *HJP* III, 457f.) as the cultic leaders in the 'Temple of the Kingdom'.

> May you attend upon the service in the Temple of the Kingdom and decree destiny in company with the Angels of Presence . . . for everlasting ages and time without end (4. 25f.).

In addition to the adoption of non-royal symbolism for the representation of the Kingdom of God, pre-Christian Pseudepigrapha also refer to the ethical dimensions of the Kingdom of God concept. Thus the Testament of Benjamin (9.1), dating in my opinion to the second/first century BC (cf. *HJP* III.2, 744f.), associates the removal of 'the Kingdom of God' from the tribe of Benjamin with their renewal of 'wanton relations with women'. The meaning of the allusion may simply refer to the deposition of the Benjaminite Saul in favour of David of

---

[11]Cf. 4Q Enoch g 1 iv in J. T. Milik, *The Books of Enoch: Aramaic Fragments of Qumrân Cave IV* (1976), 266. The restoration is rendered plausible by 4QEn Giants a 9 (ibid. 316) where the phrase *mlkwt rbwtkh* (Kingdom of thy greatness) is fairly well preserved. The royal dignity of God is repeatedly asserted in I Enoch. In 9.4 the four archangels address 'their Lord, the King: "Lord of lords, God of gods, King of kings! Your throne (endures) for all the generations of the world".' Cf. 84.2. On I Enoch, see *HJP* III, 250–68.

Judah, but it may, and probably does, imply also that divine sovereignty cannot dwell where there is sexual misbehaviour. If so, the context is spiritual/moral without being necessarily eschatological.

One more Qumran example is of particular interest for the study of the Gospels. In a wisdom poem from Cave IV, the Song of the Sage (4Q510, 1.4; cf. *HJP* III, 213, n.1), whose tone recalls the Songs of the Sabbath Sacrifice, the Kingdom idea figures in a ceremony of exorcism:

> Words of thanksgiving . . . to the God of knowledge . . . the God of gods, Lord of all the holy. [His] domini[on] is over all the powerful mighty ones and by the power of his might all shall be terrified . . . by the splendour of the dwel[ling] of the glory of his kingdom. And I . . . proclaim the majesty of his beauty to frighten and ter[rify] all the spirits of the destroying angels and the spirits of the bastards, the demons, Lilith . . .

Such an association of the Kingdom of God with the terror and fright inflicted on evil spirits is particularly noteworthy in view of Jesus' healings and exorcisms linked to the notion of the coming Kingdom of God.

Finally, an entirely different politico-religious view of the Kingdom of God arises from Josephus' account of the message of Judas the Galilean, creator of the resistance movement which caused incessant unrest in first-century AD Palestine until the first war against Rome and beyond. Named as the 'Fourth Philosophy', following the doctrine of the Pharisees, Sadducees and Essenes, Judas's proclamation strangely recalls in an exaggerated form the anti-monarchic position adopted by the Israelites in the age of Samuel (cf. above, pp. 121f.). For Samuel, the elevation of Saul to the throne was tantamount to a betrayal of God as King; for Judas, recognition of divine sovereignty was not reconcilable with the toleration of *any* 'mortal masters' (*War* ii.118).

The same idea is placed by Josephus on the lips of the rebel commander of Masada, Eleazar ben Jair, in a speech exhorting his garrison to kill themselves:

> Long since, my brave men, we determined neither to serve the Romans nor any other save God, for he alone is man's true and righteous Lord (*War* vii.323).

During and after the life-time of Jesus, that is to say, there existed a political theology among some Jews which condemned not only submission to imperial rule, but to any human authority including, it would seem, that of the King Messiah!

3. *The Kingdom of God in rabbinic literature and in synagogal liturgy*

(*a*) Rabbinic literature

In the dynamic flow of Jewish eschatological thought, the rabbinic sages of the early centuries of the Christian era view the problem of the Kingdom of God from two different viewpoints which, for want of a better distinction, may be called theoretical and practical. The first focusses on its temporal/eternal and heavenly/earthly aspects; the second, more pragmatic, is concerned with the human action that secures access to the Kingdom.[12]

As might be expected, some of the 'theoretical' rabbinic explanations are linked to, and enlarge on, teachings found in the Bible and inter-testamental writings. Thus the eschatological character of the Kingdom stands out when contrasted with the then present political reality of the Roman empire, the secular 'wicked *malkhūt*'. Its overthrow at the end of time, though less powerfully voiced throughout the Talmudic age than in the ideology in vogue during the Second Temple era, remained continuously part of the eschatological hope of the Jewish people. As an ancient homily proclaims:

> The time of the uprooting of the kingdom of wickedness is come; the time of the revelation of the Kingdom of heaven is come (Pes. R., ed. Buber, 51a).

In similar vein, the Palestinian Targums on the Song of Moses (Ex. 15.18) specify that the duration of God's Kingdom 'for ever

[12]The relevant texts have been collected and analysed in standard works and dictionaries. See, in particular, G. Dalman, *Die Worte Jesu* (2nd ed. 1930), 75–83 [ET *The Words of Jesus* (1902), 96–101]; K. -G. Kuhn, *basileus*, *TDNT* I, 571–4; *Jew. Enc.* VII, 502f. It would seem that by *theocracy*, a Greek neologism invented by him (*C. Ap.* ii. 165) which has since gained international currency, Josephus hellenizes the same idea of Kingdom of God.

and ever' is to be understood as applying to both 'worlds', the present and the future. According to the Paris Ms 110, the text reads:

> The children of Israel will say, 'The Lord's is the Kingdom in this world, and his is (the Kingdom) in the world to come.'

Again in the 'theoretical' domain, the heavenly/earthly dimension of the Kingdom, in that particular sequence, is impressively adumbrated, with special reference to human instrumentality, in the Tannaitic midrash, Sifre on Deuteronomy 32.10 (313):

> Until Abraham, our father, came to the world, the Holy One, blessed be He, was (as it were) only king of the heaven, for it is written, 'The Lord, the God of heaven, who took me . . .' (Gen. 24.7). But when Abraham, our father, came into the world, he made him king over heaven and earth, for it is written 'I will make you swear by the Lord, the God of heaven and of the earth' (Gen. 24.2).

In biblical and inter-testamental thought, when the establishment of the Kingdom of God is seen as mediated, it is usually attributed to a Messiah, victorious in battle with or without angelic support. Here it is accredited to the proselyte Abraham, the underlying idea being that the father of Israel, himself a convert from idolatry and astral worship, was responsible for the dissemination of the true religion, and with it the progressive recognition of God's dominion over mankind.[13]

Beside the theoretical question regarding the nature of the Kingdom of God, the rabbis had to face also the practical problem of how individuals could relate to it, how they were to take on 'the yoke of the Kingdom of heaven' (*'ōl malkhūt shamayīm*).

The basic rabbinic attitude seems to be that its acceptance is identical to an initial act of faith in the one, true God, and is actually achieved by the recitation of the *Shema'*, 'Hear, O Israel,

---

[13]Cf. *S & T*, 79f. Abraham as the first preacher of monotheism figures already in Josephus, *Ant*. i. 155. It is interesting to note that in Tanhuma *Lekh lekha* 6, 63, a proselyte is more cherished by God than a born Jew because the Israelites embraced the Law on Sinai only as a result of the awesome phenomena surrounding the theophany, whereas the proselyte accepts the Kingdom of God without signs and wonders!

the Lord our God, the Lord is one'. It represents positively, an acknowledgment of God's sovereignty, and at the same time negatively, a rejection of idolatry (Sifre on Num. 15.39 [116]). Rabban Gamaliel II, despite his own dispensation of the bridegroom from the obligatory recitation of the *Shemaʿ* on the 'first night', decided to ignore this exemption on the occasion of his own wedding because he did not wish to 'set aside the Kingdom of heaven even for a moment' (mBer 2.5).

It is worth stressing that recognition of God's sovereignty is not only the first and foremost act of religion, but that it has logical and chronological priority over the fulfilment of the individual precepts of the Torah. How this issue exercised the mind of the Tannaim is indicated in Rabbi Joshua ben Qorhah's discussion, in the same chapter of the Mishnah, of the link between the *Shemaʿ* and its Benedictions:

> Why does the section, 'Hear, O Israel' precede 'And if you will obey my commandments'? This is in order that one may first accept the yoke of the Kingdom of heaven and afterwards the yoke of the commandments (mBer 2.2).[14]

The same teaching is included in an anonymous Tannaitic commentary on the first of the Ten Commandments and conveyed in the form of a royal parable.

> *You shall have no other gods before me* (Ex. 20.3). Why is this said? Because He said, *I am the Lord your God* (Ex. 20.2). Here is a parable concerning a king of flesh and blood who entered a province. His ministers said to him, Issue decrees concerning them (the inhabitants)! He said to them, No. When they accept my *malkhūt*, I will issue decrees concerning them. For if they do not accept my *malkhūt*, how shall they fulfil my decrees? Likewise God said to Israel, *I am the Lord your God: you shall have no other gods*: It is I whose *malkhūt* you accepted in Egypt. They said to Him, Yes, yes. Now as you accepted my *malkhūt*, accept also my decrees: *You shall have no other gods before me* (Mekhilta on Ex. 20.3, II, 237f.)

[14]Another Tanna, Rabbi Eleazar ben Azariah, seems to propound a different view when he identifies avoidance of transgression, i.e. obedience to the commandments, with the acceptance of the yoke of the Kingdom. Cf. Sifra (ed. Weiss) 93d.

(b) The liturgy of the synagogue

If rabbinic literature echoes the ideas of the *thinking* Jew, the liturgy reflects those of the Jew *in prayer*. It is appropriate, therefore to glance fleetingly at the concepts of the divine King and Kingdom in ancient Jewish worship. Since most of the liturgical formulae have been transmitted anonymously, their dating is even more difficult than that of the sayings preserved in Talmudic literature. Nevertheless, the antiquity of a few texts concerning the Kingdom of God is reasonably sure.

Of these, the prayer known as 'Kingdoms' (*malkhiyōt* or *malkhūyōt*), a collection of ten relevant biblical verses, is the most likely to antedate the destruction of Jerusalem in AD 70. Two first-rate scholars, Adolf Büchler and Joseph Heinemann, argued that it was part of the New Year (Rosh ha-Shanah) service in the sanctuary itself.[15]

The purpose of the prayer, which is part of the so-called *'Amidah* during the New Year Festival and is discussed in the Mishnah (mR.Sh. 4.5), is the liturgical proclamation of God's supremacy over the universe. In its present form, it is a tripartite composition, including three verses from the Torah (Ex. 15.18; Num. 23.21; Deut. 33.5), three from the Psalms (22.29; 93.1; 24.7) and three from the Prophets (Isa. 44.6; Obad. 8.21; Zech. 14.9) and culminates, predictably, in the *Shema* (Deut. 6.4). Its association with the feast of Rosh ha-Shanah, the annual commemoration of the creation, is most apposite as it is in his capacity of maker of heaven and earth that God's universal Kingship is ultimately grounded.

Other ancient liturgical formulae, such as 'Our Father, our King' (*'Avīnū malkenū*) and especially the *Qaddish*, are thought to be Tannaitic in their essence, but not necessarily pre-AD 70 (Heinemann, ibid. 24, 150). The Aramaic *Qaddish*, to be dealt with again in connection with the Lord's Prayer (cf. p. 178 below), opens with a fervent appeal for the prompt institution of the *malkhūta'*. How this is to be done, by universal piety or by an eschatological act, remains unfortunately unsaid.

> May he establish his kingdom in your life and in your days and in the life of all the house of Israel, speedily and in a short while!

[15] A. Büchler, *Types of Jewish Palestinian Piety* (1922), 236–40; J. Heinemann, *Prayer in the Talmud* (1977), 94, n. 26, 128.

Finally, it should be recalled that the phrase, 'King of the universe' (*melekh ha-ʿōlam*) is an integral part of the opening of all the formulaic benedictions: Blessed art Thou, O Lord our God, King of the universe. Belief in a sovereign God would appear therefore to belong to the nucleus of traditional Jewish piety. Nevertheless, it is suggested that its absence from the ʿ*Amidah* (or Eighteen Benedictions) which, we are told, was still being reworked at the turn of the first century A D, implies that the wording post-dates the Second Temple, but by the third century no benediction lacking the mention of the Kingdom of God was acknowledged to be a genuine *berakhah* (bBer. 12a).[16]

Against Heinemann's theory, querying the regular first-century A D use of *melekh ha-ʿōlam* ('King of the universe' or 'King of the age'), it may be worth remarking that the Greek expression, 'the King *of the ages*' (*tōn aiōnōn*), literally corresponding to the Hebrew *melekh ha-ʿōlamīm* and the Aramaic *melekh ʿalmayya*, is employed three times in liturgical contexts in the New Testament (I Tim. 1.17; 6.15; Rev. 15.3), texts belonging to the late first century A D.

This bird's eye view of the 'Kingdom of God' notion has followed the historical development of the imagery from the Bible to the Tannaim. As has been seen, some of its features are confined to given periods, whereas others straddle various epochs, modifying one another in the process. It is only in a framework of this sort that the teaching of Jesus can be grasped properly as part of the evolving religious ideology of Judaism.

II   Jesus' Concept of the Kingdom of God

In the documents examined so far, divine King and divine Kingdom have appeared as reciprocal notions, with a preponderance of the concrete terms, 'King' and 'to reign'. As has been suggested, the abstract noun, 'Kingdom' is a rarity. The reverse is the case in the Gospels, and even in the New Testament as a

---

[16]Cf. J. Heinemann, op. cit., 92–94. It is curious to observe that while in the Palestinian recension of the ʿ*Amidah* the term 'King' is never applied to God, it figures eight times in the Babylonian version. A somewhat different precedent may be found in Tob. 13.1, where Tobit's prayer opens with the following benediction: 'Blessed is God who lives for ever, and his kingdom'.

whole. Jesus never addresses God as 'King'; in fact, this title very seldom appears even outside direct quotations. The customary Jewish prayer terminology, 'Lord, King of the universe', is nowhere associated with Jesus, although it figures in liturgical formulae in two late New Testament writings, I Timothy 1.17; 6.15 and Revelation 15.3.[17]

The only two designations of God as 'King' are preserved in the Gospel of Matthew, the first being in the Sermon on the Mount where Jesus dissuades his followers from taking oaths, even by using a substitute name for God, viz. Jerusalem (cf. chapter 2, pp. 34f.):

> But I say to you, Do not swear at all, either by heaven . . . or by Jerusalem, for it is *the city of the great King* (Matt. 5.34f.).

Since the italicized phrase is a free citation of the Greek version of Ps. 48.2, giving scriptural overtone to the saying, it most probably represents Matthew's learning, rather than any original wording by Jesus.

The second occurrence is in the parable of the Last Judgment (Matt. 25.31–46). In its present form it is a *Parousia* scene, with the returning Christ in the leading role. But if the interpretation proposed earlier (cf. chapter 4, p. 112) is adopted, the pristine form of the parable alludes to eschatological proceedings presided over by a divine Judge identified as 'the King' (Matt. 25.24, 40).[18]

Even if these two passages were part of the authentic teaching of Jesus, it would be difficult to argue that God *qua* King was an idea central to his thought. But since neither of them is likely to be traceable to him, the startling situation arises where a religious master, whose message centres on the preaching of the Kingdom of God, deliberately avoids, even in his prayers where it would come most naturally, the application of the commonly used royal metaphor to the Deity. This observation demonstrates the necessity to investigate the structure of a 'Kingdom' which lacks the complementary symbol of a 'King', especially since this

[17]The latter passage is attested in two forms, 'King of the ages' and 'King of the nations' (cf. p. 135 above).

[18]The remoulding of the parable by Matthew (and the Christian church) was already noticed by Bultmann (*HST*, 124).

phenomenon tallies with the conclusion presented in *Jesus the Jew* (pp. 128–56) that Jesus was not keen to identify himself as the 'King-Messiah'.

The Gospel evidence will therefore be examined under three headings: (1) the Kingdom in the parables of Jesus; (2) the Kingdom in his prophetic proclamations; and (3) the Kingdom in his sayings and commands.

1. The Kingdom in the parables of Jesus

Whilst the two notions, 'parable' and 'Kingdom of God' are often automatically coupled by New Testament interpreters, as is apparent from the title of C. H. Dodd's renowned monograph, *The Parables of the Kingdom*, the analysis which follows will be restricted to literary units in which the expressions 'the *basileia* (Kingdom) of heaven' or 'the *basileia* of God' actually figure. Since the previous chapter has already surveyed these and all the other parables in a general manner, attention will here be focussed exclusively on their 'Kingdom' aspect. The task is not as easy as might be expected because no parable sets out to define the nature of the Kingdom of God. This is perhaps not surprising. Jesus, the existential teacher, was more concerned with man's attitude and behaviour towards the Kingdom than with its essence or structure.

In a first group of texts, the common theme is the evolution which takes the Kingdom of God from latency to full revelation.

In the Parable of the Secretly Growing Seed (Mark 4.26–29), the Kingdom is neither the farmer, nor the seed, let alone the field. It is rather the concerted action of all three, the farmer's sowing, the seed's sprouting, and the field's providing shelter and nourishment for it. The three together constitute a hidden reality which is to become manifest in its own good time. Likewise the mustard seed (Mark 4.30–32, etc.), buried in the ground and burgeoning into a large shrub, secretly mirrors a paradoxical growth. As for the leaven (Matt. 13.33; Luke 13.20f.), that small piece of fermenting dough added by a housewife to a much larger amount of flour, it strangely causes the mixture to become life-giving bread.

All three parables stress the mysterious nature of the realization of the Kingdom, something already actual, yet also surreptitiously advancing towards its predetermined finale. But this enigmatically evolving reality requires human collaboration. The seed must be sown and the leaven mixed by men and women. The religious and ethical qualities demanded from those involved are not disclosed here, but they appear in other contexts.

The time factor plays a crucial role. The parables of the Weeds and the Net envisage the Kingdom in the present as opposed to the future. The good seed and the weeds coexist until the harvest (Matt. 13.24–30; 36–43); the edible and inedible fish with which the fisherman's net is filled are to be sorted out when the catch is landed (Matt. 13.47–50). In both stories, Matthew introduces what seems to be a secondary eschatological climax at the expense of the immediate existential message.

Two marriage-feast parables suggest an imminent end, but the final judgment is still awaited with an undifferentiated cast of actors. The story of the royal wedding, so Matthew 22.2, one of the rare Kingdom parables in which a king figures or, in Luke's presentation, the wedding arranged by a property owner for his son (Luke 14.16, 21), and the anecdote of the ten virgins looking forward to the arrival of the bridegroom and bride (Matt. 25.1–13), envisage the Kingdom simile as including worthy and unworthy participants. But even here, the timetable is vague. The only instance in which a specific temporal pointer is mentioned is Luke's version of the parable of the Fig Tree whose leaves reveal the closeness of summer, i.e. the onset of the Kingdom (Luke 21.29–31). Its message conflicts, as has been shown (cf. chapter 4, p. 99,n.25), with Jesus' genuine antipathy towards those hungry for signs. It is perhaps not accidental that both the terms 'parable' and 'Kingdom of God' are missing from the parallel passages in Mark 13.28f. and Matt. 24.32f.

A second group of parables focusses on the correct attitude to be adopted by the co-workers of the Kingdom. It will be noticed that all the passages come from the Gospel of Matthew. Nevertheless, though not expressly linked to the Kingdom theme, the ideas which they hold are common to every layer of Gospel tradition.

The first, and perhaps most important, moral quality is absolute devotion to the task, a willingness deliberately to concentrate every effort to it and to sacrifice all in order to achieve it, exemplified in the parables of the Hidden Treasure and the Precious Pearl (Matt. 13.44–46; chapter 4, pp. 107f.). Other explicit references to ethical and religious virtues are comprised in the parable of the Cruel Servant (Matt. 18.23–35; cf. chapter 4, p. 106), of the Workers in the Vineyard (Matt. 20.1–16; cf. chapter 4, pp. 105f.), and the parable of the Two Sons (Matt. 21.28–32; cf. chapter 4, p. 105). The first emphasizes generosity; the second conveys a double message of liberality and parallel denunciation of jealousy; in the third the key-word is repentance/*teshuvah*.

In addition to those which exhibit such explicit demands for the right moral response, many Kingdom parables contain unformulated hints at diverse aspects of correct behaviour. The most important is *emunah*, whole-hearted confidence that God will intervene: the farmer having sown the seed, the fisherman having cast the net, the woman having leavened the dough, must confidently entrust to God the successful outcome of their ventures.[19]

2. *The Kingdom in prophetic proclamations*

As will be recalled from the previous chapter (4, p. 77), the quintessence of the kerygma or preaching of both John the Baptist and Jesus was the imminence, indeed, the nascent presence, of the Kingdom of God:

Repent, for the Kingdom of heaven is at hand (Matt. 3.2 [John]; 4.17 [Jesus]).

The time is fulfilled, and the Kingdom of God is at hand; repent and believe in the gospel (Mark 1.15).

The verb, 'to be at hand', used by both Mark and Matthew (*engizein*) is part of the eschatological vocabulary of biblical prophecy (cf. Isa. 50.8; 51.5; Ezek. 7.7[4]). It expresses dramatic closeness, paralleled by Mark's 'fullness of time'. As in the parables surveyed earlier, the Kingdom, though not yet entirely present, is not envisaged as a future reality. Its prompt establishment is to be achieved by the already familiar *teshuvah*. The same note of immediacy sounds even louder in a Q saying in which

[19]The expressions 'secret(s) of the Kingdom of God/heaven' or 'word of the Kingdom' opposed to parables (Mark 4.11 par.; Matt. 13.19), and 'the scribe trained for the Kingdom of heaven', have no special contribution to make to our problem.

divinely supported exorcism is depicted as indicating the onset of the Kingdom. In a polemical context Jesus exclaims:

> But if it is by the spirit (Matt.)/the finger (Luke) of God that I cast out demons, the Kingdom of God has come upon you (Matt. 12.28/Luke 11.20).

Generally acknowledged as authentic, even by Bultmann (*HST*, 162), the statement equates charismatic mastery of the forces of evil with the sudden manifestation of divine victory and dominion, the revelation of the Kingdom of God already in action.[20]

A further 'prophetic' announcement of the arrival of the Kingdom is transmitted in another Q passage (Matt. 11.12/Luke 16.16) of some notoriety because it specifically determines the moment representing the starting-point of the new age.

> From the days of John the Baptist until now the Kingdom of heaven has suffered violence, and men of violence take it by force (Matt.).

> The Law and the Prophets were until John; since then the good news of the Kingdom of God is preached, and everyone enters it violently (Luke).

Most scholars take the phrases associated with violence in a pejorative sense, alluding to satanic or human enemies, more specifically, the Zealots/Sicarii, whose activity hinders God's royal dominion (cf. *TDNT* I, 609–14). They are probably mistaken, not recognizing Jesus' customary exaggeration in portraying his own success, and that of John before him, in proclaiming the coming of the Kingdom. The excited Jewish crowds elbowing their way towards a famous preacher suggest to Jesus the scene of warriors surging forward to conquer. Hence once more we are confronted emphatically, since the ministry of the Baptist, and especially of Jesus, with a Kingdom of God imagined as already present (cf. *JWJ*, 157f, n. 57).

[20]The verb used in the Gospels, *phthanein*, is thought to echo the Aramaic *meta'* with strong eschatological connotations. Cf. G. Dalman, *Worte*, 87f.; M. Black, *Aramaic Approach*, 211. Likewise the instruction given by Jesus to the seventy disciples, though probably a Church formulation, follows the same pattern, associating the imminence of the Kingdom and charismatic healing (Matt. 10.7; Luke 10.9). For healing as an eschatological phenomenon, cf. 1QS 4.6; 4Q521 (*JJS* 43 (1992), 303); Tg Neof, Ps-Jon on Gen. 3.15, etc.

The same idea, albeit without the imagery and with the rejection of supernatural pointers, is advanced with force in a declaration preserved in Luke alone.

> The Kingdom of God is not coming with signs to be observed; nor will they say, Lo, here it is! or There! for behold the Kingdom of God is in the midst of you (Luke 17.20).[21]

There can be no doubt that Jesus repeatedly affirmed that the Kingdom of God belonged to his own here and now, or at worst was just round the corner. If so, what are we to do with the statements ascribed to him which connote a more distant future? To begin with, Mark 9.1 and its parallels claim that, whereas the manifestation of the Kingdom was expected to occur during the life-time of Jesus' contemporaries, only 'some' of them would be privileged to witness it, thus implicitly asserting that the rest would not.

> Truly, I say to you, there are some standing here who will not taste death before they see that the Kingdom of God has come with power (Mark).

The saying is handed down without a literary-historical context, being unconnected with what precedes or follows it. Bultmann was correct in describing it as an early Christian 'community formula of consolation in view of the delay of the Parousia' (*HST*, 121), the accent being laid on the promise that at least 'some' will live long enough to see the day.

Again, Jesus' supposed mention at the last supper of not drinking wine again until doing so 'in the Kingdom of God' (Mark 14.25; cf. Matt. 26.29; Luke 22.16), strikes the reader straightaway as an unhistorical 'cult legend', to use once more Bultmann's terminology (*HST*, 265).

Finally, the establishment of the Kingdom after the Judgment, combined with the rejection of the Jews and their replacement by Gentiles, a church doctrine if ever there was one, is attested in Matt. 8.11f./Luke 13.28f.:

[21]Cf. Mark 8.12; 13.21/Matt. 24.23. Against this doctrine of no extraordinary signs other than charismatic healings and exorcism, the apocalyptic description of the return of Christ, the 'sign of the son of man', stands out as contradictory and alien with its heavenly and earthly disorders (Mark 13.24f./Matt. 24.29f./Luke 21.25f.). If proof of inauthenticity of the Parousia imagery linked to Jesus is required, there is no need to go further.

> Many will come from east and west and sit . . . in the Kingdom
> of heaven, while the sons of the Kingdom will be thrown into
> the outer darkness (Matt.).

To refuse to accept, as far as Jesus is concerned, the
authenticity of this statement does not amount to the denial of a
positive place for Gentiles in his thought. Universalistic elements
surface in the passage concerning the love of an enemy,
stereotypically a non-Jew, in imitation of God who 'makes the
sun rise on the evil and the good, and sends rain on the just and
the unjust' (5.45/Luke 6.36). A similar stance is implied in the
famous saying attributed to Hillel, Jesus' elder contemporary,
which has survived in the Mishnah where sympathy is to be
shown not towards Israel, but to all human beings:

> Be of the disciples of Aaron, loving peace and pursuing peace,
> loving mankind (*ha-beriyōt*) and bringing them near to the
> Torah (mAb 1.12).

3. *The Kingdom in the sayings and commands of Jesus*

Yet another collection of Gospel citations deals with Jesus'
thought on the attitude to be held towards the Kingdom, a subject
already touched on in some of the parables. The issue being at the
heart of the message of Jesus, the Synoptics have predictably
preserved a fair amount of instruction in this regard.

The first question to be examined is how Jesus envisaged 'entry'
into the Kingdom of God. One precondition relates to worldly
goods. Expressed negatively, it is *quasi* impossible for a rich man
to gain access to it, as is made vividly plain in the saying
concerning the passage of a camel through the eye of a needle
(Mark 10.23–25 par.; cf. chapter 4, p. 85), the genuineness of
which is as secure as any (cf. Bultmann, *HST*, 105). Positively,
actual poverty seems to be a *sine qua non*. In the first beatitude,
especially in Luke's version, Jesus declared absolutely that the
poor instructed by him were citizens of the Kingdom:

> Blessed are you poor, for yours is the Kingdom of God (Luke
> 6.20).

As is well known, the Matthean version attaches the qualifica-
tion 'in spirit' to Luke's 'poor', and turns the direct address into a
descriptive statement:

Blessed are the poor in spirit for theirs is the Kingdom of heaven (Matt. 5.3).

The change is no doubt deliberate and may have literary antecedents. Judging from Qumran parallels, the 'poor in (or of) spirit' ('*nwy rwh*) in the War Scroll (cf. 1 QM 14.7) are the meek and humble of the final age. The same phrase appears also in a fragmentary section of the Hymns Scroll reconstructed by E. Puech, which itself may represent a series of Essene beatitudes, as does also a wisdom composition from Cave 4 (4 Q Beat):

> [Blessed is] . . . with a pure heart
> and does not slander with his tongue.
> Blessed are those who hold to Thy precepts
> and do not hold to the ways of iniquity.
> Blessed are those who swear by it
> and do not burst out in ways of folly.
> Blessed are those who seek it with pure hands
> and do not seek it with a treacherous heart.
> Blessed is the man who has attained wisdom
> and walks in the Law of the Most High . . .[22]

It is worth noting that New Testament exegetes tend to attach an eschatological meaning to Matthew's version of the Beatitudes, pointing to the future tense of the subsequent verbs (the mourners, the meek, the hungry *shall* be comforted, *shall* inherit the earth, *shall* be satisfied).[23]

In sum, whereas Luke's formula – 'for yours is the Kingdom' – correctly reflects Jesus' standpoint of immediacy, the Qumran hymn supports Matthew's forward-looking interpretation.

The second essential condition for submission to the sovereignty of God is an inner attitude of mind, the simplicity of a child. In a slightly varying formulation, the message is repeated in

[22]Cf. E. Puech, 'Un hymne essénien en partie retrouvé et les Béatitudes', *Mémorial Jean Carmignac*, *RQ* 13, nos 49–52 (1988), 59–88. The main structural difference between Matthew and 4 Q Beat is that in the former each blessing is accompanied by mention of its reward, while 4 Q Beat consists of ordinary, mostly antithetic, parallelisms. Matthew (5.10) depicts also those 'persecuted for righteousness' sake' as possessors of the Kingdom.

[23]Cf. recently, W. D. Davies and D. C. Allison, *The Gospel according to St Matthew* I (1988), 445f. It should also be observed that Matt. 7.21 – Not everyone who says, Lord, lord, shall enter the Kingdom of heaven – also contains a Parousia connotation. Cf. Davies and Allison, op. cit., 711–14.

all three Synoptic Gospels, Mark and Luke prescribing a childlike attitude as a precondition for true participation.

> Truly, I say to you, whoever does not receive the Kingdom of God like a child shall not enter it (Mark 10.15/Luke 18.17).

The phrase is of interest because it mirrors a typical rabbinic expression, 'to receive [the yoke of] the Kingdom of heaven' (cf. above pp. 132f.), next to the current Gospel terminology, 'to enter'. Matthew 18.3, by contrast, substitutes for 'to receive the Kingdom of God like a child' the more concrete idiom, 'unless you turn and become like children'. But the essential message remains unaltered, namely that the trust, the *emunah*, of a child is the *conditio sine qua non* for access to the Kingdom.

If the unsophistication of the imagery concerning poverty and unconditional trust can be taken as the hallmark of Jesus' way of thinking, the speculative classification, distinguishing between 'the greatest and the least in the Kingdom' exhibits, it would seem, an ecclesiastical mentality, as is evident from Matt. 5.19f., where neglect of the least of the commandments of the Torah ranks a person as the least in the Kingdom of heaven. Yet, according to the polemic of Matt. 11.11/Luke 7.28 aimed at John the Baptist, the least in the Kingdom outranks John, the greatest 'among those born of women'.[24]

A final group of sayings defines, generally in the form of an overstatement typical of Jesus, the disposition demanded of those volunteering to labour for the establishment of the Kingdom, viz. unreserved devotion demanded by the end of time. To recall the interpretation, suggested earlier (cf. chapter 2, pp. 27–9), of the injunction, 'Leave the dead to bury their own dead, but as for you, go and proclaim the Kingdom of God' (Luke 9.60; cf. Matt. 8.22): this proverb, if it is a proverb, as well as that forbidding the ploughman to look backwards (Luke 9.62), intimates that

---

[24]The creative activity of the Matthean church should also be credited with the passages in which the mother of the apostles James and John requests privileged places for her sons in Jesus' Kingdom (Matt. 20.21), and the theological stipulation that righteousness exceeding *that of the scribes and Pharisees* qualifies for entry into the Kingdom (Matt. 5.20). This contrasts blatantly with the declaration attributed to Jesus in Mark 12.32–4 that a scribe who approved of his summary of Judaism as consisting of the *Shema'* and the combined love of God and neighbour was 'not far from the Kingdom of God'.

without an unconditional, instant and resolute self-surrender to the cause of the Kingdom of God no one is a worthy co-worker. The moral implication of the parables of the Hidden Treasure and Precious Pearl (cf. above pp. 107f.) is that entry into the Kingdom outweighs in value all possessions. The same idea is expressed in reverse when Jesus reassures those who seek the Kingdom that all their material needs will be satisfied (Matt. 6.33/Luke 12.31). Even more striking is his statement, splendidly preserved in Mark 9.47:

> If your eye causes you to sin, pluck it out; it is better for you to enter the Kingdom of God with one eye than with two eyes to be thrown to hell.[25]

But the most shockingly picturesque hyperbole depicting entry into the Kingdom is that which proposes as a means towards it the biblically forbidden act of castration (Deut. 23.1). It is appended as Jesus' rejoinder to his disciples' reaction of disappointment on hearing his ruling that divorce is lawful only on the grounds of 'unchastity' (Matt. 19.1–10).

> He said to them, Not all men can receive this saying, but only those to whom it is given. For there are eunuchs who have been so from birth, and there are eunuchs who have been made eunuchs by men, and there are eunuchs who have made themselves eunuchs *for the sake of the Kingdom of heaven* (Matt. 19.11f.).

The saying seems inappropriate in the context and it is preferable to consider it independently. If, as is usually explained, the meaning intended is that in the eschatological age the truly devout should renounce marriage, the forcefulness of the Gospel metaphor suggests an author with the originality and oratorical power of Jesus. By contrast, the unmarried Rabbi Simeon ben Azzai justified his 'unorthodox' life-style, in conflict with the commandment 'Be fruitful and multiply!', with a poetic apologia:

> My soul is in love with the Torah. The world can be kept going by others (bYeb. 63b).

[25]The parallel in Matt. 18.9 replaces the Kingdom with 'life'. In Matt. 5.29f. it is omitted altogether. In the Matthean formulation, self-mutilation is aimed at avoiding Gehenna; Jesus encourages it, by rhetorical exaggeration needless to say, in order to ensure salvation.

III   The Real Message of the Real Jesus

We move now to a brief synthesis in the form of answers to the three questions figuring in on the opening page of this chapter: 'what is the Kingdom?', 'when will it come?' and 'how is it to be entered?'.

1. *What is Jesus' 'Kingdom of God'?*

In retrospect, it is hardly necessary to stress that Jesus nowhere distinctly spells out his concept of 'kingdom'; even in the metaphorical language of the parables his approach is oblique and his outline hazy. The Kingdom of God is a mystery attainable only with human co-operation. The climax is expected, suddenly and soon, in an unheralded yet triumphal manifestation of divine power. In the mind of Jesus the *nature* of the Kingdom comes second to the *role* to be played by the actors of the drama, himself and his adepts, in ushering it in. The 'what' of the philosopher gives way to the 'when' and 'how' of the prophet and the wisdom teacher. It is therefore not surprising that the bulk of the surviving material relates to the moral and religious qualities required of those who seek the Kingdom, and the exigency of the mission facing them.

Perhaps the most paradoxical aspect of the teaching on the Kingdom of heaven which can safely be accredited to Jesus is that unlike the God of the Bible and of inter-testamental and rabbinic literature, the God of Jesus is not a regal figure, but is modelled on a smaller, hence more accessible, scale. He is conceived in the form of the man of influence familiar to Jesus and his listeners, the well-to-do landowner and paterfamilias of rural Galilee. As I have argued elsewhere, the chief characteristic of Jesus' doctrine is that it 'transforms into reality the "unreal" ingredients of the inherited imagery of the Kingdom' (*JWJ*, 36).

2. *When did Jesus expect the Kingdom to arrive?*

Since in Christian teaching the manifestation of the Kingdom of God is to coincide with the Parousia, or Christ's second coming, first believed to be imminent but progressively postponed and finally relegated to an infinitely remote end of time (cf.

JWJ, 24), one expects to discover the origins of such a doctrinal development in the Gospels themselves. Traces of it are detectable there. Jesus is not to touch wine until he can drink it anew in the Kingdom (Mark 14.25 par.); some of his followers will die without seeing the coming of the Kingdom (Mark 9.1); and still later, the Kingdom is to be inherited by the Gentiles after the Jews have been deprived of their native right to participate in it (Luke 13.27–29/Matt. 8.11f.). But these are Christian reworkings of the Gospel. The teaching genuinely traceable to Jesus testifies to a different stand.

In explicit proclamations, the Kingdom of God is not a distant reality, but one that ever since John the Baptist announced it, is 'at hand' (Mark 1.15 par.), 'has come upon you' (Matt. 12.28 par.) and is 'in your midst' (Luke 17.20f.). Its hidden but active presence underlies also the agricultural, fishing and kitchen parables. Imbued with eschatological enthusiasm, Jesus saw himself and his generation as already belonging to the initial stages of the Kingdom and called to expedite its final manifestation. The message of the texts is patent and the only obstacle preventing Christians from accepting it at its face value is that after more than nineteen hundred years it still has not happened.

Famous New Testament exegetes of this century have advanced impressive slogans in describing Jesus' eschatological doctrine relating to the Kingdom. Albert Schweitzer called it 'consistent (*konsequente*) eschatology', according to which the arrival of God's Kingdom was due in the course of the first year of Jesus' ministry, and when it failed, he slightly revised his chronology and dated the divine coming to the near future. C. H. Dodd spoke of 'realized eschatology' because he recognized the Kingdom as (potentially?) fulfilled in the life of Jesus. Joachim Jeremias sought a compromise by proposing an eschatology in the process of realization ('sich realisierende Eschatologie'), conveniently dividing the establishment of the Kingdom so that it partly fell into the life-time of Jesus and partly to the future (as far-off as need be).[26]

But the categories employed by Schweitzer and his followers do

[26]Cf. A. Schweitzer, *The Quest for the Historical Jesus* (3rd ed. 1954); C. H. Dodd, *The Parables of the Kingdom* (1935); J. Jeremias, *The Parables of Jesus* (2nd ed. 1972). For a useful discussion of these and other writers, see Norman Perrin, *The Kingdom of God in the Teaching of Jesus* (1963).

not fit the mentality of Jesus (cf. *JWJ*, 38). He and his disciples entered whole-heartedly into the eschatological age and recognized a fundamental difference between their own time with no future, and the centuries that preceded it. From the moment when Jesus obeyed the Baptist's call to repentance, time for him became the end-time demanding a decisive and irrevocable *teshuvah* which necessitated for himself and his followers a new way of life.[27]

3. *How did Jesus conceive of 'entry into the Kingdom'?*

A number of salient features, positive and negative, stand out when the ethical imperatives which Jesus bound to the Kingdom topic are investigated. Again, seen from a primitive Christian vantage-point, with the Parousia still unrealized, it is possible to identify them, or at least their most exaggerated challenges, as a morality created for the period which is to culminate with the Second Coming, an *Interimsethik* in the terminology of Albert Schweitzer, intended only for the very short and tormented period preceding 'the day of the Lord'. But such a view hardly seems compatible with what has been reconstructed as the real outlook of Jesus. It could be said, however, that even though his message remains objectively unrealized in the collective sense he intended it, on an individual level his teaching may appear as fully relevant to people of all ages.

To be brief, the survey of Jesus' preaching in parables, proclamations and sayings has shown that, the essential requisites are detachment from possessions, unquestioning trust in God and absolute submission to him. The fact that the duties imposed are generally expressed in ethical rather than 'legal' terms should not lead one to imagining that Jesus' eschatological preaching conflicts with his attachment to the Law. It is approval of his recapitulation of the Torah as love of God and love of men that brings the sympathetic scribe 'near to the Kingdom' (Mark 12.34). Perhaps even more pregnantly, in the Lord's Prayer

---

[27]In my reading of the evidence, E. P. Sanders's claim that no clear understanding of Jesus' concept of the Kingdom is possible (*Jesus and Judaism* (1985), 123–56), seems unwarranted, and I am sceptical also about Paula Fredriksen's assertion that any announcement of the Kingdom by Jesus as present must rely on later strata of Gospel tradition (*From Jesus to Christ* (1988), 101).

(Matt. 6.10) the petition, 'Thy Kingdom come', is followed by, 'Thy will be done', a divine will seen by Judaism of all ages as being expressed and manifested in the commandments received by Moses on Mount Sinai.

IV   The Kingdom Message of Jesus and Jewish Eschatology

A comparison of the Kingdom of God idea proclaimed by Jesus with the general development of Jewish eschatological thinking (cf. pp. 121–35 above) offers two positive contributions: it helps to confirm the authenticity of a few teachings attributed to him, and to place in relief the individuality of many aspects of his message.

The first negative observation concerns the total absence of one of the most distinctive features of the biblical and inter-testamental doctrine of the divine Kingdom. From the story told by Jesus, gone are the bloody eschatological battles led by a Warrior God. Nor is there any intervention on the part of angels and archangels in the final combat, so vividly depicted in Daniel, the Assumption of. Moses and especially in the Qumran War Scroll, and even in the Book of Revelation in the New Testament.

On the other hand, certain non-bellicose ideas reminiscent of Jesus' outlook, such as the Kingdom being symbolized by acts of piety, or being incompatible with a dissolute life (cf. pp. 129f. above), appear in Jubilees and the Testament of Benjamin; but the similarities are few and far between.

While the actual expressions differ, Jesus' perspective is closer to the Kingdom notion held by the Tannaitic rabbis. The cosmic view of the Bible and of the inter-testamental writings is reduced to a more manageable, individual size. Abraham is depicted as the mediator establishing the Kingdom on earth by recognizing and proclaiming God (cf. p. 132). Even more democratically, every Jew accepting 'the yoke of the Kingdom of heaven' surrenders himself to God's sovereignty. Subsequently, he puts his subordination into practice by observing the commandments. Here Jesus seems to echo the same spiritual attitude. The most remarkable coincidence lies in the role attributed to the recitation of the *Shema*ʿ as the act by which submission to the divine King is

effected, followed by the acceptance of 'the yoke of the commandments' (mBer 2.2) as seen against Jesus' formulation of the
first commandment:

> Jesus answered, The first is 'Hear, O Israel, the Lord our God,
> the Lord is one; and you shall love the Lord your God with all
> your heart . . .' The second is this, 'You shall love your
> neighbour as yourself' (Mark 12.29–31).

Since it would be unreasonable, in fact plain silly, to claim that
the Mishnah is dependent on Jesus, the only logical inference
must be that both derive from a common stream of religious
tradition which, in consequence, must be seen as established
already in the first century A D.

The common ground between Jesus and Tannaitic thinking
regarding the Kingdom is however limited. It is distinguished by
the extreme end of days fervour inspiring the entire authentic
Gospel message. Though connected both to its antecedents and to
what follows, Jesus' teaching on the Kingdom of God is a
substantially fresh creation bearing the stamp of individual
eschatology, both quietly concealed and spectacularly climactic.

Appendix: The Kingdom of God in the Rest of the New Testament

To enable the reader fully to comprehend the peculiar traits of
Jesus' own message, a brief comparison of the notion of the
Kingdom of God in the Synoptic Gospels with the other books of
the New Testament, where it plays a less eminent part, may be
useful.

In the Fourth Gospel it figures only twice, in Jesus' conversation with Nicodemus (John 3.3, 5), where the original terminology of repentance used in the Synoptics is re-styled as 'rebirth' by
means of 'water and spirit', symbolizing the Christian baptism.

The author of the Acts also follows the traditional pattern (cf.
Matt. 4.23; 9.35; Luke 4.23, etc.) in presenting the Kingdom as
the main theme of the teaching of the risen Jesus (Acts 1.3), and of
Paul (and Barnabas) in Asia Minor, Antioch and Rome (Acts
14.22; 19.8; 28.23, 31). The allusions are vague, though in the
first citation, as in II Thess. 1.5 and Rev. 1.9, entry into the

Kingdom is associated with suffering as in Matt. 5.10. In Col. 4.11, reference is made to Jews ('men of circumcision') who are Paul's 'fellow workers for the Kingdom of God'!

Charismatic activity in the Corinthian church prompts Paul to declare that 'the Kingdom of God does not consist in talk but in *dunamis*/power' (I Cor. 4.20). However, in general he pictures it in a moral context: the Kingdom is not food and drink but righteousness (Rom. 14.17); it cannot be inherited by the unjust (I Cor. 6.9f.; 15.50; I Thess. 2.12). James 2.5, echoing the first beatitude, exhorts his church to respect the poor:

> Has not God chosen those who are poor in the world to be rich in faith and heirs of the Kingdom which he has promised to those who love him?

But throughout, the Kingdom appears as a future reality, indeed the ultimate celestial reality of the eschaton:

> Then comes the end when he (Christ) delivers the Kingdom to God the Father after destroying every rule and every authority and power (I Cor. 15.24)

> And there were loud voices in heaven, saying, 'The kingdom of the world has become the Kingdom of our Lord and of his Christ' (Rev. 11.15).

Although fragments of the genuine message of Jesus survive in these texts, owing to the delay of the Parousia its urgency and immediacy have progressively faded. I think it was Alfred Loisy who first remarked that the apostles expected the return of Christ but had to put up instead with the arrival of the church.

6

'Abba, Father': The God of Jesus

As has been seen in the discussion of the Kingdom of God, the idea of a heavenly Ruler was fundamental to Jews in the biblical, inter-testamental and rabbinic ages. But so was the concept of God's Fatherhood. The two titles are coupled in the famous liturgical prayer, *Avinu, malkenu* (Our Father, our King), the origin of which is attributed by Talmudic tradition (bTaan 25a) to Rabbi Akiba's (d. *c.* AD 135) invocation before the ark of the synagogue which ended a bitter drought:

> *Our Father, our King*, we have sinned before Thee.
> *Our Father, our King*, we have no *King* but Thee.
> *Our Father, our King*, have mercy upon us.

Whereas in public pronouncements and prayers, the divine epithet, 'King', seems to predominate in ancient Jewish literature, as has been underlined, it is strikingly absent from sayings attributed to Jesus (cf. pp. 135–37). By contrast, the Synoptic Gospels depict him as addressing God, or speaking of him, as 'Father' in some sixty instances, and at least once place on his lips the Aramaic title, *Abba*. That the idea is essential for the accurate perception of the religion of Jesus is beyond question, and as usual, it goes without saying that in order to perceive his message dynamically, the Gospel evidence will have to be envisaged in perspective.

I The Heavenly Father in the Teaching of Jesus

The concept of God as Father of Jesus, of his followers, and of the whole created world, is deeply implanted in the Gospels. It figures in various literary forms – parables, sayings, prayers – and in all the layers of the Synoptic tradition – in Mark and the triple transmission, in Q, and in the separate Matthean and Lucan versions. As customary, the purpose is not mystical or theological, but existential and practical: by envisaging the Deity as a caring parent, Jesus intends to impress on his disciples their appropriate attitude towards God, and since the notions of Father and son are correlative, propose a model for the behaviour of 'brothers and sisters'.

1. The Father in the parables

Compared to the frequency of the divine Kingdom theme, the Father image is relatively rare in this literary genre, figuring only in the parables of the Two Sons and the Prodigal Son.

In the first, Matt. 21.28–32, or more exactly 28–31a (cf. p. 105), compared to the role played by the sons, the father is the less prominent character, simply issuing orders. Otherwise, the main paternal feature is unformulated forgiveness of the rebellious son when he repents. In the second, the Parable of the Prodigal Son, Luke 15.11–32 (cf. pp. 110f.), the father intuitively knows the son's regret before it is expressed, runs to meet him, embraces him, and proclaims public rejoicing for one who was lost and dead, but is now found and alive.

The restricted imagery of the God concept underlying these parables reflects love and patience towards a truly repentant child and corresponds to the spiritual yearning of the tax-collectors and sinners, Jesus' favourite clients.

2. The Father in the sayings

As is common with the sayings of Jesus, the question of their likely authenticity turns on a combined assessment of literary, redactional and ideological features, allied to coherence with his overall message and its meaning and relevance for his original, essentially Galilean audience. Bearing in mind the fact that the doctrinal content of Matthew and Luke, whether deriving from the common Q source or from their special material, considerably exceeds that of Mark, and that Matthew alone furnishes much of the significant 'Jewish' ingredient, the Marcan material will always be granted particular emphasis. Also, in the light of

Luke's insensitivity to Palestinian Jewish nuances, when his version conflicts with that of Matthew, the latter will be preferred unless there is good reason to suspect some specific bias on the part of the first evangelist.

No doubt such a stand will be considered flawed by those who see the Jewishness of the Matthean message as a deliberate Judaizing superimposed by its author or redactor on the original preaching of Jesus, which they presume to have been more universal in tenor. This view is however wholly improbable; it clashes not only with the characteristically critical tendency of Matthew towards the Jewish religious parties of Jesus' age, but also leaves incomprehensible the survival of the Jewish colouring in a writing that catered for, and has been handed down by, the Gentile church. In general, a line of development postulated by this theory is both unparalleled and unjustifiable. In consequence, the so-called 'Judaizing' traditions transmitted exclusively by Matthew will not be considered *ipso facto* as suspect.

(a) The forgiving Father

In line with the teaching of the parables, one of the salient features in Jesus' preaching is God's readiness to pardon his wayward children.

To begin with the rare Marcan saying of 11.25, one of only three examples in this Gospel where God is called Father, the shorter version, appearing in some of the oldest codices (Sinaiticus and Vaticanus) runs as follows:

> And whenever you stand praying, forgive if you have anything against anyone, so that *your Father who is in heaven* may forgive your trespasses (11.25).[1]

The longer text, which follows in 11.26, includes also a negative formulation modelled on Matt. 6.14f., itself attached as an explanatory afterthought to the relevant verse (Matt. 6.12) of the Lord's Prayer.

> For if you forgive men their trespasses, *your heavenly Father* also will forgive you; but if you do not forgive men their

---

[1] It is to be noted that these words, though originally probably independent, are appended to a logion on prayer appearing in Mark 11.24.

trespasses, neither will *your heavenly Father* forgive your trespasses.[2]

Be this as it may, there can be little doubt that the notion of pardon is one of the central ingredients of the Father image of Jesus.

(b) The caring Father

Another characteristic of the heavenly Father is his paternal solicitude, a doctrine central to the Q material and reinforced by further instances peculiar to Matthew. Once more, Luke's customary lack of appreciation of the finer points of Jesus' Jewish turn of mind is revealed several times by his substitution of 'God' for 'Father'.

In most of the examples, this benevolent divine fatherhood is linked to Jesus' Palestinian ambience and echoes the particularistic religious outlook of his age; thus concern for such essentials as food, drink and clothes is said to be the hallmark of the *Gentiles* (Matt. 6.32)![3]

In sayings preserved in the Sermon on the Mount, Jesus repeatedly reassures his anxious disciples: 'Look at the birds of the air: they neither sow nor reap nor gather in barns, and yet *your heavenly Father* feeds them' (Matt. 6.26/Luke 12.24). And again, 'Consider the lilies of the field . . . they neither toil nor spin; yet . . . even Solomon in all his glory was not arrayed like one of these' (Matt. 6.28f./Luke 12.27) . . . 'Therefore do not be anxious saying, "What shall we eat?" or . . . "What shall we

[2]The negative dictum is included also as the doctrinal summary of the Parable of the Cruel Servant (Matt. 18.35). The teaching concerning necessary reconciliation, even whilst making an offering in the Temple, is stressed also in Matt. 5.23f. without reference to a forgiving heavenly Father. The allusion to the sanctuary, which in Bultmann's opinion attests the more original form because it 'presupposes the existence of the sacrificial system in Jerusalem' (*HST*, 132) is more likely to derive from Matthew than from Jesus whose interest in Temple matters appears to have been rather peripheral.

[3]A similar allegation appears in Matt. 6.7f. where the prayer-petition of non-Jews is characterized as loquacious. It is unnecessary since 'your Father knows what you need *before you ask him*'. Even God's terrestrial agent, the miracle-worker, is portrayed as endowed with foreknowledge of the petitioner's needs. Cf. e.g. Hanina ben Dosa and the envoys of Rabban Gamaliel in bBer 34b; yBer 9d; *JJ* 75; and below n. 10.

wear?" For the Gentiles seek all these things; and *your heavenly Father* knows that you need them all' (Matt. 6.31f./Luke 12.29f.).[4]

Another *a fortiori* argument (Matt. 7.9–11/Luke 11.11–13) compares the essential benevolence of God to the attitude of human parents. Although hyperbolically described as 'evil', they would nevertheless not substitute a stone for bread for their children: 'How much more will *your Father who is in heaven* give good things to those who ask him!' (Matt. 7.11/Luke 11.13). His care for the 'little ones', whose guardian angels, according to Jesus, 'behold the face of *my Father who is in heaven*', is presented as a quintessential divine attitude in Matt. 18.10, 14.[5]

Of course, the Father in this guise appears as a rule in a human, and specifically Jewish, context, but in several sayings he is concerned also with plants and animals. However, at least one logion, in which Jesus orders his followers to love their enemies (cf. pp. 36f.), sees God's paternal loving-kindness extended to mankind as a whole.

> But I say to you, Love your enemies . . . so that you may be sons of *your Father who is in heaven*, for he makes his sun to rise on the evil and on the good, and sends rain on the just and the unjust . . . And if you salute only your brethren . . . do not even the Gentiles do the same? (Matt. 5.44–47/Luke 6.27f., 33, 35f.)

[4]The translation follows Matthew. The variants in Luke are, with one exception, of little significance. In 12.30 'your Father' replaces Matthew's 'Your heavenly Father', and in 12.24, 'God' is substituted for 'your heavenly Father' (cf. also Luke 12.6 and 12.12, compared to Matt. 10.29 and 10.20). The exception figures in 12.24 where Matthew's Semitic 'birds of the air' are identified as 'ravens'. This reading is often said to derive from Q, most recently by W. D. Davies and D. C. Allison, *The Gospel According to St Matthew* I (1988), 654, but this is highly unlikely. The term figures nowhere else in the New Testament and is abandoned by Luke in the concluding phrase of the verse ('Of how much more value are you than *the birds*'?). Moreover, the whole imagery seems to suggest seed-eaters. Finally, the raven, largely a scavenger and a bird of prey, hence an unclean animal, is not the most apposite example in the mind of a Galilean countryman of a creature nourished by a *caring* God, *pace* the frequently cited examples of Ps. 147.9 and Job 38.41, which were meaningful only in learned circles. The heavenly Father's concern for sparrows is reiterated in Matt. 10.29–31/Luke 12.6f.

[5]References to the heavenly Father in connection with an anti-Pharisee controversy (Matt. 15.13) and the future persecution of disciples (Matt. 10.20) are unlikely to be authentic on general grounds.

The model is universal. The term, 'enemy', unless otherwise defined, normally suggests an outsider to the community of Israel. Hence, although generally speaking Jesus' vision does not stretch beyond the Jewish world, an unformulated cosmopolitan and almost ecological tendency, leading to the repesentation of God as the Father of *all* the living, is not absolutely alien to it.

(c) The Father who sees secrets

Jesus' God the Father looks for inner, personal religiosity. Both the theme and its presentation in an overstated form, are fully consonant with the essence of the authentic preaching. Consequently, the fact that all the sayings belong to the material peculiar to Matthew should not be construed as evidence against genuineness.

In brief, the three central manifestations of Jewish devotion – almsgiving, prayer and fasting – must be performed without ostentation and possibly in the spirit of the ancient Hasidim, strictly in private. Generosity towards the poor must not be trumpeted; the street corner, or even the synagogue, is not the most suitable venue for inward prayer; and mortification through fasting should not be made obvious by a dismal appearance (Matt. 6.2–4; 6.5–8; 6.16–18). Those who forgo such public signals are promised that *'your Father who sees in secret* will reward you' (Matt. 6.4, 6, 18).[6]

(d) Imitatio Patris

Both Q and Matthew depict God almost always indirectly but once quite openly, as the example *par excellence* to emulate. Since Jesus' interest is primarily didactic, the theological implications of his sayings can be indirect and vague. Thus, for example, Matt. 5.9 blesses the 'peace-makers' and designates them as 'sons of God', a phrase synonymous with 'sons of the Most-High' and 'sons of your Father' (Luke 6.35/Matt. 5.45), insinuating that those who imitate the heavenly source of *shalom*, can successfully strive for peace on earth and deserve to be called 'sons of God'.

[6]For literary parallels, see *JWJ*, 164, n.33. Cf. also W. D. Davies and D. C. Allison, *Matthew* I (1988), 579.

Likewise, the 'good works' of Jesus' disciples, reflecting the generosity of the heavenly Father towards his children (cf. Matt. 7.11/Luke 11.13 on p. 156 above), are said to add to the praise of God: 'Let your light so shine before men that they may see your good works and give glory to *your Father who is in heaven*' (Matt. 5.16).

But a direct and succinct expression of the 'imitatio Patris' doctrine propounded by Jesus is patterned as will be argued in detail (pp. 200–206) on Lev. 19.2, 'You shall be holy, for I the Lord your God am holy'. This figures in a dual formulation: 'You therefore must be perfect as *your heavenly Father* is perfect' (Matt. 5.48), and 'Be merciful, even as *your Father* is merciful' (Luke 6.36). Here, Jesus and the rabbis speak with a single mouth as the Aramaic paraphrase of Lev. 22.28 impressively demonstrates: 'My people, children of Israel, as your Father is merciful in heaven, so you must be merciful on earth' (Targum Ps.-Jonathan).[7]

It should be noted that one saying of Jesus seems to conflict with the doctrine outlined here. According to that, the pre-eminence of the deity is so absolute and infinite that not only is it humanly inimitable, but even the title 'Father' is the privilege of God and any application of it to human beings is a usurpation. 'Call no man your father on earth, for you have *one Father who is in heaven*' (Matt. 23.9). The suggestion that this saying has a polemical edge criticizing rabbinic sages bearing the surname Abba carries little conviction. It appears to have been the surname of charismatics like Abba Hilkiah, grandson of Honi the Circle-maker, and his cousin Hanan, son of Honi's daughter. The latter, when requested to end a drought, (cf. p. 179), drew a neat distinction between the heavenly Abba, capable of giving rain, and himself, able only to persuade God to do so.

The saying, 'Call no man your father on earth' (Matt. 23.9), does not contradict the doctrine of the imitation of divine paternal solicitude. Its denial of the applicability to humans of attributes primarily reserved for God recalls Jesus' question to a rich young man who addressed him as '*good* Teacher': 'Why do

---

[7]There can scarcely be a better example of what I called earlier an 'ethicization' of the Law (cf. pp. 44f. above), for while the Hebrew Leviticus text reads: 'And whether the mother is a cow or a ewe, you shall not kill both her and her young in one day', the Targum elevates the rule into a universal moral command.

you call me good? No one is good but God alone' (Mark 10.18/ Luke 18.19). A similar exaggeration is contained in the words of the second-century Tannaitic Rabbi, Ishmael son of Yose, who denied the exercise of the judicial function to a single man in the following aphorism: 'Judge not alone (*yahidī*), for no one may judge alone except One' (*ehad*) (mAb 4.8). Rather than clashing with the basic Gospel message, the two sayings, stressing divine transcendence, help to redress the balance in Jesus' representation of God.

(e) The Father in apocalyptic sayings

To be brief, whether judged by Rudolf Bultmann's form-critical criteria or by my historico-religious presuppositions that the Parousia concept is a church creation, the passages figuring in this section are unlikely to be traceable to Jesus. Thus in the apocalyptic saying of Mark 8.38/Matt. 16.27/Luke 9.26, the 'son of man' atypically tells those who are ashamed of him in 'this adulterous and sinful generation' that he will reject them similarly at the moment of his solemn coming, surrounded by holy angels, in the glory of *his Father*. The same theme is repeated in the form of acknowledgment and denial in Matt. 10.32f./Luke 12.8f. Needless to say, the 'Father' image is ill-suited to the context.

Likewise the association of 'the Father', not 'the Father who is in heaven' or 'the heavenly Father', with the future eschatological Kingdom, is unnatural, and suggests editorial interference on the part of the early church. Thus Matt. 13.43, 'The righteous will shine like the sun in the Kingdom of *their Father*', is a Christian scribal commentary on the Parables of the Weeds (Bultmann, *HST*, 187). The attribution in Matt. 20.23 to the Father of the responsibility for the seating order at the eschatological banquet is an 'editorial' addition (*HST*, 326). The inheritance of the Kingdom by the blessed of the Father (Matt. 25.34) is part of the 'Christian editing' of Matt. 25.31–46 (*HST*, 125). The reference in the account of the Last Supper (Matt. 26.29) to Jesus drinking new wine 'in *my Father*'s Kingdom' (in the Kingdom of God in Mark 14.25) is qualified as a 'cult legend' (*HST*, 265), and the 'more than twelve legions of angels' whom the Father might despatch if Jesus asked for assistance at the time of his arrest counts as a 'dogmatic proof' introduced in Matt. 26.53 by the primitive church (*HST*, 284).[8]

As for the passage asserting that the 'Father' alone, not the angels or the 'Son', knows 'that day or that hour', viz. of the coming of the Kingdom in Mark 13.32/Matt. 24.36, not only is Bultmann justified in qualifying it as a Jewish saying with a Christian ending (*HST*, 159), but the idea of a father jealously guarding his privilege even from his son strikes a discordant note. Such a God is not the God of Jesus.[9]

3. The Father in the prayers of Jesus

The Synoptic Gospels contain five prayers of Jesus in which he invariably addresses the Deity as 'Father', 'our Father' or 'Abba'. They pertain to Mark, Q and Luke's special tradition. Three further passages from Matthew purport to convey Jesus' teaching on prayer, but without actually reproducing the relevant formulae. They warn against ostentation (Matt. 6.5) and insist on seclusion behind a closed door (Matt. 6.6) and on the superfluousness of presenting God, as the Gentiles apparently did, with an as it were detailed shopping-list (Matt. 6.7): '*your Father* who sees in secret' and 'knows what you need before you ask him' requires only the appropriate inward disposition.[10]

---

[8]Luke's three mentions of the Father in a similar context (Luke 12.32; 22.29; 24.49) are all correctly described by Bultmann as ecclesiastical formulations (*HST*, 111, 158, 157); so is also of course the trinitarian phrase. Father, Son and Holy Spirit, in the primitive Christian baptismal command which concludes Matthew's Gospel (28.19).

[9]The denial of divine knowledge to angels is definitely contrary to the well-established Jewish tradition according to which God always consults his heavenly court, referred to also as his 'family on high'. Cf. ySanh i, 18a; bSanh 38b; E. Urbach, *The Sages: Their Concepts and Beliefs* (1975), 179.

[10]Rabbinic literature has preserved direct and indirect parallels to the teaching of Jesus in connection with the practice of particularly devout Jews, generally referred to as the 'first Hasidim' (*hasidim rishōnīm*). The secrecy motive is mentioned apropos of almsgiving: pious 'sin-fearers' used to deposit their gifts in the 'chamber of *hashsha'īm*', i.e. surreptitious donations to enable shy 'distressed gentlefolk' (*'aniyīm benē tōvīm*) to help themselves without confronting their benefactors face to face (mShek 5.6). The advice to retire to a closed room is exemplified in the story of the first-century Galilean charismatic healer, Hanina ben Dosa, who is said to have withdrawn to his 'upper room' to pronounce a prayer through which the son of Rabban Gamaliel was miraculously cured in distant Jerusalem (yBer 9d; bBer 34b). The talmudic story suggests that Hanina

Jesus' supplication reproduced in Mark 14.36, 'Abba, Father . . . let this cup pass from me . . .' is likely to preserve his genuine mode of address to God when requesting help. The Aramaic formula was current in the primitive church, even, odd though this may seem, in the Gentile-Christian, Greek-speaking congregations of Paul (cf. Rom. 8.15; Gal. 4.6). Its significance will be discussed in the Appendix on pp. 180–83. The five surviving utterances, of which only the Mark passage and the Lord's Prayer stand a good chance of being genuine, allow a glimpse into Jesus' existential perception of God.

(a) The Lucan material

To simplify the enquiry, the two quotations from Luke – both to say the least of doubtful authenticity – may be eliminated without much ado. The prayer placed on the lips of the crucified Jesus, '*Father*, forgive them for they know not what they do.' (Luke 23.34) echoes a Judaeo-Christian missionary device, clearly formulated in Acts 3.17, namely that any potential guilt of the Jewish contemporaries of Jesus, including the authorities involved in his downfall, should be imputed to ignorance.[11]

As for Jesus' dying cry on the cross, whereas in Mark 15.37/ Matt. 27.50 it is described merely as a 'loud voice', Luke, who no doubt for theological reasons failed to include earlier the disturbing, 'My God, my God, why hast thou forsaken me?' of Mark 15.34/Matt. 27.46, introduces here a less uncomfortable quotation from Ps. 31.6, thus providing a pious ending to the sufferer's life:

Father, into thy hands I commit my spirit (Luke 23.46).

----

went upstairs, closeted himself and addressed God *before* the envoys of Gamaliel had an opportunity to speak to him, i.e. he knew in advance what they would require of him. Like the heavenly Father (Matt. 6.7), the charismatic is seen as possessing foreknowledge of the supplicants' needs.

[11]The verse is omitted from some of the oldest manuscript witnesses (P. Bodmer XIV, Vaticanus, etc.). Nevertheless, although it is improbable that the words were actually pronounced by Jesus, their deletion by the early church, which was by definition ill-disposed towards tolerating in the Gospel a prayer for divine forgiveness in favour of the hated Jews, is more likely than their later interpolation.

(b) The Q and Matthean material

Jesus' thanksgiving prayer (Matt. 11.25–27/Luke 10.21f.) has already been touched on in a previous chapter (cf. p. 50). The kernel of the passage, 'no one knows the Son except the Father, and no one knows the Father except the Son and any one to whom the Son chooses to reveal him', is generally thought to be in its redacted form an ecclesiastical, probably hellenistic-Christian creation. But the prayer itself and the underlying idea of a heavenly Father sharing his secrets with his children are genuinely Palestinian-Jewish, though contrary to Qumran ideology. Indeed, the notion of receiving and transmitting revelations, apart from the doubtfully authentic passage under discussion, is foreign to the genuine teaching of Jesus.[12]

The notion of a revealing Father, although this time the recipients are not babes, appears also in Matthew's account of Peter's confession at Caesarea Philippi: 'for flesh and blood has not revealed it (the messianic identity of Jesus) to you but *my Father who is in heaven*' (Matt. 16.17). However, compared to the Marcan and Lucan versions of the episode (Mark 8.29f./Luke 9.20f.), Matt. 16.17–19 is manifestly an apologetical supplement attributable to the early church (cf. *JJ*, 146f.).

The Lord's Prayer (Matt. 6.9–13/Luke 11.2–4), which opens with '*Our Father who art in heaven*' or 'Father', is generally held to be one of the chief sources for the study of our subject. The title is somewhat misleading since the wording, though formulated by Jesus, is not meant for recitation by himself, but by a group of disciples who refer to themselves as 'we', 'us' and 'our'. The Lucan version is shorter and, unlike that of Matthew, whose

[12]The revealed knowledge bestowed by God on the Teacher of Righteousness and communicated to the initiates of the sect lies at the heart of the theology of the Scrolls. 1QpHab 2.2f. speaks of the message he received 'from the mouth of God', identified in 7.5f. as divinely granted knowledge of 'the mysteries of the words of his servants, the prophets'. 1QS speaks of 'revealed' meaning of the commandments of the Law of Moses (5.9; 8.1); 'revelation' concerning 'appointed times' (1.9; 9.13). CD 15.13 also refers to 'revelations' regarding the Law. The sectarian beneficiaries of these revelations are several times described as 'the simple' (*peti'īm*), a term corresponding to the Greek *nēpioi* of Matt. 11.25/Luke 10.21 (cf. 1QpHab 12.4; 1QH 2.9; f15, 4). See also the non-canonical Psalm of 4Q381 1, 1f, probably antedating the Dead Sea Community, which mentions instruction, judgment, and understanding conveyed to 'the simple' (cf. Eileen M. Schuller, *Non-Canonical Psalms from Qumran* (1986), 71, 75, 77).

redaction apart from the doxology appended to 6.13 in some manuscripts, is fairly stable,[13] attests a good many Greek variants, some of them obviously intended to bring Luke close to Matthew.

This, however, is not the place for a detailed discussion of the Lord's Prayer since the present enquiry is concerned only with its contribution to Jesus' understanding of God as the Father in heaven. Nevertheless, some preliminary comments are necessary, including an assessment of the relationship between the Matthean and Lucan versions.[14]

Matt.	*Luke*
Our *Father* who art in heaven, *hallowed be thy name.*	*Father,* *hallowed be thy name.*
Thy Kingdom come,	*Thy Kingdom come.*
Thy will be done, on earth as it is in heaven.	
Give us this *day our daily bread;*	*Give us* each *day our daily bread;*
and forgive our debts,	*and forgive* us our sins,
as we also have forgiven our debtors;	for we ourselves forgive everyone who is indebted to us;
and lead us not into temptation,	*and lead us not into temptation.*
but deliver us from evil.	

In regard to the relationship between the Matthean and the Lucan versions, and irrespective of whether they are ultimately assigned to a common Q source or to the special sources (M and

[13]The doxology which is missing from the oldest manuscript tradition and from Luke, greatly fluctuates in its wording: 'for thine is the Kingdom and the power and the glory for ever. [Amen.]'/'for thine is the power and the glory for ever. [Amen]'/'for thine is the Kingdom and the glory. Amen.' Generally, and in my view rightly, considered to be a later liturgical enlargement, the phrase is nevertheless claimed to be attributable to Jesus by Joachim Jeremias (*The Prayers of Jesus* (1967), 106). Cf. M. Black, 'The Doxology of the *Pater Noster* with a Note on Matthew 6.13B', in P. R. Davies and R. T. White, *A Tribute to Geza Vermes* (1990), 327–38.

[14]For a recent examination of the problem, see W. D. Davies and D. C. Allison, *Matthew* I (1988), 590–615 with a substantial bibliography on pp. 621–24. The terms and phrases common to Matt. and Luke are printed in italics.

L), scholarly opinion tends to declare the shorter text of Luke to be the 'more original' (Davies-Allison, 592) and judges the additional material to be Matthew's creation. Underlying this surmise is the majority view that the original Lord's Prayer can actually be traced to Jesus, though no agreement has yet been reached concerning the language in which it was formulated. As a rule, Aramaic is preferred, but (Qumran) Hebrew has found a convinced partisan in the person of Jean Carmignac (*Recherches sur le Notre Père*, 1969). A strong argument can be construed in favour of the authenticity *ad sensum*, if not *ad litteram*, of the substance of both versions, not only on the basis of the general conformity of the contents with Jesus' message, but in particular because a prayer for the *coming* of the Kingdom of God without reference to the Parousia reflects better the outlook of Jesus than that of the early church.

Leaving aside for the moment the thesis that the Lucan address, 'Father', is more genuine than Matthew's, 'Our Father who art in heaven', it should be stressed that none of the Matthean extras contain anything intrinsically unattributable to Jesus. By contrast, Luke's substitution of the generic 'our sins' for the Semitic metaphor 'our debts', despite the subsequent mention of forgiving 'everyone who is indebted to us', would suggest that the shorter text is by no means necessarily the more coherent one.

A final introductory comment concerns the nature of the prayer itself which is not without implications for our appraisal of Luke's relation to Matthew. To begin with, the Lord's Prayer is both collective ('we' not 'I') and formulaic, and as such differs from the solitary petition of an individual or from one uttered behind closed doors 'in secret' (Matt. 6.6). The latter is probably meant to be spontaneous with no fixed text, such as the healing prayer of the charismatic Hasid.[15]

The Lord's Prayer was destined for a group and probably meant to be recited aloud in public though it contains nothing that would point to the context of formal worship. However, it is obvious from the addition of the final doxology, testified to by the manuscript tradition and by the Didache or Teaching of the

---

[15]According to mBer 5.5, Hanina ben Dosa knew that his intercession on behalf of a sick person was effective from a distance when he could improvise fluently. Cf. *PBJS*, 179f. Rabbinic literature (yBer v, 9c) distinguishes between an *ad hoc* and an established form of words.

Twelve Apostles (8.2), the earliest Christian ecclesiastical manual (dated between AD 60 and 150), that it soon became a liturgical and statutory prayer. The redactional introductory words in Matt. 6.9 and especially in Luke 11.1f., already foreshadow such a development.[16]

But if this is so, a further consequence has to be borne in mind. Of the five prayers of Jesus preserved in the Synoptic Gospels, all but the present one belong to the individual private class and appositely address God as 'Father'/*Abba*. In the case of a communal prayer, '*Our* Father' (*avīnū/avūnan*) [who art in heaven] seems to be more appropriate.[17] Would this imply that, contrary to the general opinion, it is once more Luke who misses the point, and that the Matthean 'Our Father who art in heaven', or more precisely 'in the heavens', is the more 'original' and meaningful opening? In any case, since we are concerned only with authenticity *ad sensum* and not with *ipsissima verba*, the original wording, the use of the longer text in an enquiry into the Father concept of Jesus appears to be unobjectionable.

This Father concept may be pieced together from an analysis of the various petitions, for the Father is believed to *be* what the Father is expected to *do*. Of the two opening prayer units, common to both versions, the first restores transcendental dignity to the familiar anthropomorphic image. The sanctification of the divine name by the worshipper echoes on earth the 'Holy, holy, holy' song of the Cherubim in the heavenly temple (Isa. 6.3). As for the second request, 'Thy Kingdom come', it associates the heavenly Father with the divine Lord, defuses the tension between the two ideas, and sets the prayer as a whole within Jesus' dominant expectation of an impending eschatological order. Both notions will be shown to be closely paralleled in the ancient Jewish prayer, the *Qaddish* (cf. p. 178 below).

Although absent from the shorter version, fulfilment of the parental wish, 'Thy will be done', is a well-attested element of Jesus' existential understanding of the Son-Father relationship

[16]On the nature of 'private and non-statutory' and the 'fixed statutory' prayer, see Joseph Heinemann, *Prayer in the Talmud: Forms and Patterns* (1977), chapters VII and IX. Heinemann explicitly classifies the Lord's Prayer as a 'Jewish private prayer' (p. 191) which could take either the 'I' form or the 'we' form (ibid.).

[17]For the 'Our Father' formula of the Jewish prayer, see above p. 152 and Heinemann, 150–55, 189–91.

(cf. above, p. 153). It is also necessary to any aspiring to belong to his spiritual family: 'Whoever does the will of *my Father in heaven* [the will of God, Mark] is my brother and sister and mother' (Matt. 12.50/Mark 3.35). The link between obedience and the idea of the coming Kingdom implies, as has been suggested that absolute filial submission to God is essential: 'Not everyone who says to me Lord, Lord, shall enter the Kingdom of heaven, but he who does the will of my Father who is in heaven' (Matt. 7.21; cf. Matt. 18.19).

That harmony between heavenly and earthly obedience is the object of supplication, the former being presented as the model of the latter. It indicates that 'this world' and 'the world-to-come' are still envisaged as distinct. A similar pattern may be observed in the prayer of R. Eliezer (ben Hyrcanus) in the Tosefta:

> Do your will in heaven and give peace of mind to those who fear you on earth (tBer. 3.11).[18]

The three remaining petitions to the heavenly Father, provision for human needs, remission of sins and protection from danger, neatly match the images of divine care and forgiveness already discovered in the parables and sayings of Jesus, and with one possible, though in my view unlikely exception, represent the disciples' temporal and spiritual necessities on the eve of the coming of the Kingdom. The exception occurs if the adjective *epiousios*, defining the 'bread' requested from the Father, is given a future connotation, as is usually the case in the contemporary exegesis of Matt. 6.11.[19]

---

[18]The same kind of parallelism figures in another prayer for peace attributed to the early fourth-century Babylonian Amora, R. Safra: 'May it be your will, O Lord our God, that you establish peace within the family on high and the family below!' (bBer. 17a). In a meta-historical Parousia context, acknowledgment or rejection of Jesus 'before men' is believed to be correlative to an acknowledgment or rejection by him 'before my Father who is in heaven' or 'before the angels of God' (Matt. 10.32f.; Luke 12.8f.; Mark 8.38; Matt. 16.27; Luke 9.26). For a strict correspondence between earthly and celestial worship in the religious thought of the Qumran Community, see G. Vermes, *QIP*, 175f.; Carol Newsom, *Songs of the Sabbath Sacrifice* (1985), 59–72. Cf. also Beate Ego, *Studien zum Verhältnis von himmlischer und irdischer Welt im rabbinischen Judentum* (1989).

[19]For a detailed study of the various meanings, see W. Foerster, 'Epiousios' in *TDNT* II, 590–99; cf. also Davies and Allison, *Matthew* I, 607–9.

The two most favoured theories, linking the Greek word to various possible Semitic originals, interpret it either as 'daily', i.e. 'today's' bread (*lahma deyōma* or *leyōma* in Aramaic), or as the bread 'of tomorrow' (*lahma delimhar* in Aramaic). The latter may indicate literally the immediate future, but is also taken by Joachim Jeremias and others as meaning 'the great Tomorrow, the final consummation'.[20] While neither of the two kinds of 'tomorrow' can be ruled out definitively, the paramountcy of the present moment in the framework of eschatological enthusiasm or desperate stress would favour the present time, i.e., 'today'. This understanding would be supported by the well-known logion which discourages the followers of Jesus from worrying about the future: 'Do not be anxious about tomorrow, for tomorrow will be anxious about itself. Let the day's own trouble be sufficient for the day' (Matt. 6.34).[21]

4. The son of the heavenly Father

To complete the study of the Father image of God in the teaching of the Gospel, the Synoptic passages describing Jesus as God's son must be re-examined briefly.[22] In doing so, it has to be borne in mind that the only witnesses depicted as claiming, first indirectly, then directly, that Jesus himself used this title are the scoffers at Calvary:

> Let God deliver him now . . . for he said, 'I am the son of God' (Matt. 27.43).

[20]Cf. *Prayer*, 100. The same exegesis may have been anticipated by Jerome (*Commentary on Matthew* 6.11) on the basis of the Gospel (now lost) according to the Hebrews: 'In evangelio quod appellatur secundum Hebraeos pro supersubstantiali pane reperi *mahar*, quod dicitur crastinum, ut sit sensus, Panem nostrum crastinum, id est futurum, da nobis hodie.' (In the Gospel called 'according to the Hebrews', for 'daily bread' I found *mahar* which means 'of tomorrow', so that the meaning is, 'Our bread of tomorrow', that is our future bread, 'give us today'.)

[21]Warning against over-optimism is part of biblical prudence ('Do not congratulate yourself on tomorrow, for you do not know what the day may bring forth', Prov. 27.1) and is echoed also in rabbinic wisdom: 'Do not be worried about tomorrow's trouble, for you do not know what tomorrow will bring forth. Tomorrow may come, but he may not be there; he is worried about the world [variant: the day] which is not his' (bYeb 63b; bSanh 100b). The switch from the second to the third person is meant to avoid the mention of the death of the addressee.

[22]For an earlier analysis, see *JJ*, 200–06, 263f.

In all the remaining passages he is called 'son of God' by others. These texts therefore do not reflect the thought of Jesus regarding the Father in heaven but rather the religious context in which this thought was transmitted. Leaving aside as anachronistic the ecclesiastical confession formula – 'Truly this was a son of God' – placed on the lips of the Roman centurion at the moment of Jesus' death (Mark 15.39) – he was moved, according to Matthew (27.54), by the extraordinary happenings occasioned by the demise of the crucified such as the rending of the curtain of the Temple, the earthquake, the risen bodies seen – the rest of the evidence falls under three headings: (*a*) messianic proclamations; (*b*) pronouncements by a heavenly voice (*bat qōl*); and (*c*) pronouncements by demons and disciples.

(*a*) Messiah – son of God

In addition to the allusion to Jesus, the son of David, as being also the son of the Most High in the Annunciation story (Luke 1.31f.), the two famous Gospel excerpts in which 'son of God' as an epithet is attached to 'Christ' are Peter's statement in Caesarea Philippi and the question asked by the High Priest when he interrogated Jesus before the council:

> Simon Peter replied, 'You are the Christ, the son of the living God' (Matt. 16.16; the Christ, Mark 8.29; the Christ of God, Luke 9.20).

> Are you the Christ, the son of the Blessed? (Mark 14.61; the son of God, Matt. 26.63).

Though manifestly deriving from Psalm 2.7, where God addresses the (messianic) king of Israel as 'my son', the full phraseology is unattested in pre-Christian Jewish literature. The oldest evidence derives from one of the readings of IV Ezra 7.28–29 ('my son the Messiah': twice in Syriac, but in Latin 'filius meus Iesus' in verse 28 and 'filius meus Christus' in v. 29, 'my Messiah' in Ethiopic and 'the Messiah of God' in Armenian), but in the course of its transmission the text may have been contaminated by Christian copyists.[23]

[23]'My son' without the mention of 'the Messiah' figures several times in IV Ezra 13.32, 37, 52; 14.9. It is encountered also in I Enoch 105.2 of doubtful

The clearest rabbinic association of the royal Messiah with metaphorical divine sonship via Psalm 2.7 is preserved in an anonymous Tannaitic teaching from bSukkah 52a:

> Our rabbis taught: The Holy One blessed be He says to the Messiah son of David who will be revealed soon in our days, as it is written, 'I will tell of the decree [of the Lord. He said to me, You are my son, today I have begotten you'] (Ps. 2.7): Ask of me and I will give it to you, as it is written, 'Ask of me and I will make the nations your heritage' (Ps. 2.8).

In short, in the specifically messianic context of New Testament and rabbinic thought, God is portrayed as the Father and Guardian of Israel's chosen redeemer. Compared with the status of the ordinary Jew, the Messiah is believed to be God's son in an elevated sense, and vice versa God is seen as his Father in a distinctive manner.[24]

----

authenticity. 'I and my son' may refer here not to God and the Messiah, but to Enoch and Methuselah. Cf. M. Black – J. C. Vanderkam, *The Book of Enoch or I Enoch* (1985), 319.

[24]The so-called 'Son of God' text from Qumran Cave 4 (4Q246, previously 4QpsDan d, now Aramaic Apocalypse), containing the phrases 'son of God' (*bereh di 'el*) and 'son of the Most-High' (*bar 'elyōn*), has been quoted by J. A. Fitzmyer in connection with Luke 1.32, 35 (*A Wandering Aramean: Collected Aramaic Essays* (1979), 93). David Flusser, by contrast, interprets the titles as applying to the Antichrist (*Judaism and the Origins of Christianity* (1988), 207–13, while F. García Martínez, *Qumran and Apocalyptic* (1992), 162–79, identifies the figure as an angelic being, Melchizedek or Michael, the Prince of Light. All these theories are built on partial evidence and depend mainly on various hypothetical restorations of lacunae.

Now that the whole text is available, it would seem that the person who calls himself, or is named by others, 'son of God' is a usurper of this title. Indeed, the kingdom governed by him is said to be characterized by internecine warfare among the nations. He is likely to be modelled on the king of Daniel 11.36 who makes himself a god. Peace is expected only after the emergence of 'the people of God', to whom 'the Great God' grants universal power and 'eternal dominion'. In short, 4Q246 is not relevant to the study of the Messiah/son of God concept. On the other hand, it may represent the earliest non-biblical evidence for the collective understanding of 'one like a son of man' of Dan. 7.13. This type of exegesis is first attested in the biblical Daniel (7.27). Cf. G. Vermes, 'Qumran Forum Miscellanea I', *JJS* 43 (1992), 301–3. Two further contributions have appeared in 1992. Emile Puech, 'Fragment d'une apocalypse en araméen (4Q246 = pseudo-Dan d) et le "Royaume de Dieu"', *R B* 99 (1992), 98–131, proposing

(b) Jesus proclaimed son of God by a heavenly voice

The *bat qōl* or heavenly voice is an intermediary device in Jewish religious speculation, replacing not only direct speech from God to man, but also divine communication through prophets. Its inauguration is dated by Tannaitic rabbis to the early post-exilic era:

> With the death of Haggai, Zechariah and Malachi, the last prophets, the holy spirit ceased from Israel, nevertheless they are made to hear (proclamations) through a heavenly voice (tSotah 13.2; bSotah 48b; bYoma 9a; bSanh 11a).

An announcement by means of a *bat qōl* often conveys divine approval of an individual or a teaching according to the rabbis, as will be demonstrated presently. The speech is in the first person and the voice is presumed to be God's.

The two Gospel examples also aim at providing celestial endorsement to Jesus' mission, though the evangelists disagree among themselves whether this was meant for Jesus alone or for other witnesses as well.

In the case of the proclamation at his baptism by John in the Jordan, the main message is clear, but its form, and to some extent even the wording, vary. In Mark 1.10–11, Jesus alone sees the open skies with the dove-like spirit descending, and hears the words revealing his election by the heavenly Father.

> And a voice came from heaven, 'You are my beloved son; with you I am well pleased'.

In Luke 3.21–22, the vision is not specifically confined to him, but he alone receives the message.[25]

---

either a royal messianic exegesis or one identifying the 'son of God' with Antiochus Epiphanes. The other figures in Robert Eisenman and Michael Wise, *The Dead Sea Scrolls Uncovered* (1992), 68–71, who opt for a messianic interpretation.

[25]The Western text of Luke (Codex Bezae, old Latin, etc.) substitutes here Ps. 2.7, 'You are my son, today I have begotten you', thus endowing the statement with a messianic overtone. It is worth noting also that in John 1.32–33, the Baptist seems to be the sole beneficiary of both the vision and the revelation.

Matthew 3.16–17, on the other hand, confines the vision to Jesus, but the voice uses a third person formula, paralleled also in rabbinic literature, implying that the revelation was directed either to John or to all the onlookers:

> And lo, a voice came from heaven, saying, 'This is my beloved son with whom I am well pleased'.

The Transfiguration accounts repeat the reference to the voice, which this time comes from the cloud, and in Mark 9.7 and Matthew 17.5, reproduce also the saying, 'This is my beloved son'. 'Beloved', however, is replaced by 'chosen' in Luke 9.35. All three Synoptics add, 'Listen to him', thus indicating that the voice addressed the companions of Jesus on the mountain.[26]

Both the Baptism and the Transfiguration narratives picture, as do the messianic passages, a loving heavenly Father bearing witness to the election of his 'son', first in a state of humility, then in anticipated exaltation. These are texts inspired by current Jewish ideas and terminology, heavily overlaid with the later theological speculation of the primitive church. The canvas depicting the appearance of the priestly Messiah in the Testament of Levi 18.6–7 contains the salient features of the Gospel passages, the unsolved question being which of the two depends on the other. The end of 18.7 in any case is generally judged to be a Christian interpolation:

> The heavens will be opened, and from the Temple of glory sanctification will come upon him [the new Priest], with a fatherly voice as from Abraham to Isaac. And the glory of the Most High will break forth upon him. And the spirit of understanding and sanctification will rest upon him [in the water].[27]

[26]The phrase is a mosaic of biblical excerpts. 'This is my beloved son with whom I am well pleased', is a combination of Gen. 22.2 ('your son . . . whom you love' – Abraham/Isaac) and Isa. 42.1 ('my chosen in whom my soul delights' – God/the Servant of the Lord). 'Listen to him' is borrowed from Deut. 18.15 (God/the prophet like Moses).

[27]The last words are inserted to amalgamate the story with the Baptism of Jesus. They are missing from most manuscripts.

(c) Son of God – exorcist and miracle-worker

The final group of texts are united within a charismatic framework and address as 'son of God' Jesus *qua* participant in the heavenly Father's dominion over the powers of evil and the hostile forces of nature. The most common context is that of exorcism narratives:

> And whenever the unclean spirits beheld him, they fell down before him and cried out, You are the son of God (Mark 3.11; Luke 4.41).

> And behold they [the two Gadarene demoniacs] cried out, What have you to do with us, O son of God? Have you come to torment us before the time? (Matt. 8.29).

> Crying out with a loud voice, he [the Gerasene demoniac] said, What have you to do with me, Jesus, son of the Most High God? (Mark 5.7; Luke 8.28).[28]

Finally, one legendary anecdote is recorded in Matthew 14.33 when on the occasion of a storm on the Lake of Galilee, the disciples acknowledge Jesus as 'son of God', i.e. one who shared God's mastery over the wind because his arrival calmed the waves and saved those in the boat.

Taken together the three representations, viz. the divine sonship of the Messiah, the testimony of the heavenly voice, and that of demons and men, clearly demonstrate that Jesus' filial relationship to God was depicted by the creators of the Synoptic tradition, not as part of the general fatherhood of God, but as a phenomenon out of the ordinary deserving special attention.[29]

---

[28]The same recognition of the son of God by Satan characterizes the Temptation account in Matt. 4.3, 6; Luke 4.3, 9.

[29]A similar tendency distinguishing Jesus' specific link with the Father from that between his disciples with God is seen by many Christian New Testament interpreters in the use of the possessive pronouns, *my* Father and *your* Father. *Our* Father figures only in Matt. 6.9. The difference is mainly stylistic and is almost certainly without doctrinal significance. It is unlikely that Jesus actually referred to God as 'my Father'. The formula never occurs in Mark, and very seldom in Q and Luke. By contrast, it is frequent in the redactional layer of Matthew and in John. John 20.18 is the only Gospel passage which may stipulate a real difference between 'my' and 'your' in 'I am ascending to my Father and your Father, to my God and your God.' On the other hand, this may simply emphasize a reciprocal relationship.

II Jesus' Teaching on the Heavenly Father in the History of Ancient Judaism

The teaching of Jesus on God the Father reflects on the one hand the religious ideas of biblical Judaism and more particularly those of his own age, but displays also identifiable individualistic traits. To distinguish the diverse elements, the history of the divine Father concept needs to be sketched and Jesus' contribution to it inserted in the right place.

1. *The divine Father in the Bible*

Although the image is not richly attested in scripture, its underlying familiarity is manifest in a variety of theophoric names containing the element *Ab* (Father).[30] They use both Hebrew divine titles, YH(W) and ʾEL and result in Abi YAH or Abi YAHU (Yah or Yahu is my Father), or YoAB (Yo is Father). Likewise we have AbiEL and ELiab (God is Father) in pre-exilic and Second Temple Jewish names. ABram and ABiram (Exalted Father and My Father is exalted), traceable to the patriarchal age, represent the same type. While the exact nuance of the term 'Father' remains hazy, there can be no doubt that even on the individual level the relationship between God and the Israelites was seen from a family point of view.

This age-old underlying attitude is explicitly voiced mostly in collective terms as applying to members of the Jewish nation. They describe God as their Father and God alludes to them as his children. The earliest attestation is in the famous passage of Exodus 4.22 where, according to the J tradition, Moses addresses Pharaoh:

Thus said the Lord, 'Israel is my son, my first-born.'

In Deuteronomy 32.6, the Song of Moses formulates the following question:

Is not he your Father, who created you, who made you and established you?

---

[30]The mythological imagery of a 'father-god' surrounded by 'sons of god' (*benē ʾelohīm* or *benē ʾelīm*), common in the Bible, seems to have largely lost its original connotations and requires no detailed examination here.

In further examples from Deuteronomy, Moses either tells the Jews, 'You are the sons of the Lord your God' (14.1), or conveys the same message by means of a simile:

> Know then in your heart that as a man disciplines his son, the Lord your God disciplines you (8.5).

The same imagery is used in Psalm 103.13 in connection with the pious:

> As a father pities his children, so the Lord pities those who fear him.

In prophetic literature, God is depicted as proclaiming the Father-son bond between himself and Israel:

> Sons have I reared and brought up, but they have rebelled against me (Isa. 1.2).

> And in the place where it was said to them, 'You are not my people', it shall be said to them, 'Sons of the living God' (Hos. 2.1 [ET 1.10].

> For I am a father to Israel and Ephraim is my first-born (Jer. 31.9).

The individual application of the Father-son reciprocity is limited to the relation between God and the king of Israel in the prophecy of Nathan to David and in the poetry of the Psalter. In the former, the divine promise of adoption concerns Solomon:

> I will be his Father and he shall be my son (II Sam. 7.14).

In the Psalms, God proclaims the king at the moment of his enthronement to be his son, a declaration endowed with messianic significance after the disappearance of Jewish political sovereignty:

> You are my son, today I have begotten you (Ps. 2.7).

Yet, whereas the metaphor seems to have been familiar, the communal reference to God in prayer form as 'our Father' occurs only relatively late, in early post-exilic passages:

> For you are our Father,
> for Abraham does not know us
> and Israel does not acknowledge us,
> You O Lord are our Father,
> our Redeemer from of old is your name (Isa. 63.16).

The parallelism between God and Abraham is most significant and the association of Father and Redeemer is also revealing.

> O Lord, you are our Father; we are the clay, and you are our Potter, we are the work of your hand (Isa. 64.7 [ET 64.8]).

As the context shows, 'Father' and 'Potter' are interchangeable. At the same time, it is not to the almighty power of the Creator, but to the love and mercy of the 'Father' that the supplicant appeals.

Still in a collective sense, but reduced from the national to the priestly level, the prophet Malachi writes:

> A son honours his father and a servant his master. If then I am a Father, where is my honour? And if I am a Master, where is my fear? – says the Lord of hosts to you, O priests (1.6).

> Have we not all one Father? Has not God created us (2.10)?

The address of God as Father by an individual is limited in the Bible to the king (Messiah?), as is apparent in Psalm 89.26–28, where God is said to quote David's confession and gives his own benevolent reaction to it:

> He shall cry to me, 'You are my Father,
> my God and the Rock of my salvation'.
> And I will make him the first-born,
> the highest of the kings of the earth.
> My steadfast love I will keep for him for ever,
> and my covenant will stand firm for him.

2. The Father in inter-testamental literature

Moving to the Apocrypha, the Wisdom of Ben Sira furnishes three examples of an appeal to God as Father: one in Greek, 'O Lord, Father and Ruler of my life' (23.1); one in Hebrew, 'I will praise you, O my God, my salvation, I will thank you my God, my

Father' (51.1), and one in both languages, 'I exalted the Lord: you are my Father' (51.10). The phrase, 'God, Father and Ruler', occurs also in the opening words of a speech by Joshua to the Jews reproduced by Josephus in *Ant.* v. 93.

Among the Pseudepigrapha, the Testament literature appears to favour the Father symbolism, though the available evidence is sparse. In the Testament of Judah 24.2, the heavens open and 'the spirit of the holy Father' is poured out on the Messiah depicted as the Star arising from Jacob and as the sun of righteousness. The Testament of Job (*HJP* III, 552–5) speaks of the splendour of Job's throne issuing from the right hand of 'the Father' (33.3) and describes his 'kingdom' among 'the chariots of the Father' (33.9); his praises too are directed towards 'the Father' (40.2). Finally, the Greek Testament of Abraham (recension A; cf. *HJP* III, 761–7) thrice couples 'God and Father' in contexts of prayer.

Philo, it should be noted in passing, regularly invests his 'Father' concept with a definitely Jewish colouring in that his God-*patēr* does not merely appear as the first cause of the Greeks, but also as 'the loving protector and helper of his children'.[31]

In Qumran writings, the Father imagery is again poorly attested. The Florilegium or Midrash on the Last Days from Cave 4 re-uses II Sam. 7.14 (cf. above p. 174) in a messianic context as pointing to 'the Branch of David who shall arise with the Interpreter of the Torah [to rule] in Zion [at the end] of time' (4Q174 1.11f.). Apart from this text, and the very fragmentary Song of the Sage from Cave 4, where God is twice called upon as 'avīnū (4Q502 39 3, 511 127 1),[32] and another passages containing the invocation 'My Father and my God' in the 4Q Joseph Apocryphon (4Q372), the only example of importance appears in a Thanksgiving Hymn (1 QH 9.34f.):

> Until I am old Thou wilt care for me;
> for my father knew me not
> and my mother abandoned me to Thee.
> For Thou art a father
> to all [the sons] of Thy truth . . .

[31]E. R. Goodenough, *An Introduction to Philo Judaeus* (1962), 38, 85f. Cf. *Moses* ii. 238–41; *Opif.* 81, 171.

[32]Cf. Eileen M. Schuller, 'The Psalm of 4Q372 1 within the Context of Second Temple Prayer', *CBQ* 54/1 (1992), 67–79.

The poet appears to compare the unkindness of his human father to the care and love of God. The most important element of this description of God as Father is the prominence given to parental, indeed maternal, affection manifest in the continuation of the Hymn: 'And as a woman who tenderly loves her babe, so dost Thou rejoice in them' (1 QH 9.35f.).[33]

3. The Father in rabbinic writings

A brief glance at the application of the term Father to God by the sages of the Mishnah, the Midrash and the Talmud will firstly consider references to 'the Father who is in heaven', and secondly, point to a few examples of the concept in hasidic, charismatic and 'heavenly voice' contexts.

Allusion to God as 'heavenly Father', determined by various possessive pronouns, is common in Tannaitic literature and is usually associated with prayer. The following are a few examples:

> Whenever the Israelites directed their thoughts upwards and subjected their heart to *their Father who is in heaven*, they prevailed . . . they were healed (m R Sh 3.8).

> On whom shall we rely? On *our Father who is in heaven* (mSot 9.15).

> Judah ben Tema said: Be strong as the leopard and swift as the eagle, fleet as the gazelle and brave as the lion to do the will of *thy Father who is in heaven* (mAb 5.20).

The formula '*my* Father who is in heaven' occurs also in Midrashic texts almost automatically in first person speech. Thus at the end of his famous exposition of Exodus 20.6, 'of them that love me and keep my commandments' as referring to Jewish

---

[33]A somewhat similar imagery may be found in the Fragmentary Targum (Vatican 440) on Exodus 15.2. 'From their mothers' breasts the babes point their fingers towards their fathers and say: This is our Father who has suckled us with [honey from] the rock and has provided us with oil from the flint stone.' Cf. Michael Klein, 'The Targumic Tosefta to Exodus 15.2', *JJS* 26 (1975), 61–67; see also idem, *The Fragment-Targums of the Pentateuch according to their Extant Sources* (1980), in loc.

martyrs of the Hadrianic persecution, after quoting Zechariah
13.6 the early-second-century R. Nathan concludes:

> These wounds caused me to be loved by *my Father who is in
> heaven* (Mekh on Ex. 20.6, Lauterbach II, 247).

Another striking example figures in Sifra on Leviticus
(ed. Weiss 93d):

> R. Eleazar ben Azariah said: Let no-one declare, 'I do not
> desire . . . swine flesh or forbidden sex, but one must say,
> although I desire them, what shall I do since *my Father who is
> in heaven* has given me such a commandment'[34]

Lastly, mention must be made of the *Qaddish*, the ancient
Aramaic prayer, definitely in existence in the age of the Tannaim
and akin in ideology to the opening part of the Lord's Prayer. The
relevant excerpts are:

> Magnified and sanctified be his great name . . .
> May he establish his Kingdom during your life . . .
> May the prayers and supplication of all Israel be
> acceptable before *their Father who is in heaven* . . .

Turning now to the Father-son relationship in the context of
holy men traditions, a subject already touched upon in *Jesus the
Jew* (pp. 206–10), seen as it were from the celestial side, it is
expressed in filial terms, and as in the New Testament accounts of
the baptism and transfiguration of Jesus, via a heavenly voice. A
Talmudic story, attested in an Amoraic tradition attributed to
Rab in the early third century, but relating to the first-century
charismatic, Hanina ben Dosa, fits the Galilean context of the
Gospels perfectly.

> Every day a heavenly voice (*bat qōl*) comes forth [from Mount
> Horeb (bBer 17b)], saying: 'The whole world is sustained only
> on account of Hanina *my son*, yet for Hanina *my son* one qab
> of carob suffices from one sabbath eve to the next (bTaan 24b/
> bHul 86a).[35]

[34]According to Joseph Heinemann, in private prayer the individual views
himself as a son, and addresses God as 'Our Father', 'Our Father who art in
heaven', 'Our Father, our King', 'Merciful Father', etc. (*Prayer in the Talmud*
(1977), 189f.).

[35]Hanina ben Dosa is depicted as the provider for mankind on account of his
prayer miraculously ending a drought. In bHag 14a, his generation is said to have
been favoured by heaven. To make plain that the voice is that of God, the
mention of Horeb is included in bBer 17b and bHul 86a.

From an earthly point of view, the hasid in prayer is portrayed almost automatically in the Mishnah as one thinking of God as his Father.

> The ancient hasidim waited an hour before praying in order to concentrate their heart on *their Father who is in heaven* (mBer 5.1).

More specifically, an Aramaic account relating to that other charismatic rain-maker, Hanan, the grandson of Honi, includes in a prayer context the form of address, Abba, directed both to God and to the holy man.

> When the world was in need of rain, our rabbis used to send school-children to him (Hanan) who seized the train of his cloak and said, 'Abba, Abba, give us rain!' He said to him (God): 'Lord of the world, do something for those who cannot distinguish between the Abba who gives rain and the Abba who does not give rain.'[36]

4. *Traditional and individual elements in Jesus' doctrine of the heavenly Father*

It is hardly surprising that the understanding of God as the heavenly Father typical of the preaching of Jesus, dovetails into the development of Jewish religious thought precisely where it is expected. In a schematic outline from the Bible to the rabbis, the idea of the divine Father moves on the collective level from the Creator/Begetter of the Jewish people (within mankind) towards the loving and affectionate Protector of the individual member of the family. The transformation starts with the Apocrypha-Pseudepigrapha from the early second century BC onwards, with Father-Creator-Master still interchangeable. By the time of the Tannaitic sages in the second century AD, the heavenly Father is the providential God, distinct from God the King-Judge-Ruler, and the paternal image is clearly very familiar in the hasidic-charismatic milieu. The majestic liturgy of the Temple of Jerusalem is the genuine home ground of the august notion of the righteous and almighty Lord of the universe.

[36]bTaan 23b. Cf. *JJ* 211. See also above, pp. 16,n.6 and 158.

In seeking to place Jesus' teaching within the religious history of Judaism, it cannot fail to be noticed how much closer the former is to the ancient hasidim and even the rabbis of the age of the Mishnah than to the ideology of the Qumran community. As has been shown, the entire Dead Sea Scrolls literature yields hardly any direct use of the divine Father idea, and only a single example of a loving Father. None of the Qumran hymns, although most of them are individual prayers, is addressed to the Father, but they start as a rule with, 'I thank Thee O Lord'. Scholars who still insist that Qumran is the chief comparative source for the study of Jesus' message should bear in mind this crucial issue of the respective concepts of God.

A negative, but significant feature, repeatedly emphasized in the previous pages, of Jesus' representation of God consists in the absence of any royal figure, and of a corresponding self-deprecation and abasement before a divine Lord. On the contrary, the piety practised and preached by Jesus, like that of the hasidim of old, is characterized by a simple trust and expectation. Before the tremendous majesty of a divine Judge was foreseen as following the coming of the Day of the Lord, Jesus and his co-workers in the establishment of the Kingdom turned for inspiration, help and strength of purpose to the heavenly Abba.

Needless to say, the picture of a loving and solicitous Father does not tally with the human experience of a harsh, unjust and cruel world. Then as now, fledglings fell from the nest, little ones perished and, as Jesus himself was soon to experience, the innocent suffered. It would be a mistake to imagine that he offered to his followers a kind of sentimentally anthropomorphic image. But what lies at the heart of his intuition and gives individuality and freshness to his vision is the conviction that the eternal, distant, dominating and tremendous Creator is also and primarily a near and approachable God.

Appendix: Abba isn't Daddy![37]

In *Abba. Studien zur neutestamentlichen Theologie und Zeit-geschichte* (1966), republished in substance in English under

[37]The words of this heading reproduce the ironic title of an excellent paper published by James Barr in *JTS* 39 (1988), 28–47.

the title, *The Prayers of Jesus* (1967), Joachim Jeremias put forward several innovative theses which have made a profound impression on New Testament scholarship during the last quarter of a century. His fairly complex argument which, according to Barr (p. 30), 'shows certain signs of inconsistency', may be summed up as follows:

(*a*) The Aramaic term *abba* is 'a pure exclamatory form', viz *Father!*, and not an emphatic state corresponding in English to a noun with a definite article (= *the* father) (*Prayers*, 58).

(*b*) It originated in the babbling of 'children's speech'. The gemination *ab-ba* ('Dada') is modelled on the baby's more frequent call to *im-ma*, ('Mama') (ibid.).

(*c*) This form of invocation is so familiar in tone that its association with the Deity would have struck ordinary Aramaic-speaking Jews as 'disrespectful' (p. 62). Hence 'there is no instance in Jewish prayer literature of the vocative *abba* being addressed to God' (p. 60).

(*d*) Its use by Jesus was 'something new and unheard of' (p. 62).

(*e*) *Abba* in Palestinian Aramaic became an all-purpose phrase. The various expressions in the Greek Gospels, viz. 'the Father', 'Father!' (vocative), but also 'my/his/our Father' (noun with a possessive pronominal suffix) (pp. 58f.) are all traceable to Jesus' *Abba*.

This theory, and especially the derivation of the phrase from child language, has greatly influenced recent New Testament literature despite the fact that Jeremias himself had second thoughts on the subject.[38]

In a random glance at books published between 1979 and 1991, I have come across the following explanations of the term 'Abba': 'The familiar address of a child to his earthly father' (C. Rowland); 'Abba implies "father dear"' (I. M. Zeitlin); 'my own dear Father' (J. P. Meier); 'Jesus' term . . . is Abba . . .

---

[38]'One often reads (and I myself believed it at one time) that when Jesus spoke to his heavenly Father he took up the chatter of a small child. To assume this would be a piece of inadmissible naivety' (p. 62). Yet on pp. 59 and 109 he writes: '. . . it was never forgotten that *abba* derived from the language of small children', and '. . . it is a vocative form, originally a piece of childish chatter, which then came to be used generally . . ., *although the memory of its humble origin was never lost*' (my italics).

which can also connote the familiar "Daddy"' (J. H. Charles-worth); 'Abba, "Papa"' (C. Perrot).[39]

The implications are momentous for, if Jeremias is correct, Jesus' habitual style in addressing God and speaking of him would be peculiar to the point of being idiosyncratic. From the historico-critical point of view this would mean that Jewish doctrinal tradition would be unable to shed any light on the Gospel usage.

In the light of the foregoing scrutiny, it may be said that Jeremias definitely misunderstood, and perhaps even wrong-headedly misinterpreted, the evidence. In a summary fashion I have already argued (*JWJ*, 42) that in Jewish Aramaic the term *Abba* belonged not only to the style adopted by children, but could also be used in the solemn, 'religious' context of an oath, as for example in Targum Neofiti on Genesis 44.18, where the furious Patriarch Judah swears 'by the life of the head of *abba*' (= Jacob) that he will put to death all the Egyptians, or in the even more explicitly 'adult' speech of the daughters of Lot, planning a second incest with 'father' according to Targum Neofiti on Genesis 19.34.

> On the following day, the elder daughter said to the younger one, 'Behold I slept with *abba* yesterday. Let us make him drink wine also tonight. Go in and sleep with him and let us raise sons from our father.

Quite independently, James Barr, in his painstaking philological enquiry, has reached the same basic conclusion. He ironically observes that Jeremias's theory linking *abba* with children envisages a situation antedating Jesus by 'some millennia'. 'As an account of '*abbā* in New Testament times, infantile babbling is nonsensical' (p. 34).[40]

---

[39] Cf. C. Rowland, *Christian Origins: An Account of the Setting and Character of the most important Messianic Sect of Judaism* (1985), 255; I. Zeitlin, *Jesus and the Judaism of his Time* (1988), 62; John P. Meier, *A Marginal Jew: Rethinking the Historical Jesus* (1991), 175; J. H. Charlesworth, *Jesus within Judaism: New Light from Exciting Archaeological Discoveries* (1989), 134; C. Perrot, *Jésus et l'histoire* (1979), 280. The revised Luther Bible renders Abba in German as 'lieber Vater'.

[40] A similar attitude is revealed in Jeremias's thesis that the Talmudic rabbis copied Jesus when shaping their narrative parables. Cf. *The Parables of Jesus* (1972), 12. Cf. above p. 97.

Barr's second argument against Jeremias stresses that the testimony of the followers of Jesus indicates no awareness of anything extraordinary in Jesus' address of God. The Greek Gospels regularly employ (*ho*) *patēr*, i.e. (the) father, and not the diminutive *papas* or *pappas* (dad or daddy). Such words never figure in the New Testament because they are 'quite unsuitable for biblical style' (p. 38).

Thirdly, Jeremias's claim – cf. (*e*) above – that *abba* has a vocative function, and that it stands for 'father!' as well as 'my father!', etc., is also mistaken. In all three New Testament passages where the Aramaic term figures (Mark 14.36; Rom. 8.15; Gal. 4.6), and is followed by its Greek translation, the rendering is always *ho patēr*, i.e. the nominative preceded by the definitive article, and not the Greek vocative, *pater* (p. 40).

Finally, since Jeremias himself accepts that the phrase 'Our Father who art in heaven' was current in the first century AD, his 'strenuous' assertion that addressing God as 'Father' was extremely rare before Jesus loses all significance (p. 45). In consequence, Barr writes, 'one cannot help feeling that Jeremias has made the non-use of *'abbā* . . . into an apologetic matter' (p. 46).

In brief, Jeremias's hitherto popular theory is without philological foundation. Its literary-historical conclusion, viz. that before Jesus Jews did not appeal to God as *Abba*, is not only unproven, but also unlikely.

7

Jesus the Religious Man

We are so accustomed . . . to make Jesus the object of religion
that we become apt to forget that in our earliest records he is
portrayed not as the object of religion, but as a religious man.
(Thomas Walter Manson, *The Teaching of Jesus* (1935), 101)

This striking statement by a renowned British New Testament
scholar appositely defines the angle from which the synthesis of
the religion preached and practised by Jesus must be approached.

The essential elements of this religion have been identified and
analysed in the preceding chapters. All that remains now is to
piece together, without undue repetition, the various threads, to
supplement them where necessary, and to bring into relief the
central inspiration of Jesus and the salient traits of his teaching
and action.

The religion of Jesus is authentically Jewish. Nevertheless, his
own kind of Judaism displays specific features partly attributable
to the eschatological-apocalyptic spirit which permeated the age
in which he lived, and partly, on the subjective level, to his own
turn of mind. To bring out as clearly as possible the differences,
I will sketch first-century AD mainstream Judaism, which, if
allowances are made for the changed circumstances (e.g. the
destruction of the Temple), is in line with the religion of the later
rabbis, and its parallel eschatological version embraced by the
Qumran or Essene community.

1. Late Second Temple Judaism is summarized with remarkable concision in a saying attributed to Simeon the Righteous,
probably the Zadokite High Priest Simeon II (*c.* 200 BC). He
was praised by the sage Jesus Ben Sira (Ecclus. 50), and defined in
Pirke Abot as the final link in the chain binding the men of the
Great Synagogue, starting with Ezra and Nehemiah, to the

proto-Pharisees of the second century B C. According to Simeon, the pillars on which the world stands are the Torah, the cult and acts of mercy (mAb 1.2), in other words, the threefold Jewish practice of obedience to God's commandments, the performance of the Temple ritual, and moral action summed up as loving-kindness.

As regards Temple worship, it is important to emphasize that although considered the holiest of all religious pursuits by the priestly authorities, such as Simeon the Righteous, and their partisans, it was of the least tangible significance for lay Jews residing away from Jerusalem. For the inhabitants of the Holy Land, visiting the Sanctuary was, in theory, a thrice-yearly event, each of one week's duration. How many actually attended is impossible to ascertain especially when it is borne in mind that the journey to and from Jerusalem could, for many, more than double the time spent away from field or workshop; and for that majority of the Jewish people which lived in the Diaspora and were as such exempt from obligatory pilgrimage, it must have appeared as a dream hoped to come true perhaps once in a lifetime. This should be taken into account when Jesus' lack of particular interest in Temple worship is considered, and *a fortiori* in any serious attempt to comprehend the relative ease with which late first- and early second-century Jews overcame the crisis created by the destruction of the Sanctuary.[1]

Jewish writers, such as Philo and Flavius Josephus, who lived at the beginning of the common era, and were roughly speaking the contemporaries of Jesus or the evangelists, perceived their religion as an *historical* phenomenon. They saw it foreshadowed in the story of the patriarchs before being revealed to Moses on Sinai. Envisaged as rooted in the biblical past, it was expected to continue as long as the present age of the world. Yet, when they sought to describe it briefly, they instinctively and regularly summarized it as the fulfilment of a divinely ordained and transmitted code of behaviour towards God and men. Destined for the individual and society alike, this Torah/Instruction or *Nomos*/Law was conceived of as essential Judaism, the most excellent of all religious systems. Ideally, such a knowledge of,

---

[1]Here I strongly dissent from the thesis advanced by E. P. Sanders both in *Jesus and Judaism* and in *Judaism: Practice and Belief*, where the importance of the role of the Temple is, in my judgment, vastly overestimated.

and obedience to, God's laws constituted the Jew's second nature.

Thus Josephus writes:

> For it is good that these laws should be so graven on their hearts and stored in the memory that they can never be effaced . . . Let your children also begin by learning the laws, most beautiful of lessons and a source of felicity (*Ant.* iv. 210f.).

> Above all, we . . . regard as the most essential task in life the observance of our laws and of the pious practices based thereupon (*C.Ap.* i. 60).

Josephus asserts that familiarity with the Torah was so profound that it was as it were written on the heart of every Israelite and the ensuing religious action was seen as almost instinctive.

> Should anyone of our nation be questioned about the laws, he would repeat them all the more readily than his own name. The result, then, of our thorough grounding in these laws from the first dawn of intelligence is that we have them, as it were, engraven on our souls (*C.Ap.* ii. 178).

The same idea expressed in nearly identical words appears already in Philo.

> Holding that the laws are oracles vouchsafed by God and having been trained in this doctrine from their earliest years, they (the Jews) carry the likenesses of the commandments enshrined in their souls (*Legat.* xxxi. 210).

Both authors stress that the whole life of the Jew is an uninterrupted religious act of obedience to divine commandments from the cradle to the grave (*Legat.* xvi. 115).[2]

---

[2]Josephus boasts of his precocious learning. 'While still a mere boy, about fourteen years old, I won universal applause for my love of letters; in so much as the chief priests and the leading men of the city used constantly to come to me for precise information on some particular in our ordinances' (*Life* 9). Compared to this, the legend of the twelve-year old Jesus in the Temple, where he sat among the teachers, listening to them, asking them questions and amazing them by his understanding and his answers (Luke 2.46f.), seems to be a semi-cliché, couched in moderate terms.

This ceaseless concern with divine statutes was clearly not understood, *pace* Paul of Tarsus, as a mere performance of the 'works' of the Law. Josephus infuses all the commandments with an overwhelming religious-moral content,[3] and Philo, as is well known, discovers profound spiritual mysteries in the most prosaic statutes. Yet even he, the arch-allegorizer, emphasizes a practice of Judaism which, while seeking transcendental truth, observes also the plain meaning of the Torah. In his ponderous style, the Alexandrian sage insists on the dual reality of the Jewish religion.

> There are some who, regarding laws in their literal sense in the light of symbols of matters belonging to the intellect, are overpunctilious about the latter, while treating the former with easy-going neglect. Such men I for my part should blame for handling the matter in too easy and off-hand a manner: they ought to have given careful attention to both aims, to a more full and exact investigation of what is not seen and in what is seen to be stewards without reproach (*Migr.* xvi. 89).

Apart from the presupposition of an urban learning, normal in Jerusalem or Alexandria, but unlikely among the fishermen and day-labourers in Galilean villages, what distinguishes this outlook from the religious vision of Jesus is the absence of an *eschatological* perspective. The Judaism of Philo and Josephus, foreshadowing that of the post-70 AD rabbis, was primarily approached from a *communal* angle, and was distinguished by a *nomocentric* piety, viz. one founded on the Torah/Law, rather than on the Temple.[4]

2. As for the Qumran or Essene variety of Judaism, its essence was equally communal and *nomocentric*, but as it was also imbued with a spirit of eschatological expectation, its attitude to the Torah took on a peculiar shape. For if the sectaries believed

---

[3] Cf. G. Vermes, 'The Summary of the Law by Flavius Josephus', *NT* 24 (1982), 289–303.

[4] The superiority of the Law over the Temple is all the more remarkable since Josephus was certainly, and Philo possibly, of priestly descent. Cf. Josephus, *Life* 1; Jerome, *De viris illustribus* 11: 'Philon . . . de genere sacerdotum'. See *HJP* III, 814f.

that Moses' message was the only path leading to God (1 QS 1.1–3), that admission into the Community was conditional on a whole-hearted return to the Mosaic Law (1 QS 5.8), and any deliberate or even inadvertent transgression of a single commandment resulted in irrevocable expulsion (1 QS 8.21–23), they were also convinced that genuine obedience to the Torah was possible only by means of additional and indispensable end-of-time revelations received, and transmitted, either by the Priests, the sons of Zadok (1 QS 5.9) or by the Congregation (4 QSd).[5] Without the eschatological key to the closed book of the Law, and in particular to the religious calendar, any obedience was thought to be specious, a snare presented by Satan as a kind of righteousness (CD 4.15–17) to catch unenlightened Jews. And while the Scrolls clearly state the necessity of inward devotion, they lay substantial stress, as does Pharisaic and rabbinic orthodoxy, on matters relating to ritual purity of cultic origin. In sum, the Community taught that the only piety leading to the Kingdom of God was that inspired by divine revelations supplementary to the commonly-known Torah, granted to the Teacher of Righteousness and the other charismatic Essene masters. The prophetic ingredient, conspicuous in the Dead Sea writings, served to enrich and strengthen the Mosaic kernel of Qumran Judaism.

Finally, it is worth noting that no doubt owing to historical circumstances which had created a temporary breach between the sect and the Jerusalem sanctuary prior to the actual onset of the ultimate (eschatological) phase of the present age, the offering of sacrifice, that integral part of Second Temple religion, was symbolically replaced by prayer, 'the offering of the lips' (1 QS 8–9), as it was to be also, after AD 70, in rabbinic and later Judaism.

I   Jesus' Eschatological Judaism

The enquiry carried out in chapter 2 has demonstrated that in his religious teaching and observance, Jesus not only was not hostile

[5]Cf. G. Vermes, 'Preliminary Remarks...', *JJS* 42 (1991), 250–55; 'Qumran Forum Miscellanea I', *JJS* 43 (1992), 300f.

to the Torah in principle or refused to abide by it in practice, ready when necessary to choose between conflicting obligations, but that he acknowledged the Law of Moses as the foundation-stone of his Judaism. This general attitude does not imply, however, that his concern matched that of mainstream Jewish thought and practice or Qumran Essenism. He was not preoccupied with particular precepts and their specific limits, with their traditional, or rational, or scriptural, or revelation-based exegesis, but focussed his attention on the overall impact of the Torah on individual piety.

As for the relevant vocabulary, the term *nomos* figures 195 times in the New Testament corpus, but in the Synoptic Gospels it is completely absent from Mark, appears only twice in Q (Matt. 5.17, 11.13; Luke 16.16, 17), six times in Matthew, and if the five occurrences of the word in the Lucan Infancy gospel are discounted, twice in Luke. Most of the attestations come from the so-called Pauline writings (135 if Hebrews is included), followed by Acts (18), the Fourth Gospel (15) and James (10). The very distribution of the examples indicates that, while the role of the Law was central to the doctrinal polemics of the Pauline church with Pharisee-led Judaism in the post-AD 70 period and with Torah-abiding Judaeo-Christianity, its function in Jesus' eschatological version of the impending Kingdom of God was of quite another kind.

This difference in perspective may be due to a concatenation of causes, but eschatological vision is probably the chief one. A religion such as Judaism has a social dimension at its heart and envisages a *continuing future* for both the group and its members so that they can right existing wrongs and strive towards perfection along a timeless, divinely pre-established path. In a real eschatological atmosphere the change is total. The future to all intents and purposes is abolished and replaced by imminence, immediacy and urgency. In its absence, the collective is fragmented into its constituent parts, and instead of a search for society's progress and improvement, single men and women have to face up at once to an ultimate choice and decision. There is no second chance for one convinced that the Kingdom of God is at hand. Quiet optimism has no place in the final age of crisis and upheaval. Peace is deceptive: it is just a lull before the final war.

Eschatological enthusiasm[6] inevitably loses its intensity when the end is delayed. The interpretation of divine procrastination is that it is either a period intended to try people's patience and perseverance, or an act of favour granting more time for repentance. Thus the Qumran sectarian interpreter of the prophecy of Habakkuk describes the prolongation of the final age as stretching beyond all prophetic expectation and impresses on the members of the Community that they must not slacken in the 'service of truth', in the sure knowledge that 'all the ages of God will reach their appointed end as he determines for them in the mysteries of his wisdom' (1QpHab 7.7–14). This Essene acquiescence foreshadows a similar disappointment linked to a renewed, if revised, hope in the late New Testament era, magnificently portrayed in chapter 3 of the Second Letter of Peter:

> First of all you must understand this, that scoffers will come in the last days with scoffing ... and saying, 'Where is the promise of his coming?' ... But do not ignore this one fact, beloved, that with the Lord one day is as a thousand years, and a thousand years as one day. The Lord is not slow about his promise ..., but is forebearing toward you, not wishing that any should perish, but that all should reach repentance. (II Peter 3.3–9).

Thereafter, with the day of the Lord still unrealized, the dying flames of expectancy fade, and whereas in theory God's epiphany was still awaited, only lip service was paid to eschatological belief. In practice, life returned to normal and religion reverted to its customary secure social reality. Ecclesiastic Christianity represents this final state of the evolution. The religion of Jesus the Jew is a rare, possibly unique, manifestation of undiluted eschatological enthusiasm. Whether his mission lasted three years, or two, or more probably just one, it was too short to allow room for a slow development of doubt, let alone disenchantment,

---

[6]The phrase is a free rendering of Martin Buber's 'enthusiasm of eschatological presence' (Enthusiasmus eschatologischer Gegenwärtigkeit) coined in *Zwei Glaubensweisen* (1950) in *Werke* I (1962), 707. Norman P. Goldhawk's English translation renders it as 'enthusiasm of eschatological actuality'. Cf. *Two Types of Faith: A Study of the Interpenetration of Judaism and Christianity* (1961), 76.

regarding the imminence of God's decisive intervention in the affairs of this world.

II   The Corollaries of Jesus' Eschatological Enthusiasm

If Jesus *truly* believed that the Kingdom of God was at hand – and all the available evidence points to his not having hedged his bets – his conviction that very little time remained for people to alter their course and devote themselves unreservedly to 'seeking the Kingdom', permeated his whole action and defined the specific nature of the piety he sought to inculcate. Unlike the religious vision which takes the future for granted and envisages life in a solidly established group context, eschatological ardour demands a complete break with the past, exclusively concentrates on the present moment, and does so not from a communal but from a personal perspective.

1. *Eschatological individualism*

Pure eschatological religion being thus personal in nature, starts with an essential and decisive individual act: repentance. In the Semitic mentality of Jesus the Jew, it implied not a change of mind as the *metanoia* of the Greek Gospels would suggest, but a complete reversal of direction away from sin, in accordance with the biblical and post-biblical Hebrew dual concept of 'turning', viz. 'turning away from' or 'returning to', conveyed by the verb *shuv* and the noun *teshuvah*.

The precondition of any true religious act, whether his own baptism of repentance in the Jordan, or his disciples', is that oft-mentioned *teshuvah*, the genuine turning away from all non-God-centred pursuits and 'conversion' to the 'Kingdom of heaven'. Jesus never defined the essence, requirements and consequences of *teshuvah*. Having little familiarity with Temple matters, he is hardly expected to have elaborated on whether divine pardon was preceded by, or followed, the offering of a 'sacrifice for sin'. In his world-view, such particulars were insubstantial.[7]

[7]It may be taken for granted that people, even the simple country folk, who obeyed his call, and earlier that of John, instinctively knew what was expected of

Unlike the communal act of repentance, an integral part of liturgy such as the Qumran ceremony of the renewal of the Covenant, the *teshuvah* displayed by Jesus at his baptism by John was personal.[8] So also was Jesus' appeal to repentance. It would even appear as an anti-community move since it was to be obeyed if necessary at the price of conflict within the family or the social group as the Gospels in the wake of biblical prophecy clearly intimate (Matt. 10.21, 34–37; Luke 12.51–53; 14.26; cf. Micah 7.6). Jesus' underlying message is that every man devoting himself to a whole-hearted search for God's Kingdom is essentially alone.

Teshuvah being personal, the ensuing pardon was also naturally so. Jesus' own role here, namely that he claimed for himself God's right to forgive sins, has been misunderstood by such strange bedfellows as hostile Galilean scribes and pious Christian theologians of all ages. The former accused him of blasphemy while the latter have used the same words of Jesus in support of their claim concerning his divinity. But the matter need not detain us for long. The principal relevant passage in the Synoptic Gospels, the healing of a paralytic in Capernaum, depicts Jesus, not as forgiving, but as declaring that the sick man's sins were forgiven. Employing a passive, impersonal turn of phrase, which in the Semitic thought of his time was automatically accredited to God, he certainly does not arrogate to himself a divine status.

———

them and acted accordingly. The question of the causal relationship between repentance and forgiveness did not bother them greatly. It has been queried whether Jesus departed from the orthodox path by declaring a man's sins forgiven without *prior* repentance, not to speak of the prescribed 'sin-offering', but although the Temple priests out of class solidarity and self-interest would certainly have insisted on the latter (such sacrifices formed an important part of their income: cf. *HJP* II, 260), for Jesus' Galilean disciples the issue was of scholastic rather than real significance.

[8]The Essene confession of sins is formulated in the first person plural: 'We have strayed! We have [disobeyed!] We and our fathers before us have sinned and done wickedly in walking [counter to the precepts] of truth and righteousness' (1 QS 1.24–26). It should be noted, however, that the Qumran entry into the Covenant in the form of an oath obliging the new member to 'return' to the Law of Moses (1 QS 5.8), and accompanied, it seems, by some kind of Essene baptism (1 QS 3.9–11; 5.13f.), is also by definition an individual commitment, but one taking place, like the *Confiteor* of the Catholic mass, within the formalized framework of a public ceremony.

Underplaying his part as a charismatic healer, he attributes the cure to the faith of the paralytic. His sudden ability to walk after years of immobility is proof that his sins have been pardoned (by God).[9]

2. *Eschatological urgency*

In a religion animated by true eschatological zeal, time becomes focussed on the present. It is true that eschatological *literature* is replete with speculation aimed at determining the stages that lie ahead. Chapter 9 of the Book of Daniel claims that the age of its readers belongs to the last 'week' (i.e. seven year period) of the seventy weeks of years of the end of the world era, and that this is patently marked by the introduction of the 'abomination of desolation' into the Jerusalem Temple (cf. also Mark 13.14; Matt. 25.15). Paul's eschatological vision, outlined in II Thess. 2.3–8, is even more detailed. But what seems to be the genuine message of Jesus is inimical to signs (Luke 17.20). It declares futile the careful plans of the wealthy farmer concerning the rich harvest he expects (Luke 12.16–21) and places the coming of the Kingdom first, insisting on an exclusive concentration on the needs of today (Matt. 6.33f.; Luke 12.31).

In a world in which the *now* is sacrosanct, all dawdling is banned. Duties connected with the Kingdom of God are to be performed at once and the dead are to be left to bury their own dead (Matt. 8.22; Luke 9.60). The eyes of the seeker must gaze forward: 'No one who puts his hand to the plough and looks back is fit for the Kingdom of God' (Luke 9.62).

3. *Eschatological absoluteness*

Jesus' eschatological devotion is absolutely single-minded, unstinting and decisive. As has been shown apropos of the

[9]This passage, (Mark 2.1–12; Matt. 9.1–8; Luke 5.17–26; cf. also Luke 7.47) and a remarkable Qumran parallel from the Prayer of Nabonidus, in which a Jewish exorcist is said to have forgiven the sins of the king and *thereby* delivered him from a long illness, are discussed in *JJ* 67–69, 240f. in the context of the relationship between devil/sin/sickness and healer-exorcist/forgiveness/cure in inter-Testamental charismatic Judaism. Note that in the two Gospel stories, those of the paralytic and of 'the woman of the city who was a sinner' (Luke 7.37), Jesus' declaration that their sins have been forgiven scandalizes the conventional Jews.

parables of the precious pearl and the treasure hidden in a field (Matt. 13.44),[10] not only must they be purchased without delay, but also at any price. Their discoverer must give for them all that he has. Such unreserved generosity characterizes the poor widow referred to by Jesus who in putting her fortune of two ha'pennies into the Temple treasury, gives all her possessions to God (Mark 12.41–44; Luke 21.1–4). Leading his recruits towards the dawning Kingdom, Jesus commands them to renounce all self-interest and be ready to lose their lives in order to reach their ultimate goal (Mark 8.34–9.1; Matt. 16.24–28; Luke 9.23–27).

III   Jesus' Eschatological Religious Action

From these premises of urgency and total devotion follow the eschatological qualities of religious action. As has been clearly demonstrated in chapter 2, Jesus made no attempt to restrict, or interfere with, the Torah; he rather embraced it as the recognized framework of Judaism. What he strove to emphasize was inward piety for the individual devotee of the Kingdom of heaven. In brief, he adopted, intensified and sought boldly to inject into the Judaism of ordinary people the magnificent prophetic teaching of the religion of the heart (cf. Isa. 29.13).

By way of an introductory digression it should be made plain that the representation of Judaism in the wake of Paul – and nearly two thousand years of Christianity – as a *legalistically motivated religion of works* contrasted with Jesus' prophetic religion of loving-kindness is a caricature, and a poor one at that. It all depends on how blinkered the observer is. There are Jews who derive genuine spiritual enrichment from the observance of the commandments, in the same way as there are Christians whose piety is married to a persistent, even scrupulous, concern for the drawing of a precise boundary between the licit and the illicit. Old fashioned Catholics, in particular monks and nuns, and sabbatarian Protestants, live according to a *halakhah* not unlike that of a strictly orthodox Jew.

---

[10]The Copper Scroll from Qumran (3Q15) lists sixty-four locations of buried gold, silver and other valuables. According to rabbinic law, no doubt in force already in the first century, the buyer of a field and 'all that is in it' (mBB 4.9) would become the legal owner of such a treasure trove.

The definition of the nature of an ancient religious system depends, furthermore, on the choice of the literary sources on which the diagnosis relies. If Judaism is described exclusively on the basis of such legal or near-legal documents as the Mishnah, the Talmud or the *Shulhan Arukh*, it will appear more legalistic and casuistic than spiritual; but so would Christianity if seen one-sidedly mirrored in the codes of canon law, penitential books or manuals of moral theology of the various churches. Even the extremely strict variety of Second Temple Judaism reflected in the Dead Sea Scrolls regularly mixes down-to-earth practicalities of organized religion with elevated counsels of holiness, ethics and wisdom. Its teachers may on the one hand be keen on specifying the minimum quantity of water required to render a ritual bath valid (CD 10.10–13), but they insist on the other hand that no ceremony of purification is effective unless coupled to an authentic act of inner renewal: 'for they shall not be cleansed unless they turn from their wickedness' (1 QS 5.13f.).

Unlike the rabbis and the Essene teachers who insisted on both the letter and the spirit of the Law, Jesus marched in the footsteps of the great prophets of Israel in placing an almost exaggerated accent on the *inward aspects* and *root causes* of the religious action, impassioned as he was to foment the eschatological fervour of the individual. Instead of solemnly laying down directives for an orderly social, cultic and moral life within a community of the elect, he sought to perfect their inner spiritual persona.

There is no reason to presume that he was opposed to formal worship and formulaic prayer. Yet rather than exhort his disciples to concentrate their minds so that they might focus their attention on God before reciting a benediction or participating in worship, he enjoined them to withdraw to a hidden room (Matt. 6.6) away from the public gaze where each could commune alone with the heavenly Father. As has been observed in chapter 2, in stark contrast to the behaviour of the apostles who continued to visit the Temple at times set for services (Acts 2.46; 3.1; 22.17), Jesus is portrayed as a man of solitary prayer.[11]

---

[11]In rabbinic literature, ancient hasidim like Abba Hilkiah, grandson of the charismatic Honi, and Hanina ben Dosa are pictured as retiring to pray on the flat roof of the house or in the upper chamber (bTaan 23b; yBer v, 9d; bBer 34b). These portraits lack an eschatological ingredient. Likewise, the Therapeutae or

The same purity is prescribed for almsgiving and fasting. Both are to be performed 'in secret', observed only by God, not just to ward off the temptation of publicly appearing devout, which is counselled by the rabbis too, but also to transform charity and self-mortification exclusively into steps towards the Kingdom of heaven.[12]

IV   The Well-Springs of Jesus' Religion

Such a description of the eschatological Judaism of Jesus, unavoidably theoretical to some extent, is a far cry from the existential reality of his attitude both to God and to man. Throughout these pages it has been shown that it was not his custom to build towers of wisdom or cathedrals of theology; instead, he unreservedly addressed himself to furthering the work of God and his Kingdom, and to kindling, or at least endeavouring to implant, his own ardour in the hearts and minds of his followers. But to achieve a reliable grasp of his cast of mind, an attempt must be made to identify the well-springs of his religion.

1. Faith

If repentance (*teshuvah*) with its corresponding reliance on divine forgiveness is its *conditio sine qua non*, trusting faith (*emunah*),

———

contemplative Essenes are said by Philo (*Vit. Cont.* 25) to have spent their praying hours in a 'sanctuary' (*semneion*) or 'closet' (*monastērion*). According to mBer 5.1, the attention of the men of piety (*hasidim*) was so powerfully concentrated on prayer that even being greeted by the king or having a snake twisted around their ankle would remain unnoticed. Cf. *JWJ*, 164f.

[12]Generosity is hailed as praiseworthy by Jesus ben Sira (Ecclus. 31.11), and the branch of the Essenes represented by the Damascus Document openly taxed its members for charitable purposes (CD 14.10–16). But clandestine almsgiving appears also in the Testament of Job 9.7f. and mShek 5.6. Both cases are presented from the standpoint of the shy poor: they are to be allowed to help themselves without facing their benefactors. In the case of formal fasting, the Mishnah (Taan 1.6) prescribes outward manifestations of penance: no washing, no anointing and no footwear (and also no sexual intercourse). The builders of the Kingdom of God by contrast were advised by Jesus to disguise their fasting under a clean and well-kempt appearance (Matt. 6.17).

entailing a complete surrender of the self to God, is its life-blood. Manifest in the healing narratives, in the parables as well as in the sayings of Jesus, it pervades the whole Gospel message as a confident expectation which he recommends to his followers and praises when encountering.

Everything he does is animated by *emunah*. Central to his work as healer-exorcist, he expresses it poignantly in an answer to a man on the brink of despair he witnesses the failure of Jesus' disciples to deliver his son from the 'demon' of epilepsy (Mark 9.14–27; Matt. 17.14–18; Luke 9.37–43). 'If you can do anything,' – the father begs Jesus, 'Have pity on us and help us!' (Mark 9.22). The answer, which embraces both the suppliant and the charismatic healer, constitutes one of the principal tenets of the religion of Jesus, one that seems to exclude any need for a Mediator or Redeemer:

All things are possible to him who believes (Mark 9.23).

Yet the close circle of Jesus' followers often fail in *emunah* and are castigated as 'men of little faith'. By contrast, its presence in the rare Gentiles whom Jesus is reported to have treated, such as the paralysed servant of the Judeophile Roman centurion from Capernaum, apparently a benefactor of the local synagogue (Matt. 8.5–13; Luke 7.1–10), and the woman from the district of Tyre and Sidon (Southern Lebanon today) with the possessed daughter (Mark 7.24–30; Matt. 15.21–28), evoke his baffled approval:

I tell you, not even in Israel have I found such a faith (Matt. 8.10; Luke 7.9).

O woman, great is your faith! (Matt. 15.28; cf. Mark 7.29).[13]

The religion preached by Jesus exudes confidence. People are enjoined incessantly to ask, search and knock on the door (Matt. 7.7f.; Luke 11.9f.). Constantly he opts for the hyperbole to emphasize the overall importance and power of *emunah*. Faith as small as a mustard seed – proverbially the tiniest quantity – can lift a mountain (Matt. 17.20), or better still, lift it and cast it into

---

[13]The woman's trust is all the more admirable since Jesus apparently first tried to shrug her off: 'It is not right to take the children's bread and throw it to the dogs' (Mark 7.27).

the sea (Mark 11.23; Matt. 21.21).[14] Again, trust in God's willingness to answer pleas in cases of extraordinary need inspires and justifies prayer which amounts to importuning (Luke 11.5–8).[15]

Emunah demands the total commitment of the self to God even at the price of risk. To serve two masters is self-contradictory: one has to choose either God or Mammon (Matt. 6.24; Luke 16.13). Even when the master's service entails the use of money, as in the parable of the talents (Matt. 25.14–30; Luke 19.12–27), confident risk-taking is enjoined. To look for fool-proof protection against risk in the form of hiding the 'seed'-talent ruins the enterprise and is tantamount to a lack of piety. Similarly, an unhesitating acceptance of risk is stressed in the parables of the acquisition of the hidden treasure or the precious pearl (Matt. 13.44–46), and even more so in the story of the shepherd who leaves ninety-nine sheep unguarded and exposed to danger while looking for a single lost animal (Matt. 18.12f.; Luke 15.4–7). Indeed, when ultimate values are at stake, Jesus recommends, once more hyperbolically speaking, as has been pointed out earlier (pp. 144f.) the ready offering of a hand, a foot or an eye (Mark 9.43–48; Matt. 5.29f., 18.8f.):

> It is better for you to enter the Kingdom of God with one eye than with two eyes to be thrown into hell (Mark 9.47).

More dramatically still, self-castration with all that it symbolizes is suggested for the single-minded at the approach of the eschaton, the consummation of the ages:

> There are eunuchs who have made themselves eunuchs for the sake of the Kingdom of heaven (Matt. 19.12).[16]

[14]Once more Luke (17.6) mixes the metaphors and speaks of a fig tree being planted in the sea by faith!

[15]However, it still falls short of the petulant threat of the first-century BC charismatic Honi, or Onias the Righteous as he was called by Josephus, who told God that he would not move from the circle which he had drawn around himself unless his request for the ending of a drought was granted. Cf. mTaan 3.8. The Josephus passage is in *Ant.* xiv. 22; see also *JWJ* 49 and p. 108 above.

[16]The obviously metaphorical import of this saying did not stop Origen, the greatest biblical scholar of the early church from applying these words to himself literally in an excess of ascetic enthusiasm at the beginning of the third century!

Jesus' tendency to accentuate a message by means of over-statement is, as has been noted many times, an essential constituent of his popular rhetoric. In addition to the passages just cited, the list should include the overturning of existing hierarchies, the first becoming the last and vice versa (Mark 10.31; Matt. 19.20; 20.16; Luke 13.30), the exalted being humbled and the humble exalted (Matt. 18.4; 23.12; Luke 14.11; 18.14); and the leaders being changed into servants (Mark 10.43f.; Matt. 20.26f.; Luke 22.26). The same logic has pro-duced the equation of signs of sexual interest (or divorce) with adultery, and of anger with murder (Matt. 5.27–30; Mark 10.2–12; Matt. 19.3–10; Matt. 5.32; Matt. 5.21–23). The claim that scribes exploit widows (Mark 12.40; Luke 20.47); the command that a charitable person's left hand must not know what the right hand does (Matt. 6.3); that one must turn the other cheek (Matt. 5.39; Luke 6.29) and must love one's enemies (Matt. 5.39–48; Luke 6.20–23), complete the canvas of Jesus' best-known exaggerations.

The reverse of *emunah* is anxiety, careful forethought, precau-tion, planned provision for the future. These ingredients of ordered social and family life have no place in a world fired by eschatological zeal. Thus one who practises the religion preached by Jesus prays only for the day's need (Matt. 6.11; Luke 11.3). If God can provide for the birds and wild flowers, *a fortiori* for those humans who have faith (Matt. 6.25–33; Luke 12.22–31). Contrary to modern wisdom, Jesus declares that no careful planning can add 'one cubit' to a man's span of life (Matt. 6.27; Luke 12.25). Hence:

> Do not be anxious about tomorrow, for tomorrow will be anxious for itself. Let the day's own trouble be sufficient for the day (Matt. 6.34).

A final Gospel pointer to one infused with Jesus' concept of *emunah* is that such a person must come to resemble a little child, entirely dependent, not on the mother as we would say, but on the heavenly Father, sure that, like Galilean lake-side people them-selves, he will not offer a snake to a son or daughter who clamours for fish (Matt. 7.10; Luke 11.11).

Like the charismatic Hanan, probably known as Abba Hanan, mentioned earlier (p. 179), who told the children demanding rain after one of the many long droughts, that their prayer should be addressed to the other (heavenly) Abba (bTaan 23b), Jesus' representation of genuine childlike spirituality goes hand in hand primarily with one of the Deity as a loving and caring Father. His religion is of one piece. He and his followers are to call on God as Abba. The awesome Lord of heaven, the *Rex tremendae majestatis*, lies beyond the limit of his vision, being part of the new age of the Kingdom which is to come.

2. *Imitatio Dei*

In my last Riddell Memorial Lecture delivered at the University of Newcastle in 1981 I raised the question which must be confronted again at this moment: What in the last resort was the principle, embraced by Jesus and impressed on his followers, which was to enable them in the final days to live perfectly as children of their heavenly Father?[17]

The answer given then still strikes me as valid. Initiated by *teshuvah* and nourished by *emunah*, the religion of Jesus can ultimately be summed up as an untiring effort to follow God as a model, a constant *imitatio Dei*. The doctrine is an essential part of one of the streams of biblical, inter-testamental and rabbinic Judaism, and as such constitutes the apogee of our description of the religion of Jesus the Jew.

This notion of shaping human action on a pattern established by the Deity is both easy and difficult to comprehend, and as will be shown, elicited conflicting reactions among the rabbis.[18] It has a double biblical foundation. The first is contained in the creation story, with its assertion that man is made in God's image (Gen. 1.27) and is consequently capable of 'godly' behaviour. The second is entailed in the solemn injunction issued by Moses on God's behalf: 'You shall be holy; for I the Lord your God am

[17]*The Gospel of Jesus the Jew* (1981), 43; *JWJ* 52.
[18]Cf. S. Schechter, *Some Aspects of Rabbinic Theology* (1909), 199–218 ('Law of Holiness and Law of Goodness'); A. Marmorstein, 'The Imitation of God (Imitatio Dei) in the Haggadah', Jeschurun 14 (1927), reprinted in *Studies in Jewish Theology* (1950), 106–21; G. F. Moore, *Judaism in the First Centuries of the Christian Era* (1930) I, 441; II, 109–11; M. Buber, 'Imitatio Dei', *Israel and the World* (1963), 66–77; *Encyclopaedia Judaica* 8 (1971), 1292f.; E. E. Urbach, *The Sages: Their Concepts and Beliefs* (1975), 383–5; Pamela Vermes, *Buber on God and the Perfect Man* (1980), 141–44.

holy' (Lev. 19.2). This lofty ideal is to be achieved by 'loving . . . God', and 'walking in all his ways' (Deut. 11.22).

Second-century Tannaitic sages showed great interest in the problem of 'imitation'.[19] Their positive formulation of the issue is akin to the piety of Jesus. The doctrine is anchored, in the name of the early second-century master, Abba Sha'ul, to Leviticus 19.2, 'You shall be holy as I the Lord your God am holy' in Sifra on this verse:

> What is the duty of the king's household (*pamilyah* – familia)? To follow in the footsteps the king.

The same Abba Sha'ul proclaims an identical teaching in interpreting the Song of Moses in Exodus 15.2,

> This is my God *we'anwehu*.

Instead of understanding the Hebrew word, in conformity with common exegetical tradition, as 'and I will praise him', Abba Sha'ul substitutes for it *'ani wa-hu*: 'This is my God, *I and he*'. The last, odd-sounding clause is then further developed in the direction of the *imitatio Dei*:

> Resemble him, please! Just as he is merciful and gracious, you too must be merciful and gracious (Mekh. on Ex. 15.2 [Lauterbach II, 25]).

More directly, an anonymous Tannaitic teacher provides a much fuller exegesis attached to the midrash Sifre on Deuteronomy 11.22, 'that you may walk in his ways'.

> These are the ways of God: 'The Lord, a God merciful and gracious' (Ex. 34.6). It is also said, 'All who shall be called by the name of the Lord shall be saved' (Joel 3.5 [ET 2.32]). But how can a man be called by the name of the Lord? Just as God is called merciful, you too must be merciful. The Holy one blessed be he is called gracious, so you too must be gracious, as it is written, 'The Lord is gracious and merciful . . .' (Ps. 145.8), giving presents freely. God is called righteous, as it is written, 'For the Lord is righteous, he loves righteous deeds'

[19] Solomon Schechter pertinently notes that they often present a kind of *imitatio hominis* by God. Cf. 'God and the World' in op. cit. [in the previous note], 37.

(Ps. 11.7), so you too must be righteous. The Lord is called *hasid* (loving, devoted), as it is written 'For I am *hasid*, says the Lord' (Jer. 3.12), so you too must be *hasid*. This is why it is written, 'All who shall be called by the name of the Lord shall be saved' (Joel 3.5 [2.32]).[20]

The fullest description in Hebrew of the *imitatio Dei* comes from a third-century Palestinian Amora, Rabbi Hama, son of R. Hanina. Expounding Deuteronomy 13.5, 'Follow the Lord, your God', he teaches:

Is it possible for a man to follow the Shekhinah? Is it not written, 'The Lord your God is a devouring fire' (Deut. 4.24)? But follow the attributes (qualities) of the Holy one blessed be he. Since he clothes the naked, as it is written, 'And the Lord God made for Adam and his wife garments of skin and clothed them' (Gen. 3.21), you too must clothe the naked. Since the Holy one blessed be he visited the sick, as it is written, 'And the Lord appeared to him (Abraham after his circumcision) at the Oaks of Mamre' (Gen. 18.1), you too must visit the sick. Since the Holy one blessed be he comforted the mourners, as it is written, 'After the death of Abraham God blessed his son Isaac' (Gen. 25.11), you too must comfort the mourners. Since the Holy one blessed be he buried the dead, as it is written, 'And he buried him (Moses) in the valley' (Deut. 34.6), you too must bury the dead (bSotah 14a).

No less detailed is an Aramaic recital of the ways of God taught to Israel which is appended in the Pseudo-Jonathan Targum to Deuteronomy 34.6, the story of the burial of Moses by God. While there are many overlaps, the targumic account is not a pure repetition of R. Hama's teaching.

Blessed be the name of the Lord of the world who taught us his right ways. He taught us to clothe the naked by his clothing of Adam and Eve. He taught us to join bridegrooms and brides by joining Eve to Adam. He taught us to visit the sick by revealing himself in a vision of the Word (Memra) to Abraham when he was sick. He taught us to comfort mourners by

---

[20](Sifre on Deut 11.22 [49], ed. L. Finkelstein, 114). Note the subtle difference between God being *called*, but man must *be* merciful, gracious, etc.

revealing himself again to Jacob on his return from Padan at the place where his mother had died. He taught us to feed the poor by causing bread to descend from heaven for the children of Israel. He taught us to bury the dead through Moses to whom he revealed himself by his Word (Memra) and with him companies of ministering angels.[21]

Finally, in a double version, Pseudo-Jonathan most succinctly formulates the law of *imitatio Dei* either as spoken by Moses or by God himself. The first, contained in Brian Walton's London Polyglot Bible (1654–57), on Lev. 22.28, runs:

My people, children of Israel, as *our Father* is merciful in heaven, so you shall be merciful on earth.

The second figures in the British Library manuscript (Add. 27031) on the same verse:

My people, children of Israel, as *I* am merciful in heaven, so you shall be merciful on earth.

All these texts agree in accentuating the positive aspects of the divine Model who is repeatedly depicted as merciful and gracious, even though actual experience may not always show him so. Negative qualities are only occasionally singled out, e.g. men must not steal because God *hates* robbery (bSuk 30a), but they are clearly less attractive than his virtues. Moreover, it is never proposed that a man should seek for his own use the divine prerogative of justice, let alone vengeance.

On the other hand, some rabbis of the Amoraic period, finding the idea of the imitability of God dangerous since it might place in question his transcendence, lay down certain caveats. They hasten to emphasize that human imitation is merely a pale

---

[21]A sequence of divine acts of loving-kindness towards the patriarch Joseph, prefiguring the rabbinic lists, appears in the Testament of Joseph 1.4–7, where God's actions are contrasted with the corresponding misdeeds of the brothers of Joseph. 'These my brothers hated me, but the Lord loved me. They wanted to kill me, but the God of my fathers kept me safe. They let me down into a pit, but the Most High brought me up again. I was sold into slavely, but the Lord set me free. I was taken into captivity, but his strong hand supported me. I was assailed by hunger, but the Lord himself fed me. I was alone, but God gave me comfort. I was ill, but the Most High came to my help. I was in prison but the Saviour showed me favour. In bonds, and he released me. Slandered, and he pleaded my cause. Reviled by the Egyptians, and he delivered me.'

shadow of the original: 'Do you think that you can be as holy as I am? No I alone am holy' (LevR 24.9). Elsewhere they even hint at the impossibility of any imitation of God, arguing that only one capable of creating can be recognized as an imitator of the Creator (Tanh.B. iii. 111).

Needless to say, with the possible exception of Matt. 23.9, where the title, Father, is reserved for God alone (cf. p. 158 above), the extant Gospel evidence discloses no sign of such theological worries on the part of Jesus, nor would one expect a popular teacher imbued with eschatological zeal to pay regular attention to doctrinal refinements of this sort. Amid what was believed to be the death-throes of the age, trust in a God envisaged as benevolence, made good sense, the only sense.

The kernel of Jewish teaching on the imitability of God's loving-kindness and the duty to follow him in his ways forms the quintessential quality of the religion of Jesus and can be reduced – like the six hundred and thirteen commandments of Moses – to the single precept:

Be perfect as your heavenly Father is perfect (Matt. 5.48).

Yet even this concept of 'perfection' may be seen as far too abstract. Therefore, Luke's concrete formulation of the same instruction, which anticipates the words of Abba Sha'ul and the Palestinian Targum, is more likely to be genuine:

Be merciful as your Father is merciful (Luke 6.36).

Thus the core of Jesus' religion is not Torah *observance* as such – though it is by no means excluded and prompts inner spirituality. It is not a search for purity – ritual or ethical. It is not self-sanctification in the form of a life of prayer and worship – in the Temple or the synagogue. It seems not even to have been a pursuit of God for his own sake, but by means of devotion to his brethren after the pattern of a merciful heavenly Father. He goes so far as to assert that at the Last Judgment, the divine King's single criterion will be whether or not a person imitated him in his deeds of love. In the original parable of the Judgment (cf. above, 112), the prize of salvation is awarded to those who have acted with generosity towards a God in disguise:

> I was hungry and you gave me food.
> I was thirsty and you gave me drink.
> I was stranger and you welcomed me.
> I was naked and you clothed me.
> I was sick and you visited me.
> I was in prison and you came to me (Matt. 25.35f.).

To the question of when God has met with such kindness, the reply comes that it was when it was shown to persons of no importance, to 'the little ones' (Matt. 25.40). Both the twist in the narration, *imitatio Dei* being seen as graciousness towards God and extending a loving hand to the distressed, are all typical of the teaching style and religious outlook of Jesus and constitute a coherent whole.

These 'little ones' are also those unable to reciprocate. When Jesus sent his disciples to 'heal and exorcize', they were, when seen as successful, usually offered a donation, but he forbade them to accept anything. 'You received (your charismatic powers) without paying, give without payment!' (Matt. 10.8). Also, according to the well-known parable, no true loving-kindness, untainted by hope of a return invitation, is possible except when the guest list includes only 'the poor, the maimed, the lame and the blind' (cf. Luke 14.12–14) – precisely those who are banned from the messianic assembly according to the Qumran Rule of the Congregation, apart from 'the poor' who are not mentioned there (1 QSa 2.5f.).

Finally, nothing better illustrates Jesus' true vision of goodness than the hyperbole *par excellence*, in which he extends the biblical commandment to love one's neighbours to include also one's enemies. Without wishing to rehearse the discussion of Matt. 5.39–45; Luke 6.27–35 (cf. above pp. 36f.), it is enough to observe that this being the purest form of altruism, it is verifiable in the case of God who makes the sun shine and the rain fall over the just and the unjust (Matt. 5.46). More concretely, Jesus' doctrine of the *imitatio Dei* culminates in a loving embrace of God's 'enemies', such as the tax-collectors, and indirectly even the Gentiles (Matt. 5.45f.; Luke 6.32–34), who are seen as foes of the righteous also.

Jesus showed compassion not merely to the unfortunate, the sick and the helpless commended by the biblical prophets, but to the pariahs of his society shunned by the well-thinking and the respectable. The Gospels present him regularly in contact with the 'unclean', i.e. persons afflicted with contagious diseases, or 'possessed by demons' whom as healer-exorcist he was not to avoid, but also the social, political and moral outcasts, known in the New Testament as 'publicans and sinners', whose 'friend' he was accused of being (Matt. 11.19; Luke 7.34). He not only welcomed their attendance at his teaching (Luke 15.1), but chose a tax-collector, or rather a customs official, Levi-Matthew, as one of his apostles, and sat at his table surrounded by Levi's colleagues and other 'sinners' (Mark 2.14f.; Matt. 9.9f.; Luke 5.27–29). Luke (19.1–6), probably trying to improve on the other Synoptics, shows Jesus inviting himself to the home of the diminutive Zacchaeus, Jericho's *architelōnēs*, or publican-in-chief. These often extortionate civil servants, employed by the Romans in Judaea and Herod Antipas in Galilee,[22] are regularly referred to in the Gospels as 'sinners'. So also, in an anecdote which may be of Luke's creation, probably on a factual basis, is the city woman usually identified as a whore who, deeply moved by repentance, washed the feet of Jesus with her tears. His readiness to receive them with warmth shocked bourgeois Jews not attuned to the needs of the last days which call for the devoted physician and the pastor to seek out those who have strayed from the straight path (Mark 2.17). The healthy and conventionally good were not his concern. 'There will be more joy in heaven over one sinner who repents', Luke (15.7) gives him to say, 'than over ninety-nine just'.

V   The Holy Man Jesus

Here in a nutshell is the religion of Jesus the Jew.

A powerful healer of the physically and mentally sick, a friend of sinners, he was a magnetic preacher of what lies at the heart of the Law, unconditionally given over to the rescue, not of communities, but of persons in need.

He was always aware of the approach of the end of time and, at the moment known only to God, of the imminent intervention of our Father who is in heaven, who is to be

---

[22]Cf. *HJP* I, 374–76; see also E. Badian, *Publicans and Sinners* (1972).

revealed soon, the awesome and just Judge, Lord of all the worlds.

The Kingdom of God which Jesus firmly believed was 'at hand' did not come during his brief life span. He was not at the head of his adepts, to pay homage to the King of Kings and be welcomed by him. He died, instead, on a Roman cross, in agony, betrayed by all his pusillanimous disciples apart from – we are told – a few women, and mocked by the cruel and mindless onlookers who might well have spoken the taunting words placed on their lips by the evangelists:

> He saved others, he cannot save himself . . . He trusts in God; let God deliver him now if he desires him (Matt. 27.42f.; Mark 15.31f.; Luke 23.35).

Without presuming to know what went on in the dying Jesus' mind, it cannot be far wrong to surmise that even on the way to Golgotha, even on the cross, his *emunah* held firm until the terrible moment when he saw that God had abandoned him, and groaned:

> *'Eloi, Eloi, lama sabachtani?'*, which means, 'My God, my God, why hast thou forsaken me?' (Mark 15.34)

With this cry of despair, uttered from the broken heart of a man of faith, he 'breathed his last' (Mark 15.37).

Despite the overwhelming blow dealt to his followers by his execution, they soon convinced themselves that Jesus was not dead but lived on, since it was in his name they were achieving success as healers, exorcists and preachers. Awaiting his imminent return in glory, for his eschatological message remained alive, and assisted before being overshadowed by the foreign genius of Paul of Tarsus, they enthusiastically continued what they believed to be Jesus' own mission, preaching their gospel as though it were his, and founding the religion which came to be known as Christianity.

8

The Religion of Jesus and Christianity

The adherents of the teaching propagated by the apostles and disciples of Jesus began to be known by the early AD forties as 'Christians' (Acts 11.26), not only within their own communities (I Peter 4.16), but also among outsiders (Acts 26.28). If, as I believe, part of Josephus' *Testimonium* is genuine, his allusion to the 'tribe of the Christians' which at the time of writing the Jewish Antiquities in the nineties of the first century had 'still not disappeared' (*Ant.* xviii. 63), would represent the earliest attestation of the title outside the New Testament. Ignatius, bishop of Antioch, called the religion to which he belonged, and for which he gave his life in *c.* AD 107, *Christianismos*. From the second century onwards, the new faith spread and flourished further and further beyond the confines of Judaism, mostly, though not exclusively, among the slaves and the down-trodden of the Mediterranean world in the first instance. Persecuted repeatedly for over two centuries by the Roman state, it eventually became from the fourth century onwards, first the dominant, and later the official religion of the empire. Now, at the end of the twentieth century, the various churches of Jesus, or rather Christ, continue to command the real or nominal allegiance of a substantial portion of mankind. The journey from the first name to the second, i.e. the representation of the evolution of the christological images in the New Testament, is penetratingly analysed and splendidly sketched by Paula Fredriksen in *From Jesus to Christ* (1988).

The complex reality which still constitutes, after nearly two millennia of development, today's Christianity has been formulated in authoritative creeds, and since the churches of the East and the West continue to recite in their liturgies one of these almost timeless confessions, I give below the Nicene-Constantinopolitan Creed, composed in the fourth, and re-worked in the fifth century, as a short-hand expression of ecclesiastical orthodoxy. The English text is borrowed from the *Book of Common Prayer* of the Church of England.

I believe in one God the Father Almighty,
Maker of heaven and earth,
And of all things visible and invisible:

And in one Lord Jesus Christ, the only-begotten Son of God,
Begotten of his Father before all worlds,
God of God, Light of Light,
Very God of very God,
Begotten, not made,
Being of one substance with the Father,
By whom all things were made:
Who for us men and for our salvation came down from heaven,
And was incarnate from the Holy Ghost of the Virgin Mary,
And was made man,
And was crucified under Pontius Pilate.
He suffered and was buried,
And the third day he rose again according to the Scriptures,
And ascended into heaven,
And sitteth on the right hand of the Father.
And he shall come again with glory to judge both the quick and
   the dead:
Whose kingdom shall have no end.

And I believe in the Holy Ghost,
The Lord and giver of life,
Who proceedeth from the Father and the Son,
Who with the Father and the Son together is worshipped and
   glorified,
Who spake by the Prophets.

And I believe one Catholick and Apostolick Church.
I acknowledge one Baptism for the remission of sins.
And I look for the Resurrection of the dead,
And the life of the world to come. Amen.

The historical Jesus, Jesus the Jew, would have found the first three and the final two lines of the Christian creed familiar, and though not theologically minded, would have had no difficulty in assenting to them, but he would no doubt have been mystified by the remaining twenty-four lines. They appear to have little to do with the religion preached and practised by him. Yet the doctrines they proclaim, Christ's eternal divine status and bodily incarnation, the redemption of all mankind achieved through his crucifixion, his subsequent exaltation and, above all, the Trinity of the Godhead, Father, Son and Holy Ghost, form the basis of the faith of which he is supposed to be the architect.

Today as in past centuries, the believing Christian's main New Testament source of faith lies, not so much in Mark, Matthew and Luke and their still sufficiently earthly Jesus, as in centuries of speculation by the church on the theological Gospel of John with its eternal Word become flesh, and perhaps, even more on the letters of Paul with their drama of death, atonement, and resurrection. The Christ of Paul and John, on the way towards deification, overshadows and obscures the man of Galilee.

The disappearance of the Master called for a radical re-thinking and re-orientation during the years and decades following Golgotha, when Jesus' disciples had to explain to themselves, and then to their listeners, the significance of the cross and the 'resurrection'. Being Jews, and at first addressing only Jews, they fell back on the standard explanation of Jewish religious innovators: these events had all been foreordained by God and were the fulfilment of biblical prophecy. Their task was not easy, as I have outlined in *Jesus the Jew*, because of the absence of contemporary evidence of an expectation of a suffering and dying Messiah, or of one executed but resurrected before the final Judgment. Peter's laborious effort to discover the forecast of Jesus' rising from the dead in Psalm 16.8–11 [15.8–11 in the Greek Bible] must have carried little weight, so Paul cleverly abstained from specifics and assured the Gentile Christians of Corinth, who would not have known the difference in any case, that Christ died for man's sins, was buried and raised on the third day *kata tas graphas*, 'according to the scriptures' (I Cor. 15.3), without giving book, chapter and verse.

However, unable to envisage Jesus in any context other than that of the awaited Messiah, first-generation Christians re-interpreted the notion of Israel's redeemer, the Anointed of God, in the light of the life of Jesus, a crucified and risen Christ who, after a short and esoteric post-'resurrection' existence on earth ascended to his heavenly throne.[1] Jews in Judaea and Galilee must have found this new kind of Messiah alien, untraditional and . . . unappealing, and it can cause no surprise that apart from cosmopolitan Jerusalem with its substantial immigrant population from the Diaspora, the New Testament is silent on any progress of the new movement in the Palestinian homeland.

Another important element of the religion of Jesus, his teaching concerning the *eschaton*, the day of the Lord, the coming of his Kingdom, required significant recasting. As has often been underscored in the foregoing pages, the great event which Jesus was convinced would happen in his life-time failed to materialize, but since first-generation Christianity was still imbued with eschatological enthusiasm, the end had to be rescheduled to coincide with the impending Parousia, the triumphant return of the exalted Christ from heaven, surrounded by the host of angels. Although the fresh scenario was no more successful than the first, in fact it opened the door to unending postponements and the practical extinction of the real eschatological hope, nonetheless, Christ's 'coming again in glory' to inaugurate *his* Kingdom is still on the lips of every eucharistic worshipper.

Such a revised edition of Jesus' message entails also a total shift in religious thought. Jesus' eyes were fixed on God and his Kingdom. Those of his followers, in particular Paul, focussed on the risen and glorified Lord. The purely theocentric religion of Jesus became a christocentric faith in which the heavenly Father plays practically no role. For Jesus, *teshuvah* and *emunah*

---

[1]The claim that a Dead Sea Scrolls fragment alludes to a slain Messiah is ill-founded. It is now advanced with greater caution by R. Eisenman and M. Wise, *The Dead Sea Scrolls Uncovered* (1992), 24–29. For a case arguing in favour of a triumphant messianic interpretation, see G. Vermes, 'Seminar on the Rule of War from Qumran Cave 4 (4Q285)', *JJS* 43 (1992), 85–90. The notion of a risen Messiah seems to be unknown in extant ancient Jewish literature. Hence there can be no question of the fulfilment of a traditional expectation, and if it were true that Jesus repeatedly foretold his death and subsequent rising, the profound bewilderment of his closest companions before and after the crucifixion would need some explanation. Moreover, what does the claim of Jesus' *bodily* resurrection add to the belief in his spiritual survival if the 'risen Lord' is seen only by those who have faith in him and appears under such a strange guise that none can recognize him until he identifies himself! By contrast, the less emphasized doctrine of Jesus' ascension to heaven, prefigured in the Bible by Enoch and Elijah and in post-biblical literature by Moses and Isaiah, evoked familiar resonances in first-century Jewish ears.

rendered everything possible; no mediator was needed. In Christianity, nothing is possible, not even *teshuvah* or *emunah*, without the atoning death of Christ bringing salvation to the world. Jesus' immediacy in practising and commending *imitatio Dei* is also diluted, and whilst it still appears as a spiritual counsel in, 'Be imitators of God as beloved children' (Eph. 5.1), the man from Tarsus presents himself as an imitator, not of God, but of Christ, and as such offers himself for imitation to the members of his churches (I Cor. 11.1).

Paul's powerful, brilliant and poetic imagination creates a magnificent drama, echoing the mystery cults of his age, in which through baptism into the death and resurrection of Jesus-Christ the new initiate enters into communion with the great act of salvation by means of which the New Adam removes from human nature that universal sinfulness which resulted from the fall of the first man in the garden of Eden.

The migration of Christianity from the Jewish to the Graeco-Roman world, another consequence of Paul's masterly apostolate, necessitated a further drastic interference with Jesus' religion. Since the obligatory imposition of the Torah on Gentiles, including circumcision, would have stopped many from joining the church, the Jewish Law, the innermost source of Jesus' piety, was not only made optional, but had to go, be abolished in the name of Christ. In 'Paulinism', which is largely identical with Western Christianity, the Torah is perversely metamorphosed from a well-spring of life into an instrument of death: 'While we were living in the flesh our sinful passions, aroused by the Law, were at work in our members to bear fruit of death. But now we are discharged from the Law . . .' (Rom. 7.5f.). 'Christ is the end of the Law' (Rom. 10.4). Is it an exaggeration to suggest that oceans separate Paul's Christian Gospel from the religion of Jesus the Jew?

The place of Israel whose lost sheep Jesus was sent to save had to be reappraised in this new world-view. The unbelieving Jews, blinded by their Torah, were judged and found guilty of obstinacy and deprived of their privileges *qua* chosen people in favour of the new 'Israel of God' (Gal. 6.16). To be fair, it has to be said that Paul, despite many harsh polemical comments against Judaism, shies off in the end from damning his people for ever. His inventive poetic mind imagines that the rejection of

Christ is a dreadful but only temporary lapse. The apostle of the Gentiles by attempting to graft the whole converted non-Jewish world on to the Jewish stock, thus making them the heirs of all the divine promises granted to Abraham and his posterity, secretly hoped that elevation of the Gentiles would excite the jealousy of the Jews, and bring them to *teshuvah* and submission to Christ so that 'all Israel' might be saved (Rom. 11.26).

The author of the Fourth Gospel had no such Judaeophile sentiments. The term, *Ioudaioi*, originally applying perhaps just to Judaeans, but by the time of the redaction of the work at the end of the first century incorporating all the evangelist's 'unconverted' fellow countrymen, i.e. the near totality of the Jewish people, acquired ominous overtones. In John's account of the life of Jesus, the Jews are a blood-thirsty gang who seek to kill Jesus from the outset and do not desist until they have succeeded in their deadly plan. John's Christ, who had nothing in common with the real Jesus, declares to his compatriots:

> You are of your father the devil, and your will is to do your father's desire. He was a murderer from the beginning . . . (John 8.44).

Here is the origin of the Christian tendency to demonize the Jews, the source of all mediaeval and much modern religious anti-Judaism, which directly or indirectly led to the Holocaust. Tragically, it took six million lives to persuade the largest of the Christian churches to annul the charge of deicide levelled for so long against the people of Jesus.

The de-Judaization of the pristine gospel in the Graeco-Roman world was no doubt unintentionally helped by the underlying universalism of Jesus' doctrine of *imitatio Dei*, a God whose providence includes all, and his primary concern for the individual, thus permitting an easier dispensation from the mostly communal and social aspects of the Law of Moses. This went also hand in hand with the decline of Judaeo-Christianity of the first vintage, consisting of Torah-observing Jews who followed the teaching of Jesus without such 'Christian' accretions as the doctrine of the virgin birth or the deification of Christ. These people were unpopular both in the Jewish camp, and among the members of the Gentile church; though they probably remained closest to Jesus, the Jews considered them as Christians and the

Christians as heretics. 'While they wish to be both Jews and Christians', wrote Jerome to Augustine, 'they are neither Jews, nor Christians'.[2] They vanished from the scene, the few surviving pockets having no doubt reverted to the Jewish fold. With it, the last, and by then no doubt distorted, vestiges of the religion practised by Jesus and preached to Jews disappeared, allowing a free run for the triumphal progress of Hellenized Christianity in the non-Jewish world of Late Antiquity.

Despite all this, in fairness, it must be emphasized that notwithstanding all its alien dogmatic and ecclesiastical features, Christianity still possesses fundamental elements of the piety of Jesus, such as his emphasis on purity of intention and generosity of heart, exemplified in a Francis of Assisi who relinquished wealth to serve the poor, and even in our century, an Albert Schweitzer, who abandoned fame to heal the sick in God-forsaken Lambaréné, and a Mother Teresa who, age-old, cares for the dying in the filthy streets of Calcutta.

Shortly before his death, the great British New Testament scholar, C. H. Dodd, produced an excellent little book on the life of Jesus. But if the thesis developed in the present study is even partly true, the title Dodd chose, *The Founder of Christianity* (1970), must be judged a misnomer. Though admittedly not *totally* unconnected, the religion of Jesus and Christianity are so basically different in form, purpose and orientation that it would be historically unsafe to derive the latter directly from the former and attribute the changes to a straightforward doctrinal evolution.[3]

It would seem no less unjustifiable to continue to represent Jesus as the establisher of the Christian church (or churches?). For let it be re-stated for a last time, if he meant and believed what he preached – and I for one am convinced that he did – namely that the eternal Kingdom of God was truly at hand, he simply could

---

[2]'Dum volunt et Iudaei esse et Christiani nec Iudaei sunt, nec Christiani' (*Epist.* 89 to Augustine, Patrologia Latina XXII). These so-called Ebionites or Nazarenes cannot be compared with present-day 'Messianic Jews' or 'Jews for Jesus', who under the disguise of the ordinary observances of Judaism seem to be plain, fundamentalist, evangelical Christians.

[3]No doubt, on a meta-historical level, Christian faith and theology attribute these changes to the work of the 'Holy Spirit': 'When the Spirit of truth comes, he will guide you into all the truth' (John 16.13).

not have entertained the idea of founding and setting in motion an organized society intended to endure for ages to come. A great challenge, perhaps the greatest of them all, which traditional Christianity of the Pauline-Johannine variety has therefore still to confront does not come from atheism, or agnosticism, or sheer materialism, but from within, from the three ancient witnesses, Mark, Matthew and Luke, through whom speaks the chief challenger, Jesus the Jew.

Whether this challenge is accepted will be seen in the decades, even centuries, to come, though faint signs indicate that the most perceptive Christian New Testament scholars are already conscious of the task awaiting them. But it would seem also that muted sounds are audible in Jewish scholarly circles suggesting that the antique taboo on Jesus, mistakenly held responsible for Christian anti-Semitism, is beginning to fade and that hesitant steps are being made to re-instate him among the ancient Hasidim in initial fulfilment of Martin Buber's 'prophecy': 'A great place belongs to him in Israel's history of faith.'[4]

Nor is this all. For the magnetic appeal of the teaching and example of Jesus holds out hope and guidance to those outside the fold of organized religion, the stray sheep of mankind, who yearn for a world of mercy, justice and peace lived in as children of God.

[4]*Two Types of Faith: A Study of the Interpenetration of Judaism and Christianity* (1951), 13.

Abbreviations

Ab.	Abot
ANRW	*Aufstieg und Niedergang der Römischen Welt*, ed. H. Temporini and W. Haase
Ant.	*Jewish Antiquities* by Flavius Josephus
AOT	*Apochryphal Old Testament*, ed. H. F. D. Sparks
apGen	Genesis Apochryphon
ar	Aramaic
Arakh.	Arakhin
ARN	Abot de-Rabbi Nathan
AZ	Avodah Zarah
b	bavli (Babylonian Talmud)
BB	Bava Batra
Beat	Beatitudes
Ber.	Berakhot
BM	Bava Mesiʿa
BQ	Bava Qamma
BR	Bereshit Rabbah (cf. GR and GenR)
C. Ap.	*Contra Apionem* by Flavius Josephus
CBQ	*Catholic Biblical Quarterly*
CD	Cairo Damascus Document
CHB	*Cambridge History of the Bible*, ed. P. R. Ackroyd and C. F. Evans
Decal.	*De Decalogo*, by Philo
DJD	*Discoveries in the Judaean Desert*
DSSE	*The Dead Sea Scrolls in English* by G. Vermes
Er.	Eruvin
Ex.R.	Exodus Rabbah
Flac.	*In Flaccum* by Philo
fr.	Fragment
GenR/GR	Genesis Rabbah (cf. BR)

Gitt.	Gittin
H	Hodayot (Thanksgiving hymns)
Hag.	Hagigah
HJP	*History of the Jewish People in the Age of Jesus Christ*, by E. Schürer-G. Vermes-F. Millar-M. Black-M. Goodman
HST	*The History of the Synoptic Tradition* by R. Bultmann
HUCA	*Hebrew Union College Annual*
Hul.	Hullin
IDBS	*Interpreter's Dictionary of the Bible*: Supplementary Volume
Iss.	Issachar
JBL	*Journal of Biblical Literature*
J & J	*Jesus and Judaism* by E. P. Sanders
JJ	*Jesus the Jew* by G. Vermes
JJS	*Journal of Jewish Studies*
JSJ	*Journal for the Study of Judaism*
JSS	*Journal of Semitic Studies*
JTS	*Journal of Theological Studies*
JWJ	*Jesus and the World of Judaism* by G. Vermes
Jub.	Jubilees
LAB	Pseudo-Philo's Liber Antiquitatum Biblicarum
Legat.	*Legatio ad Gaium* by Philo
Lev.R.	Leviticus Rabbah
Life	Josephus' Autobiography
LXX	Septuagint
m	Mishnah
M	Milhamah (War Scroll)
Mak.	Makkot
Mekh.	Mekhilta
Men.	Menahot
Mid.	Middot
Migr.	*De migratione Abrahami* by Philo
Moses	*De vita Mosis* by Philo
MS	Manuscript
Ned.	Nedarim
Neof.	Neofiti
Ohol.	Oholot
Opif.	*De opificio mundi* by Philo

OTP	*The Old Testament Pseudepigrapha* ed. by J. H. Charlesworth
p	Pesher
PBJS	*Post-biblical Jewish Studies* by G. Vermes
Pes.	Pesahim
Pes.R.	Pesiqta Rabbati
PL	Patrologia Latina
PRK	Pesiqta de-Rab Kahana
Ps-Jon	Pseudo-Jonathan
Q	Qumran (1Q, etc. Qumran Cave 1, etc.)
Q [NT]	Hypothetical Gospel source from 'Quelle'
QIP	*The Dead Sea Scroll: Qumran in Perspective* by G. Vermes
R.	Rabbi
RB	*Revue Biblique*
RQ	*Revue de Qumrân*
S	1QSerek (Community Rule); 4QSa,b,c, etc. = various manuscripts of the Rule from Cave 4
Sa	Rule of the Congregation or Messianic Rule
S & T	*Scripture and Tradition in Judaism* by G. Vermes
Sanh.	Sanhedrin
Sb	1QS Benedictions
Shab.	Shabbat
Shebu.	Shebuot
Shek.	Shekalim
Sot.	Sotah
Suk.	Sukkah
t	Tosefta
Taan.	Taanit (Fast)
Tanh.	Tanhuma
TDNT	*Theological Dictionary of the New Testament*
Tg	Targum
Th–A	Genesis Rabbah, ed. J. Theodor – H. Albeck
TS	Temple Scroll
V.C.	*De vita contemplativa* by Philo
War	*Jewish War* by Flavius Josephus
y	yerushalmi (Jerusalem or Palestinian Talmud)
ZNW	*Zeitschrift für die neutestamentliche Wissenschaft*

Bibliography

Abrahams, I., *Studies in Pharisaism and the Gospels* II, 1924

Allegro, J., Anderson, A. A., *Discoveries in the Judaean Desert of Jordan V: I (4Q158–4Q186)*, 1968

Avigad, N., Yadin, Y., *A Genesis Apocryphon*, 1956

Bacher W., *Die Agada der Tannaiten* II, 1890

Badian, E., *Publicans and Sinners*, 1972

Baillet, M., *Discoveries in the Judaean Desert VII: Qumrân Grotte 4 III (4Q482–4Q520)*, 1982

Baillet, M., Milik, J. T., Vaux, R. de, *Discoveries in the Judaean Desert III: Les petites grottes de Qumrân*, 1962

Barr, J., 'Abba isn't Daddy!', *JTS* 39 (1988), 28–47

Barrett, C. K., *Jesus and the Gospel Tradition*, 1967

Barthélemy, D., Milik, J. T., *Discoveries in the Judaean Desert I: Qumran Cave I*, 1955

Black, M., *Aramaic Approach to the Gospels and Acts*, [3]1967

— 'The Doxology of the *Pater Noster* with a Note on Matthew 6.13B', in P. R. Davies and R. T. White, *A Tribute to Geza Vermes*, 1990

— Vanderkam, J. C., *The Book of Enoch or I Enoch*, 1985

Blank, S. H., 'The Death of Zechariah in Rabbinic Literature', *HUCA* 12–13 (1937–38), 327–46

Blumberg, C. L., 'Interpreting the Parables of Jesus: Where are we and where do we go from here?', *CBQ* 53 (1991), 50–78

Bosker, B. M., 'Wonder-working and Rabbinic Tradition. The Case of Hanina ben Dosa', *JSJ* 16 (1985), 42–92

Bornkamm, G., *Jesus of Nazareth*, 1956

Brock, S. P., 'Psalms of Solomon' in H. F. D. Sparks (ed.), *The Apocryphal Old Testament*, 1984

Buber, M., *Zwei Glaubensweisen*, 1950 [ET *Two Types of Faith: A Study of the Interpenetration of Judaism and Christianity*, 1961]

— 'Imitatio Dei', *Israel and the World*, 1963, 66–77

— *Kingship of God*, 1967

Bultmann, R., *Jesus*, 1926 [ET *Jesus and the Word*, 1934]

— *The History of the Synoptic Tradition*, 1963

— *Theologie des Neuen Testaments,* [5]1965

Burrows, M., *The Dead Sea Scrolls of St Mark's Monastery I: The Isaiah Manuscript and the Habakkuk Commentary,* 1950; II/2 *The Manual of Discipline,* 1951

Büchler, A., *Types of Jewish Palestinian Piety,* 1922

Caird, G. B., *Saint Luke,* 1963

Camponovo, O., *Königtum, Königsherrschaft und Reich Gottes in den frühjüdischen Schriften,* 1984

Carlston, C. E., Art. 'Parables', *IDBS,* 641f.

Charlesworth, J. H., *Jesus within Judaism: New Light from Exciting Archaeological Discoveries,* 1989

— (ed.), *The Old Testament Pseudepigrapha* I–II, 1983–85

Collins, J. J., 'Sibylline Oracles' in J. H. Charlesworth, *OTP* I

Cranfield, C. E. B., *The Gospel according to Saint Mark,* 1959

Crossan, J. D., *The Historical Jesus: The Life of a Mediterranean Jewish Peasant,* 1991

Dalman, G., *Jesus-Jeshua: Studies in the Gospels,* 1929

— *Die Worte Jesu,* [2]1930 [ET *The Words of Jesus,* 1902]

Daube, D., *The New Testament and Rabbinic Judaism,* 1956

Davies, P. R., White, R. T. (ed), *A Tribute to Geza Vermes,* 1990

Davies, W. D., Allison, D. C., *The Gospel according to St Matthew I,* 1988

Dequeker, L., 'The "Saints of the Most High" in Qumran and Daniel', *Oudtestamentische Studiën* 18 (1973), 108–87

Derrett, J. M. D., *The Law in the New Testament,* 1979

— 'Law and Society in Jesus' World', *ANRW* 25.1 (1982). 477–564

Dihle, A., *Die goldene Regel. Eine Einführung in die Geschichte der antiken und frühchristlichen Vulgärethik,* 1962

Dodd, C. H., *The Parables of the Kingdom,* 1935, 1961

Ego, B.., *Studien zum Verhältnis vom himmlischer und irdischer Welt im rabbinischen Judentum,* 1989

Evans, C. A., *To See and not Perceive: Isaiah 6.9–10 in Early Jewish and Christian Interpretation,* 1989

Falk, Z. W., *Introduction to Jewish Law in the Second Commonwealth* II, 1978

Feldmann, A., *The Parables and Similes of the Rabbis, Agricultural and Pastoral,* 1927

Feldman, L. H., *Josephus and Modern Scholarship 1937–1980,* 1984

Fiebig, P., *Altjüdische Gleichnisreden und die Gleichnisse Jesu,* 1904

— *Die Gleichnisse Jesu im Lichte der rabbinischen Gleichnisse des neutestamentlichen Zeitalters,* 1912

Fitzmyer, J. A., 'The Matthean Divorce Texts and some new Palestinian Evidence', *Theological Studies* 37 (1976), 197–226

— *A Wandering Aramean,* 1979

Flusser, D., *Die rabbinischen Gleichnisse und der Gleichniserzähler Jesus*, 1981
— *Judaism and the Origins of Christianity*, 1988
Foerster, W., Art. 'Epiousios' in *TDNT* II, 590–99
Forkman, G., *The Limits of the Religious Community: Expulsion from the Religious Community within the Qumram Sect, within Rabbinic Judaism and within Primitive Christianity*, 1972
Fredriksen, P., *From Jesus to Christ*, 1988
Freyne, S., *Galilee from Alexander the Great to Hadrian*, 1980
— *Galilee, Jesus and the Gospels*, 1988
Furnish, V. P., *The Love Command in the New Testament*, 1973
García Martínez, F., *Qumram and Apocalyptic*, 1992
Goodenough, E. R., *An Introduction to Philo Judaeus*, 1962
Goodman, M. D. *State and Society in Roman Galilee, AD 132–212*, 1983
— *The Ruling Class of Judaea*, 1987
Green, W. S., 'Palestinian Holy Men: Chrismatic Leadership and Rabbinic Tradition', *ANRW* ii. 19.2 (1979), 619–37
Harvey, A. E., *Jesus and the Constraints of History*, 1982
Hauck, F., Art. 'Parables' in *TDNT* V, 747–51
Heinemann, J., *Prayer in the Talmud*, 1977
Hengel, M., *The Charismatic Leader and His Followers*, 1981
Jeremias, J., *Abba. Studien zur neutestamentlichen Theologie und Zeitgeschichte*, 1966
— *The Prayers of Jesus*, 1967
— *The Parables of Jesus*, 1972
Jülicher, A., *Die Gleichnisreden Jesu*, I–II, 1886–1910
Käsemann, E., *Essays on New Testament Themes*, 1964
Kilpatrick, G.D., *The Origins of the Gospel according to St Matthew*, 1946
Kittel, G., Friedrich, G. (eds), *Theological Dictionary of the New Testament* I–X, 1964–1976
Klausner, J., *Jesus of Nazareth: His Life, Times and Teaching*, 1925
Klein, M., 'The Targumic Tosefta to Exodus 15:2', *JJS* 26 (1975), 61–67
— *The Fragment-Targums of the Pentateuch according to their Extant Sources*, 1980
Lagrange, M. J., *L'évangile de Jésus-Christ*, 1929
Lindenberger, J. M., 'Ahiqar' in *OTP* II, 479–507
Manson, T. W., *The Teaching of Jesus*, 1931
— *The Sayings of Jesus* [1937], 1979
Marmorstein, A., 'The Imitation of God (Imitatio Dei) in the Haggadah', *Jeschurun* 14 (1927), repr. in *Studies in Jewish Theology*, (1950), 106–21
Meier, J. P., *A Marginal Jew: Rethinking the Historical Jesus*, 1991
Moore, G. F., *Judaism in the First Centuries of the Christian Era* (1930) I–III
Mowry, L., Art. 'Parables', *IDB* III, 649–54
Meyer, A., *Jesu Muttersprache*, 1896

Milik. J. T., *The Books of Enoch: Aramaic Fragments of Qumrân Cave IV*, 1976

Neusner, J., 'Types and Forms in Ancient Jewish Literature: Some Comparisons', *History of Religions* 11 (1972), 354–90

— *A History of the Mishnaic Law of Purities, Part XIII*, 1976

Newsom, C., *Songs of the Sabbath Sacrifice*, 1985

Otto, R., *The Kingdom of God and the Son of Man*, 1938

— *The Idea of the Holy*, 1959

Pallais, P., *Exegesis of Lev. 19:18 and the Love Command in Judaism: Variations on a Theme* (Oxford MPhil. thesis, 1988)

Perles, F., 'Zur Erklärung von Mt 7.6', *ZNW* 25 (1926), 163f.

Perrin, N., *The Kingdom of God in the Teaching of Jesus*, 1963

— *Rediscovering the Teaching of Jesus*, 1967

— *Jesus and the Language of the Kingdom*, 1976

Perrot, C., *Jésu et l'histoire*, 1979

Puech, E., 'Un hymne essénien en partie retrouvé et les Béatitudes', *Mémorial Jean Carmignac*, *RQ* 13, Nos 49–52 (1988), 59–88

Renan, E., *La vie de Jésus*, 1863

Rabinowitz, L. I. and Scott, R. B. Y., Art. 'Parables', *Enc. Jud.* 13, 72–77

Rad, G. von, Kuhn, K. G., Schmidt, K. L., Art. *basileus* in *TDNT* I, 564–93

Rowland, C., *Christian Origins*, 1985

J. Saldarini, *The Fathers according to Rabbi Nathan*, 1975

Sanders, E. P ., *Jesus and Judaism*, 1985

— *Jewish Law from Jesus to the Mishnah*, 1990

— *Judaism: Practice and Belief: 66 BCE – 66 CE*, 1992

Sanders, E. P. and Davies, M., *Studying the Synoptic Gospels*, 1989

Sanders, J. A., *Discoveries in the Judaean Desert of Jordan IV: The Psalm Scroll of Qumran Cave 11*, 1965

Schechter, S., *Aboth de Rabbi Nathan*, 1887, repr. 1967

— *Some Aspects of Rabbinic Theology*, 1909

Schiffman, L. H., *Sectarian Law in the Dead Sea Scrolls: Courts, Testimony and the Penal Code*, 1983

— (ed.), *Archaeology and History in the Dead Sea Scrolls*, 1990

Schlosser, J., *Le règne de Dieu dans les dits de Jésus*, 1980

Schuller, E. M., *Non-Canonical Psalms from Qumran*, 1986

— 'The Psalm of 4Q372 1 within the Context of Second Temple Prayer', *CBQ* 54 (1992), 67–79

Schürer, E., Vermes, G., Millar, F. Black, M., Goodman, M., *The History of the Jewish People in the Age of Jesus Christ* I–III, 1973–1987

Schweitzer, A., *Von Reimarus zu Wrede*, 1906

— *The Quest of The Historical Jesus*, 1910

Segal, J. B., *The Hebrew Passover from the Earliest Times to AD 70*, 1963

— 'Popular Religion in Ancient Israel', *JJS* 27 (1976), 1–22

Smith, M., 'Matt. v.43: "Hate Thine Enemy"', *HTR* 45 (1952), 71–3

— *Jesus the Magician*, 1978

Sparks, H. F. D. (ed.), *The Apocryphal Old Testament*, 1984

Stendahl, K., *The School of St Matthew*, 1954

Stern, D., *Parables in Midrash: Narrative and Exegesis in Rabbinic Literature*, 1991

Strack, H., Billerbeck, P., *Kommentar zum Neuen Testament aus Talmud und Midrasch*, 1922–28

Strugnell, J., 'Moses Pseudepigrapha at Qumran' in L. H. Schiffman, *Archaeology and History in the Dead Sea Scrolls*, 1990, 221–56

Sukenik, E. L., *The Dead Sea Scrolls of the Hebrew University*, 1955

Sweet, J. P. M., 'Assumption of Moses' in H. F. D. Sparks, *AOT*, 1984

Tov, E., 'The Unpublished Qumran Texts from Caves 4 and 11, *JJS* 43 (1992), 101–36

Urbach, E. E., *The Sages: Their Concepts and Beliefs*, 1975

Vermes, G., *Scripture and Tradition in Judaism*, 1961, [2]1973

— 'Bible and Midrash', *CHB* I (1970), 199–231 [= *PBJS*, 59–91]

— *Jesus the Jew*, 1973

— *Post-Biblical Jewish Studies*, 1975

— *The Dead Sea Scrolls: Qumran in Perspective*, 1977, [2]1982

— *The Gospel of Jesus the Jew*, 1981

— 'A Summary of the Law by Flavius Josephus', *NT* 24 (1982), 289–307

— Jewish Studies and New Testament Interpretation', *JJS* 33 (1982), 361–76

— *Jesus and the World of Judaism*, 1983

— 'Scripture and Tradition in Judaism: Written and Oral Torah', in G. Baumann (ed.), *The Written Word: Literacy in Transition*, 1986, 79–95

— *The Dead Sea Scrolls in English*, [3]1987

— *The Jesus Notice of Josephus Re-examined*, *JJS* 38 (1987), 1–10.

— 'Josephus' Portrait of Jesus Reconsidered', in *Orient and Occident: A Tribute to the Memory of A. Scheiber*, 1988, 373–82

'Bible Interpretation at Qumran', in *Yigael Yadin Memorial Volume*, Eretz-Israel XX, 1989, 184*–191*

— 'Biblical Proof-Texts in Qumran Literature' [*Edward Ullendorff Festschrift*], *JSS* 34 (1989), 493–508

— 'Preliminary Remarks on Unpublished Fragments of the Community Rule from Qumran Cave 4', *JJS* 42 (1991), 250–55

— 'The Oxford Forum for Qumran Research: Seminar on the Rule of War (4Q285)', *JJS* 43 (1992), 85–90

— 'Qumran Forum Miscellanea I' *JJS* 43 (1992), 301–3

Vermes, P., *Buber on God and The Perfect Man*, 1980

Weber, M., *From Max Weber: Essays in Sociology*, ed. H. H. Gerth and C. Wright Mills, 1979

Weiss, J., *Die Predigt Jesu vom Reiche Gottes*, 1990

Weiss Halivni, D., *Midrash, Mishnah and Gemara*, 1986

Wilcox, M., 'Upon the Tree – Deut. 21:22–23 in the New Testament', *JBL* 96 (1977), 85–99

Winton, A. P., *The Proverbs of Jesus: Issues of History and Rhetoric*, 1990

Würthwein, E., *The Text of the Old Testament*, 1980

Yadin, Y., *The Scroll of the War of the Sons of Light against the Sons of Darkness*, 1962

— *The Temple Scroll* I–III, 1983

Young, B. H., *Jesus and his Jewish Parables: Reconsidering the Roots of Jesus' Teaching*, 1989

Zeitlin, I. M., *Jesus and the Judaism of his Time*, 1988

Ziegler, J., *Die Königgleichnisse des Midrasch*, 1903

Index of Names

Index of References

BIBLE

APOCRYPHA

PSEUDEPIGRAPHA

QUMRAN

PHILO

JOSEPHUS

NEW TESTAMENT

MISHNAH

TOSEFTA

PALESTINIAN TALMUD

TARGUMS

DATE DUE
